For Uncle Nowell

The Lone Pine
PICNIC
GUIDE
To British Columbia

Nancy Gibson
John Whittaker

LONE
PINE

First printed in 1989 5 4 3 2 1

Printed in Canada

The Publisher:
Lone Pine Publishing
#206, 10426-81 Avenue
Edmonton, Alberta, Canada
T6E 1X5

Canadian Cataloguing in Publication Data
Gibson, Nancy.
    The Lone Pine picnic guide
    to British Columbia

    Bibliography: p.
    Includes index.
    ISBN 0-919433-59-6

    1. British Columbia - Description and travel - 1981-
- Guide-books.* 2. Picnicking. 3. Outdoor cookery.
I. Whittaker, John, 1940- II. Title.
FC3807.G52 1989   917.11'044   C89-091091-X

Cover design: Yuet Chan
Front cover photo: Martin J. E. Ross
Editorial: Mary Walters Riskin
Printing: Hignell Printing Limited

Publisher's Acknowledgement
The publisher gratefully acknowledges the assistance of the Federal
Department of Communications, Alberta Culture and Multicultural-
ism, the Canada Council, and the Alberta Foundation for the Liter-
ary Arts in the production of this book.

QUEEN
CHARLOTTE
ISLANDS

Atlin

BRITISH COLUMBIA

*(Each number on the map corresponds to
the picnic number in the book.)*

Cassiar

Liard

Fort Nelson

Fort Nelson

River

Williston

Lake

Fort St. John

Dawson
Creek

Kitimat

Fort
St. James

Prince
George

38

39

River

Williams
Lake

Fraser

35 36

40

33

37

Revelstoke

32

Lillooet

Kamloops

34

30

ort Alice

VANCOUVER
ISLAND

7   13

3

8

20

19

Merritt

23

Vernon

26 25

27

Kimberley

28

VANCOUVER

11

9

Kelowna

31

2

Nanaimo

1

10

Chilliwack

21   22

24

Nelson

29

4

5

VICTORIA

6

12 14 — 18 are in Vancouver

Table of Contents

Acknowledgements

This book reflects the willingness of many people to tell us about their favourite picnic spots. There were the unknown family in the pick-up truck near Wildhorse Creek; Winn Weir at Invermere; and Jim Gibb at Canal Flats, all of whom stopped what they were doing in response to our usual opening, "We are looking for special places for picnicking.... What would you suggest?" They all spent several hours showing us spots we'd never otherwise have found, and telling us local stories that you would never otherwise be reading. We would like to thank Dave and Nina Saxby, whose house served as our Vancouver base, who fed us our first sushi, who lent us their books and even took us on a picnic — the one where John broke his ankle; and Uncle Ross Whittaker who has spent many years showing us the beauty and the history of the Kootenays, and where to pick huckleberries; and Terrie Cappello with whom we organized the first annual North Cooking Lake Community Picnic so long ago; and Marion the Librarian, who could always find the missing recipe, poem or place; and her husband, Denis Saffron, whose repertoire is never limited by circumstance.

Once we had drafted the 40 picnics, we wanted each to be read by someone else who was thoroughly familiar with the area — we do not profess to be experts on all these places, and some errors are inevitable. Some picnics reflect the generosity of people who have lived in the area for a long time, and who are proud to share their knowledge, people like Dave Ritchie and Florence Boyes at Craigellachie; Lorna Robb in Barkerville; Captain Ted Kennedy of the Phoebe Ann, who spent time showing us the boat, and Gordon Mackie, the owner, who edited the picnic; Roger Wheelock at Butchart Gardens; and Len and Sheila Bland who helped select the correct Victoria park. We are grateful to the many people at provincial Travel InfoCentres, national, provincial and municipal park offices, historical associations and chambers of commerce throughout the province, who kindly helped us at the research stage and at the proof-reading stage. Our thanks to M.D. Ballard, Tom Bell, G.D. Bower, Evan Bueckert, M. Bumney, Karen Garland, Jim Gibb, H.F. Hambleton, Ingred Lehwald, Bruce K. Mason, Dale Mumford, Collette Murrell, Carrie Namislo, Otren Seger, B.J. Theriault, Don Turner, Joan Verschuren, and Alayna Wilton. There are many more people who will know that they have helped us to write this book — to all of you, our sincere thanks.

Acknowledgements

We are grateful to Jim Wilson at the British Columbia Ministry of Tourism and Provincial Secretary for the photographs which accompany the Capilano Canyon and Fort Langley picnics, and to the British Columbia Provincial Archives for the historical photographs. The references to Pauline Johnson's stories and the poem, "Lines and Squares," from A.A. Milne's *When We Were Very Young* appear with the kind permission of McClelland and Stewart.

Many people have helped us to gather just the right recipes for their favourite picnic, and here we thank Isabel Butler and Kathleen Butler Elder, Barbara Allen, Anna Franklin and Mike Sich.

We are deeply grateful to our editors: Uncle Nowell Sadlier-Brown who reviewed the manuscript, giving us the benefit of his extensive knowledge of the English language and of British Columbia history, and a bed any time we were near the Shuswap; Helen and Hugh Lavender who reviewed the manuscript, took us gold panning, and always had a hot cup of coffee ready when we needed it; and Mary Walters Riskin at Lone Pine Publishing whose enthusiasm, encouragement, and incisive editorial eye carried us through to the end.

Despite the willing assistance of so many people, there will be some errors in the text, and these are clearly our own. In some cases facilities change over time, and these changes will conflict with information here. We sincerely regret any inconvenience.

Picnics have always been a family enterprise with us, and so is this book. Although Carolyn and Diana have worked closely with us on the writing and art work, each and every one of our nine children has, over the years, introduced major innovations and refinements to our picnicking. Thank you Michael, Carolyn, Diana, Steven, Ginger, Justin, Jason, Annthea and Katy.

There have been so many friends who have taken us on picnics, lent us their books, and shared their ideas, which we have shamelessly adopted — thank you all.

And finally, we would like to thank Grant Kennedy, President of Lone Pine Publishing, for taking serious picnicking seriously!

Key to Symbols

 Picnic Tables

 Water Source

 Toilets

 Shelter

 No Pets Allowed

 Boat Launch

 Swimming

 Fires Allowed (stoves ,or pits,
and wood available)

 Telephone

INTRODUCTION

Picnic Preamble

In our family a picnic is a very special thing. It is a delicate blending of the right people, the right setting, a suitable menu, interesting activities and conversation, and nice weather. When all these elements coincide, the result is inevitably a delightful memory for the participants. Our picnics are recorded in "memory pictures" by one of our daughters, and in photographs by some of the rest of us. Many a family reunion at Christmas is peppered with each of us remembering a different, but splendid picnic, and revitalizing the memories for each other with the full colours of both kinds of pictures.

This book is designed to help you make your picnics memorable occasions, replete with historical anecdotes, legends, adventurous menus and recipes, things to see and do nearby, and a touch of magic here and there. There is no particular logic to the selection of places we simply followed our whims and instincts. Occasionally we sought the settings for history we already knew; a place with a strong aura of the past is Craigellachie, for example, where the last spike of the transcontinental railway was driven in 1885. Sometimes we were overcome by the natural beauty of a site, like the Keremeos Grist Mill or Cascade Falls. Often our sense of whimsy led us to a spot to stop and sit and enjoy, and Granville Island is that kind of place. Several of our picnics reflect the history of native Canadians, since we are aware that they have been visiting or living in many of the best picnic sites for at least 10,000 years. And sometimes our sense of fun triumphed, and the result is exemplified in the Sasquatch picnic.

A picnic is usually a celebration of some sort. Although most picnics are held outside, indoor picnics should not be overlooked, especially in winter. They require less planning, and transportation is easy especially if the picnic is on your living room floor, or in the middle of your king-sized bed. A formal picnic, with cold cuts, potato salad and an appropriate libation, served on the floor in front of the fire, can be great fun for the whole family or for a couple (and there are no mosquitoes, either).

Pages of Picnics

Everyone loves a picnic, so we selected spots which are easily reached by car, usually involving no more than a hundred metres of walking so that each picnic would be accessible to most senior citizens and to little kids. Thus, with reluctance we turned down the wonderful site that required 8 kilometres of steep hiking, and islands accessible only by private boat. Most of the picnics are small-scale, meant for friends, couples, and families. We have, however, included a chapter on planning picnics for large groups, and this includes a few recipes for 100, and the rules to some games which we remember playing in our youths. The picnic at Kimberley includes recipes for 40 people, in case your large groups aren't so large.

Most of our picnic places were discovered as we explored our own region on weekends and in the summer. We found that theme picnics were a great way to educate ourselves and our kids, and the kids quickly became experts in identifying magic picnic places some of them in the heart of the city.

Each of the 40 picnics included in this book has a theme, as do all of our own picnics. The theme may be suggested by the place, the history, or the name, but sometimes the connection is a bit far-fetched, as you will see.

Picnics in Perspective

Why would any sane person leave all the comforts of a modern home to venture off to a wild, untamed place to eat a meal prepared over a campfire, sitting on an old blanket or a rough bench amid ants and mosquitoes, when the most meticulous preparation might get rained on anyway?

Anthropologists tell us that the human species is driven to interact with the elements, to conquer nature, to reaffirm dominance in the natural order of things. This urge to control the wilderness leads to isolated episodes wherein the human species attempts to "civilize" the wild by using propane stoves, deck chairs, plastic canopies, battery-operated fire starters, and in extreme cases, recreation vehicles, to establish a crude replica of the suburban homestead upon a piece of unsettled land.

The first picnics weren't imitations of anything — people ate out and cooked over campfires on nice days because it got stuffy in the caves. As technology went along, cooking methods became refined, and with the concept of the chimney, moved permanently indoors in most societies, ending forever the annoyance of trying to start a fire in the rain.

But not forever. It has been speculated that the notion of picnicking crossed the channel to England from France in the 19th century along with the "cult of nature" influence spawned by Jean Jacques Rousseau and fueled by the Romantic Poets. By now people were living comfortably inside relatively permanent dwellings with such conveniences as indoor plumbing and windows. The simple life of the past was idealized, and living in harmony with nature took on a certain romantic appeal. Romantic idealism is rarely pragmatic, but the adoption of picnicking by the British is either an example of monumental blindness or determined self-deception, given the usual climate of the British Isles. In the never-ending contest between people and nature, it is during the act of picnicking that people are most vulnerable to the elements; to be "rained out" means that nature remains dominant despite technology.

There are several other sociological explanations for the peculiar behaviour displayed by picnickers. These outings can be interpreted as an attempt to escape from the urban industrial environment, an escape from artificiality. Picnic participants may be seeking temporary informality to balance the enforced rigidity of modern daily life. Alternatively, picnics can be seen in a positive light as the reaffirmation of a social unit. For example, making a morose 14-year old son attend a family picnic reaffirms parental power within the family. (But is it worth it?)

The Spanish carry this group affirmation to an extreme, collecting 10,000 people for a week once a year on a mountain top, or alternatively in a swamp, and picnicking and dancing day and night for the duration, without even a Port-a-Potty in sight! During this religious picnic, called a romeria, rain does not diminish the festivities, but is simply ignored; dancing continues, parades march on, masses are held, and fires miraculously continue to burn. Our equivalent of the romeria is the community picnic or agricultural fair, but unlike the Spaniards, we usually go home at night.

Pique-Niques Past

According to the Oxford dictionary the word picnic did not occur in English in literature before 1748. The word is most likely derived from the French *pique-nique*. In England, nineteenth century picnics were a pastime of the rich involving an outing to a pastoral setting and a meal composed of contributions of food from each participant. Hence the rarely used word, picnickery, which implies "a collection of things from various sources, like the provisions at a picnic." The Picnic Society in London was a group of people whose gatherings were characterized by dramatic presentations and other social entertainments to which each member of the Society contributed. Finally, a picnickian is a person who takes part in a picnic. With this broader sense of the word picnic, our readers, fellow picnickians all, will understand our concept of the compleat, or in more contemporary terms, the magic picnic, the components of which are not limited to victuals, but must include an appropriate setting, congenial company, and a mystique. This last component is intangible, but essential. It provides the theme — and the magic part of the picnic. A magic picnic is one in which all components are in place and are savoured and enjoyed by each picnickian.

The art of picnickery is flexible, limited only by the standards and requirements of the particular picnickians. Some issues may be taken for granted, and remain unspoken, such as clothing. What to wear on a picnic is a personal question. It has been addressed by some of our greatest minds at some length, and here we refer you to the famous painting by Edouard Manet entitled "Dejeuner sur l'herbe" (less elegant in English — Lunch on the Grass) in which one of the female picnickians elected to wear nothing at all. We leave these delicate issues to the reader, although we discuss clothes in a general, objective way in our chapter on equipment.

Particularly Precious Picnics

Our family tradition of picnicking was elevated to an art form one day beneath the ruins of an old Spanish fort as we sat (fully dressed) in the shade of a silvery olive orchard, transported by the beauty of the afternoon, the compelling history of the place, and the wonderful tastes of the Andalucian foods and wines which composed our seven course feast, complete with china and crystal! After our return to Canada we continued to seek out "magic" picnics at home, picnics which had the right combination of elements   and we have discovered many such places.

Some of our picnics are less serious than others. The first of these began when we tried to find Black Forest Cake to eat in the German Black Forest. After many stores and bakeries let us down, we finally found a frozen cake in a supermarket and then drove back into the Black Forest from the village to thaw the cake and have our picnic. This sort of theme picnic challenges everyone's imagination, and permits the corny members of the group to display the full range of their talents.

We would be dishonest if we didn't acknowledge a debt to James Michener, who expounded on the art of picnicking before we did in his book on Spain, Iberia. He had discovered the Spanish penchant for picnicking, and later so did we, as we meandered through Spain with our five children in an ancient but loyal Volkswagon van called Vincent (see photo on back cover). This van carried all seven of us, our packs and the thirteen boxes of books that always seem to accompany us throughout Europe, at a steady but slowish speed. Vincent took us to many picnics throughout Spain as we read bits of Michener aloud. The van was probably the best-equipped picnic-mobile in

Europe — carrying a portable table, a portable propane paella cooker, cutlery, china and linens, and a couple of pretty vases for flowers for table settings.

We have developed and refined our picnic equipment since then, and our suggestions are offered in the next chapter of this book. Many picnic sites are equipped with tables and grills and shelters, but some of the sites that we especially like have no amenities whatsoever, other than the magic of the place. You may choose to have an elaborate formal picnic, complete with your own portable table, or you may choose to have a sandwich on a blanket. In some of our picnics we offer both options. We have provided an index of the recipes from all the picnics at the back of the book so that you can mix and match.

Proximate Proportions

Our picnic recipes are expressed sometimes in metric units, sometimes English, and sometimes both. Indeed, it is in the kitchen that Canada's conversion to metric is at its most confusing. Exact conversion produces ridiculous quantities: for example, 1 cup is equal to 236.6 millilitres. The usual way that a Canadian cook copes is by having measuring devices calibrated in both cups and millilitres. Then it is easy to switch systems to match the recipes. The important thing is to stick to the same system throughout the recipe, as it is generally proportion that is more important than actual quantity. For those who have only one kind of measuring cups, the following approximate conversion table is offered.

Approximate Metric Conversions

1/4 tsp	1 ml
1/2 tsp	2 ml
1 tsp	5 ml
1 Tbsp	15 ml
1/4 cup	50 ml
1/2 cup	125 ml
1 cup	250 ml
4 1/2 cups	1 L

Pursuing Picnic Perfection

We expect our readers to fall into two groups: those who already picnic seriously and want to compare their spots with ours; and those who want to become serious picnickers, and just need a little push.

We must acknowledge the suggestions from friends, many of whom will recognize elements of their own picnics in these pages. Our friends did help us as we went along, although they flatly refused to take us seriously as we described the magnitude of the task of picnic-book-writing facing our family. In fact, the most empathetic comment came from our publisher. "Ah, a tough job but someone has to do it!" he said. But was that compassion or envy in his tone?

Everyone has a favourite picnic. As we wandered the province doing our research we found that people who had been strangers to us a moment before had warmed to the word "picnic" and were suddenly confiding intimate family picnic secrets to us in exhaustive detail! There was the family in the pick-up truck who, when asked if there were any good picnic spots in the area, turned the truck around, yelled, "Follow us!" and led us along a logging road part way up a mountain to a favourite place. They told us vignettes of local history that wouldn't be found in reference books, but which added the "magic" to the picnic. This wasn't an isolated example. When we asked one man in a small town museum about the local history he quickly telephoned to his wife to ask her to make up a picnic basket, drove us to his farm to pick her up, and took us all on one of the best picnics we've ever had.

We know that we have not seen, discovered nor even heard of all the great picnic places in B.C. In fact, we would find it very distressing if we had, for much of the fun comes with the joy of discovering a new site, and this is our challenge to our readers. A picnic is an adventure that you share; we invite — nay, we encourage — readers to share their special picnic places for possible future editions of this book. Write to us, care of the publisher. All letters will be answered and suggestions acknowledged.

And now, let's go on a picnic!

Picnic Paraphernalia

In this chapter we provide a checklist which progresses from the very basic kit for the occasional picnicker to the sophisticated gear of the serious dilettante. There is also discussion of the relative merits of different items which reflects our personal biases, but acknowledges other points of view, so that you can make your own informed selections. The following sections are arranged in a progression from a simple picnic kit to a more elaborate set-up.

The Absolute Basics

Also known as the "Boy Scout" or the "Be Prepared" kit, this consists of one Swiss army knife carried at all times in the jacket pocket. This isn't as simple as it seems. Care must be taken when selecting a Swiss army knife because they come with such a delightful array of pop-up gadgets that one is tempted to get the one that does everything including pick teeth, darn socks and yodel. This is unfortunate because knives with all those attachments, if they can still be called knives, weigh so much that they can no longer reside in a pocket but require a belt pouch or pick-up truck to carry them around. Fortunately, the Swiss have priced these knives beyond the reach of most wage-earning picnickers and so, while the temptation may be there, the where-with-all is often not. Our knife, which serves us well, has attachments that:

     flip bottle caps,
     pull corks,
     open cans,
     slice cheese, and
     get the onion pickles from the bottom of the jar.

These are the essential functions, since smacking bottles against rocks to open them is ecologically unsound and potentially dangerous, and an inaccessible can of paté de foie gras can spoil your whole day. These knives are still available for less than $20.

The Basic Picnic Kit

Do you travel much in your car, and do you like the occasional "impromptu" picnic? In that case, in your trunk along with the jumper cables, tire chains, and the half-filled bottle of windshield fluid should be a basic picnic kit. This kit can be kept in a small box, taking up very little space, but permitting spontaneous picnicking without frills. It will do very well for the occasional picnicker, and you can add more equipment if you find you need to.

First there are the basics, the:
> can opener,
> bottle opener,
> cork screw,
> knife suitable for cheese.

While the all-purpose Swiss army machine will do, it also may introduce bits of cork into the wine, spray soda pop all over from punctured tops, and leave nasty jagged edges around the lips of tins. Thus we progress to special purpose devices. The cost is truly a function of what you want to spend, with corkscrews and can openers varying in price from $1.98 to $20 each. Electric can-openers are non-functional, of course, at most picnic sites, so purchase one of the more primitive manual models (or reclaim the old one from the back of the kitchen drawer).

Other convenient — and sometimes essential — bits of equipment that can be tucked into your picnic box are:

Bread knife: Although it may be fashionable to tear chunks of French bread from the loaf, there will be times when you want smooth slices, and this requires a knife with a serrated edge and a least an eight inch (20 cm) blade. We prefer a serrated edge to a sharp French or German chef's knife because it tends to stay sharp longer, and is not quite so lethal when you are fishing around in the picnic kit for something else. This knife is also useful for slicing onions and tomatoes.

Insect repellent: Deep Woods Off is among the best.

Sun tan lotion: It doesn't always rain on picnics. Get a high protection lotion, especially if near lakes, glaciers or the ocean.

Band-aids: Place a few in a plastic bag.

Matches: In the old days when smoking was socially acceptable, matches or other forms of fire-starting apparatus, like lighters, were always available. Now they are not, and one must make a special note to remember them. Bring lots, in a water-proof plastic bag or box. If you really want dependability, most camping stores sell waterproof matches.

Toilet paper: In Boy Scout camping days, this used to be referred to as 1001 because it has 1001 different uses. Keep in an old coffee can, with a tightly-fitting plastic lid to keep it dry.

Garbage bags: Always pack out what you bring to any site.

Flashlight: It doesn't matter what time the picnic starts, at some point in the season you may find yourself stumbling around in the dark, possibly looking for something like car keys or a child's tooth retainer. Check the flashlight occasionally to make sure the batteries are not dead.

Binoculars: Whether you prefer the big field glasses, or one of the small but powerful sets, these are invaluable for spotting birds, looking at mountains, and spying on other picnickers.

Although it probably won't fit in your kit box, you will want a

Blanket: Any old blanket will do, but there are good woolen blankets in matching zipper cases which are sold as car blankets. These have the advantage of doubling as a pillow in the car for tired picnickers.

The final, but essential ingredients of a basic picnic kit are:

Flower, bird and tree identification books: Invaluable aids when wading through swamps, or wandering mountain meadows. There is something nice about knowing that the fuzzy pink plant is really "Rosy Pussytoes."

Standard Equipment Package

Once you get beyond the impromptu picnic and onto a planned, or at least semi-planned, occasion there are certain items that become standard equipment. These items tend, in our case, to live in a cardboard box in the garage, where they can be quickly found. It is the presence of these items that moves picnicking from rustic ad-hockery to a pleasant art form. Since much of the picnicking takes place in parks, which usually have some of the rudiments of civilization such as toilets and fire pits or grills, the equipment package is directed at making the maximum use of those environments. These items, used in addition to the basic kit outlined above are:

Simple first aid kit: Antiseptic ointment; Lanacaine, to treat a cut, burn or bite; tweezers to remove the sliver or nettle; Dettol to kill the germs; an elastic bandage for the sprained or broken ankle; some Tylenol or Aspirin for pain or headache; and some anti-histamines in case of that unlikely instance where someone stirs up a hornets' nest.

Fire makers: It is possible that someone else always gets to picnic spots just before we do and takes all the good wood; or maybe park staff have never tried to burn the firewood they supply. For whatever reason, our dominant impression of the firewood provided in parks is that it is green, impossible to split, and unwilling to burn. To alleviate the distress we take fire starter: nice little white squares of petroleum product that will eventually ignite the most stubborn of firewoods.

Splitting maul: We were originally of the opinion that little hatchets were a potential disaster, best left in the hardware store window, and that a 3-pound, long-handled axe would look after most eventualities. Several frustrating years of trying to split the wood at parks has changed our minds, and we now carry a 6-pound splitting maul (found in most hardware stores, about $25) which adequately serves the purpose. Although all of us can wield it when necessary, it is best to bring along a son still experiencing his "macho" period. Daughters' boyfriends are a satisfactory substitute.

The kitchen cupboard: A number of things which are always available in the cupboard or the fridge are rarely thought of until you are on a picnic and realize that you don't have them. Our little supply box contains: salt, pepper, soya sauce, Worcestershire sauce, mustard, sugar, ground coffee, a small bottle of cooking oil, and a small bottle of dish washing detergent.

Pots and pans: The absolute minimum implements include: a cast iron frying pan, which will turn an uneven fire into an even heat; a pot for boiling things; a coffee pot; and a large plastic basin which does double duty as a food preparation basin and a washing-up bucket. Other items, woks and double boilers and the like, depend on the menu you propose to use but are not part of the standard equipment. Our coffee pot is an old enamel camp coffee pot into which we throw water and grounds; it sits directly upon the fire. We did experiment for a while with a Melita pot, and one of those fancy Italian jobs that has a spring-mounted plunger to push the grounds to the bottom. These were unsuccessful because you want coffee the most when both you and the weather are cold and miserable. The fancy European jobs have no facility for re-warming the coffee, whereas the old pot can just be set, or left, among the coals. In addition, coffee from the fancy systems just doesn't have that nice chewy texture we associate with campfire coffee.

The kitchen sink: Basic items that make life over the coals more bearable are: an old glove for picking hot pots off the stove; a flipper for turning things in the pan; some tongs for grabbing things; a slotted spoon for fishing, and a serving spoon. Remember also to bring a dish rag, scouring pad, and some dish towels.

Coffee cups: Coffee cups merit a listing of their own since they are still an item that is in dispute in this family. There is a faction that likes the tin or enamel cups like the old miners had. Such a cup has the added appeal that when the coffee is cold, the cup can be placed directly on the grill to reheat. The other faction claims that tin cups burn your hands and lips initially, that the coffee cools down too fast, and finally that there is always a chip in the enamel right where your lips meet the rim. This second faction favors a simple Melmac cup (they are used in hospitals) which the first faction feels are ugly. A third faction has been attempting to introduce earthenware mugs, which are, of course, breakable.

The above list should reduce or eliminate most of the preparation hassles associated with picnics. Planning can then focus directly on the menu and on the central — and usually remembered — items such as the disposable plastic plates, cups and cutlery, the plastic table cloth, and the coffee Thermos.

The Garage Sale Picnic Kit

If you begin to picnic more frequently you may prefer not to use plastic disposable equipment. You may progress to the Garage Sale Picnic Kit, which includes:

Old, hard-sided suitcase: This will be your storage and carrying case, so give some thought to the size you want. It isn't an irrevocable decision, however, since these suitcases cost between about $1 and $5. Your sales resistance should prevent you from spending more than that.

Dishes: Select some that please you from the wide variety available at garage sales and flea markets. You may merely upgrade to a classier set of plastic dishes, or you may choose dinner plates of different, but complementary, antique patterns.

Glasses: Select some good glass or crystal goblets. After extensive research, supplemented by numerous field trials, we have discovered that wine tastes terrible when sipped from plastic glasses.

Table cloth: Linen or cotton, not plastic -- and only occasionally found at garage sales. You may have to buy a length of pretty fabric and hem it.

Table cloth clips: Available in camping supply stores, these hold your table cloth down in a breeze (or even a gale force wind).

Spices: In a small box in your suitcase/picnic kit place small quantities of your favourite fresh spices. Use the little bottles they come in, or save old pill containers or small jars.

Bread board: Picnics often involve slicing and serving cheeses, cucumbers, paté, tomatoes, and chunks of smoked salmon. Picnic tables, although they may contain interesting graffiti, sap drippings, and remnants of previous picnics, are not the most hygienic surfaces on which to work. We suggest that you bring your own bread or cheese cutting board. A slab of wood will likely do, but plastic cutting boards are lighter and easier to clean.

The Abercrombie and Fitch Picnic

We feel that we would be doing our readers an injustice if we did not mention that symbol of Yuppie Splendour, the Abercrombie and Fitch Picnic Basket.

This will cost close to $300 for two, and almost $500 for the set for four. It comes with four dinner plates in an exclusive china pattern, a Thermos, stainless steel cutlery, plastic mugs, glass wine glasses, plastic-covered storage containers, a table cloth, and salt and pepper, all neatly placed in a wicker and leather basket.

Although basically a good idea, with a few first rate features (we especially like the china pattern), the selection has a few flaws which must be overcome if it is to be a truly functional picnic basket. We suggest that you throw out the plastic mugs and replace them with china or pottery mugs; replace the stainless cutlery with silver flatware; and replace the glass wine glasses with crystal.

One final accompaniment, absolutely essential if you expect to achieve recognition commensurate with the Yuppie status, is:

The matching table cloth, picnic blanket and helium filled balloon. The balloon is anchored to your picnic table and enables friends and relatives to locate you on a crowded picnic turf. It also helps if the balloon is coordinated with your sports clothes and to the upholstery of your BMW.

Quest for Fire

The metal grills and firewood provided at parks present a continuing challenge to the patience and resourcefulness of the picnic devotee. These pits can be used to cook the occasional hot dog and marshmallow, but for serious cooking they offer frustration, angst, and burned salmon. Thus, as your picnic menus move beyond hot dogs, we suggest you upgrade your fire sources to include some of the following items.

The coleman naphtha gas stove: It's the sportsman's companion, the traditional camp cooker, the burner that always dies when you are not paying attention to it, and the one which causes you to bang your knuckles when pumping it up. The Coleman is cheap to operate, reliable, and reasonably safe. The problem is that you must love and understand your Coleman, know how much to pump it up, always have the little funnel for filling it, and generally pamper it. If you do, it will give you years of dependable service.

The portable hibachi: Shishkabobs grilling over a bed of coals . . . a picture postcard picnic. Our problem is that we never seem to be able to get the charcoal going properly and so the meat takes too long, or is still raw at serving time, and the beautiful bed of coals finally appears just about the time we are packing up to go. Also, we have not yet mastered the problems of transporting charcoal so that it doesn't make a mess in the trunk of the car.

Propane appliances: Fuel from a bottle. We must confess that we tend to like the neat, simple, reliable heat that comes from a propane fire. We do not believe that half the fun of a picnic is fiddling with a fire source; we prefer to transport the close control of a modern kitchen stove to our picnic table. The first of these devices we acquired was the single burner propane gas ring which is a little tripod with the propane bottle forming one leg. This works well for one-dish items like stir-frys in a wok, or frittatas, or soups. It's also great for making coffee. It can change from simmer to boil instantly, and as long as you have a spare bottle, the heat goes on. We have been so happy with this little burner that for cooking multipot meals, instead of going to a two- or three-burner stove, we take two or three single-burner units. This is, however, probably the most expensive means of cooking, since the little propane bottles cost about $5 each.

Propane portable barbecue: Recently introduced, this table-top item weighs about 20 pounds (9 kg), sells for about $50, and runs on propane. The control it offers means that steaks and chops can be grilled — not sacrificed — and since the lid closes, baking is now possible at a picnic.

Dutch oven: There is one historic cooking artifact that is great fun, and a source of excellent meals. This is the traditional Dutch oven which is neither Dutch, nor an oven, but rather is a big cast iron pot with a lid like a pie plate. The Dutch oven can be buried in a fire pit, with coals stacked up on the lid, and left to cook bread, casseroles, or stew.

Gilding the Lily

There are some items which may, by some, be judged as frivolous or decadent, but could still find their way into your picnic kit. These include:

Folding lawn chairs: For many these are not an extra, but are rather a basic necessity. The picnic table that is comfortable to sit at for long periods of time has yet to be developed, and a few lawn chairs provide excellent thrones for elders.

The portable picnic table: Plastic folding picnic tables which seat four and can be easily carried are available for approximately $100. Ours folds into a flat case which remains in the trunk of our car and is useful in underdeveloped picnic spots.

Ice bucket: Used for serving chilled wine or champagne. It is also possible to get pottery bottle containers (they look like a plain flower vase) which you supercool in your freezer or in ice. The wine bottle (white or sparkling wine) rests inside the chilled container on the table, and the wine remains cold throughout the meal.

Portable blender: Battery-operated blenders are fairly new on the market and may take a bit of hunting, but they are perfect for mixing margueritas, daquiris, or sauces and salad dressings at the picnic site.

First aid kit: By the time you become a regular picnicker you will need to have a reliable first aid kit. Accidents do happen: ankles get twisted, fingers get cut, wrists get sprained, and people get bitten by all manner of insects. Many such ailments can be treated without spoiling the picnic. We have with us on all picnics a waterproof plastic case containing the following items:

band-aids
3" tensor bandage — extra support for sprains and twisted limbs
Dettol — disinfects wounds

Lanacaine   removes sting from burns and bites
several packages 4 x 4 gauze bandages
several packages 2 x 2 gauze bandages
1 roll 2" gauze bandage
1 roll low-allergy adhesive tape
Scissors
Q-tip swabs
finger splint — to immobilize a sprained or broken finger
   butterfly bandages — to pull together the edges of a cut after it
has been cleaned
Tylenol or Aspirin
A mild antihistamine
   A pocket guide to first aid — for the moments when you panic
and can't remember what to do.

Clothing

Some people wear funny hats, others have a favourite jacket that
is worn only on picnics. Fun and comfort are both important. Picnics
are not to be confused with serious hikes, for which clothing can be
prescribed. Picnics vary widely — what might be right for a city park
picnic might not be right for a ghost town picnic in the mountains.
Still, there are a few general considerations. A light plastic jacket or
poncho that folds up into a tiny pack will be appreciated time and
time again during unexpected showers. Rubber boots are a good idea
if there is a hike near the picnic ground, especially if it passes through
boggy land. Generally we find that on a picnic there is no shortage of
carrying space, as there is on a hike or a longer trip. There is usually
lots of space in the trunk of the car, so the extra pair of boots or
flippers are not a major inconvenience even if they are not used.

Food Storage and Handling

Food storage is an important issue, even if you are only moving
the food a short distance. The danger of food poisoning is serious,
although easily avoided by taking some sensible precautions. The
simplest rule of all is: keep hot foods hot and cold foods cold.
   This caution will require a bit of special equipment, and a little
foresight. For example, if you prepare a lasagna at home for the
picnic, cook it just before you leave, wrap it in newspapers or other
insulation material, and transport it in a box or, ideally, in a picnic
cooler with other hot foods. A cooler can be used to transport both hot
and cold foods, but not together. A cooler, after all, is only an
insulated box with handles. The point is to keep the meal as hot as
possible during transfer. Similarly, if a potato salad is included in
your menu, make it the day of the picnic and chill it thoroughly in the

refrigerator. Just before leaving, place it in an ice-filled cooler, or otherwise insulate it to keep it well-chilled all the way to the picnic table. It is a good idea in packing the cooler to place ice blocks or refreezable sacks on top of the food as well as in the bottom of the cooler.

Protein foods require special attention; eggs, meat and milk must be kept cold during transfer. This also applies to foods derived from dairy products, such as yogurt, mayonnaise and cheese. Here Thermos or vacuum bottles, long the mainstay of the hot coffee drinker, can also be used to keep milk, yogurt or a cold soup cold.

Foods containing acid should not be stored or transported in metal containers or pans, even if they have been prepared in them. Although the result is not dangerous, it is displeasing, as the acid will react with the metal to discolour the food, and there will be a slight metallic taste. Vinegar is dilute acetic acid, wine contains acid, and most fruits and vegetables contain acid, especially oranges, lemons, tomatoes and rhubarb. Store and transport these foods and their sauces and juices in plastic or glass containers.

Meat is one of the most dangerous sources of bacteria, and deserves a separate discussion. Buy only fresh meats. Keep them cold during transport and processing. Make sure that all meat is well cooked — rare steaks should be served only if the meat was freshly purchased just before the picnic and then transported at 4 °C (40° F) or less. Your control of temperatures is much less accurate on a picnic, so it is easier to estimate doneness on pieces of meat that are about the same size and thickness.

Chicken is especially hard to judge, but as a precaution, ensure that there is no pink meat near the bones, and that all juices are white, before you serve the meat.

Cooking eventually kills the bacteria in meat, but there is a certain range of warmth, 40° to 140°F (4°C to 60°C), during which bacteria flourish. Be very sure that all meat has been cooked until it reaches a higher temperature than this. If you can't measure with a thermometer, carefully examine the meat before serving.

A word about cutting boards. You may have a nice clean piece of wood or plastic in your picnic kit which you then use to prepare the meat for barbecuing. If you later prepare vegetables or anything else on the cutting board, you will contaminate this food with the bacteria from the uncooked meat. There are two solutions: first, have two cutting boards, one for preparing raw meat and the other for everything else; second, carry with you a solution of Javex and water for washing down the cutting board each time it is used for preparation of raw meat.

One way to avoid some of the dangers of bacterial contamination of picnic meats is to use a marinade. The acid in the marinade slows the growth of bacteria. The marinating container (plastic or glass) should still be kept cold in transit.

This completes the summary of the results of our years of experimenting with picnic equipment. Undoubtedly everyone has his or her own personal preferences, and new gadgets continually appear on the market. We are fairly selective because we still want to keep spare tires in the trunk, and occasionally even carry loads of groceries. We only acquire what will fit in our existing picnic suitcase. A picnic kit is an expression of personal taste — give full rein to yours, to make your picnics easy and fun to organize.

VANCOUVER ISLAND

1 Petroglyph Park / Yellow Point Nanaimo

A Petroglyph Picnic

  🏊

Contrary to what most teenagers believe, Rock Artists were here long before the invention of the electric bass and the moog synthesizer. We know they were here, but we don't know when, nor do we know who they were. It may be hundreds or even thousands of years since people began to chisel and paint the rocks to create this rock art.

How to get there

Birds, wolves, lizards and sea monsters await visitors to Petroglyph Park on the southern outskirts of Nanaimo on the east side of Highway 1. Because of a median strip dividing the road, you cannot get to the park when going south on

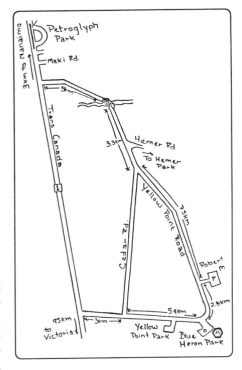

the highway; instead you must overshoot to the next intersection and enter the park driving north. The petroglyphs are the reason for this picnic, but there is no suitable place in the park to eat.

We suggest a lovely little picnic spot called Blue Heron Park on Yellow Point. This park is an isolated oceanside bit of magic that makes it well worth the 17 km drive. The short, direct way to the park is to drive south on Highway 1 from the Petroglyph Park for 14 km (9 mi.), to Yellow Point Road. Turn left (east) on Yellow Point Road, and find Blue Heron Park about 8.5 km (5 mi.) farther on the right. An alternative, and more scenic route, is to turn left on Cedar Road, 3 km south of the Petroglyph Park, and follow it to Yellow Point Road.

Petroglyphs

A petroglyph is a picture or pattern which has been carved, chipped or hammered into the rock face by human hands. A pictograph is a painting on a rock-face, usually done with ochre or other natural substances. Both are sometimes referred to as 'rock art.' These images were carved in rock, usually sandstone, by prehistoric native people. Experts believe that these carvings date back several hundred years. It is difficult to date the carvings because, unlike other archaeological artifacts, they are not lying in the ground in association with other things that can be easily dated, such as tools or the remains of an ancient fire.

The images are usually thought to be of religious significance to early peoples in the region. Figures of animals or people can often be discerned, although some part of the figure may be exaggerated, or extra limbs added. Some of the images are thought to be representations of spirits.

The Nanaimo site, a great sandstone ridge overlooking the harbour, has numerous figures of humans, animals, birds and fish. It has been suggested that the ridge was a site of ancient rituals, and some of the figures suggest puberty rites. Alternatively, it could be that this was just a nice piece of soft flat rock where people came who liked to draw.

British Columbia is especially rich in petroglyph sites; over 50 have been identified. Unfortunately many have been damaged by vandals, environmental chemicals, or real estate development, and the government now protects some of the sites. The petroglyphs in Petroglyph Park are casts of original carvings: the originals were deteriorating rapidly, and had been badly vandalized. The casts reveal the original clarity, and permit an observer to wonder at the purpose of these pictures in stone. What sort of magic did they work?

Things to do and see

1. Take home a "rubbing" suitable for framing and hanging in the living room. Rubbing is what we all did as children when we stretched a piece of paper over a coin and scribbled over the area with a soft lead pencil: an image of the coin was our reward. Rubbing became especially popular in the 1960s and 1970s as many North American youths (our children included) toured Europe and found the beautiful medieval funeral brasses in the ancient churches. A few hours spent on your knees in a cold church and you were rewarded with a rubbing of a memorial likeness of a medieval knight. This same technique can be used to record and reproduce petroglyphs.

The actual petroglyphs at this site are priceless historic monuments and so, to protect them from further deterioration, they have been placed under protective covers. However, casts have been made of the petroglyphs and these casts are available and accessible for making rubbings.

To make a petroglyph rubbing, stretch a piece of cotton cloth across the casting. Fasten the cloth firmly down with masking tape, then rub crayon or cobbler's wax (heelball) lightly across the area of the carving. The design of the grooved lines underneath will emerge in white on the cloth. Stretch and frame your rubbing, and when it is hanging in your living room you can speculate on who did it, and why, and what it really means, anyway.

2. At Ladysmith, 29 km (18 mi.) south of Nanaimo, visit the Crown Forest Industries Arboretum and Museum. It contains early logging equipment, and trees from around the world including an English yew, and a Chinese dawn redwood. It is on Highway 1, and open daily.

3. If you are in Nanaimo in mid-July, check at the local tourist infocentre for the time of the World Famous Bathtub Race from Nanaimo to Vancouver's Kitsilano Beach.

Things to eat

Cold salmon cakes and "Indian ice cream" make this picnic unforgettable. Traditional Indian ice cream has been, and still is, a very popular treat. It is made from soapberries, which are combined with water and whipped to a light, frothy foam with the consistency of a beaten egg white and the colour of pale pink salmon. Traditionally the mixture was beaten with a bundle of inner cedar bark or a sala branch and sweetened to a sweet-sour taste. You can make a treat of similar taste with raspberries, yogurt, sour cream and honey.

MENU

Salmon Cakes
Tossed Green Salad
Assorted Pickles
Indian Ice Cream

Salmon Cakes

(Serves 6)

1 pound canned salmon with liquid
1/3 cup flour
2 eggs, slightly beaten
salt and pepper, to taste
1/2 cup milk, or enough to make a mixture that can be handled without
falling apart
parsley and tarragon to taste
bread crumbs

Mix all the ingredients except the bread crumbs. Shape into flattened cakes. Roll in bread crumbs and place onto a well-greased cookie sheet. Bake in a moderate oven, 350 °F, for 20-30 minutes, or until done. You may also fry these cakes at the picnic site in a frying pan that has been lightly greased.

Indian Ice Cream

(Serves 10-12)

1 quart fresh raspberries or 1 pkg. frozen berries
1 tub plain yogurt
1 small tub sour cream
honey to taste

If using frozen berries, thaw and drain. Mix the berries with the yogurt, the sour cream and honey to taste. Remember that this dessert must have a slightly sour taste, so do not add all the sour cream at once. Add the sour cream and honey alternately until you get the desired taste. Using an electric or hand mixer, beat well until mixed and frothy. Keep cool until served.

2 Wikaninnish Beach Pacific Rim Park
An Ocean Picnic

Land's End is the name given to a point on the southwest corner of England, where a rocky headland juts out into an angry Atlantic Ocean; an appropriate name from a people who knew that to go farther was folly. Pacific Rim National Park, a thin strip along the west coast of Vancouver Island, is a similar sort of place. It is a desolate place of sand, bog and rain forest where sea lions frolic, whales keep watch, and the waves hammer away at the shore. It is a place of great beauty, and a place where we feel humble when confronted by nature's raw power.

How to get there

The picnic site we have chosen is at Wickaninnish Beach on the Long Beach unit of Pacific Rim National Park. Long Beach is reached by driving about 115 km on a winding mountain highway (# 4) from Port Alberni. The picnic table we prefer is found by turning right into the parking lot and then finding the sign that says Trail D. The table is about 15 m (50 feet) beyond. Dress warmly and bring sweaters and other warm things. Although our friends tell us that the weather out on the rim can be warm and glorious, our experience tells us it can

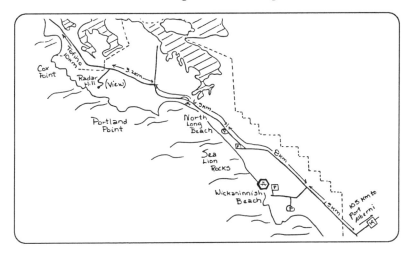

also be wet and miserable. The water is swimmable, if you avoid the rip tides, but it is cold so you can't stay in it long. Beware of hypothermia — a wetsuit is a good idea. Since the beach is so far from anywhere, the trip takes on aspects of an expedition, so try to plan for all varieties of weather: you will probably get them. Remember your binoculars, as the scenery along the trip is really worth it, even in inclement weather.

Whales and Lions

In the spring the migrating gray whales swim past the beach on their annual journey from Baja, Mexico, to the Arctic. The first ones are seen in late February, with the bulk passing between mid-March and mid-April. Although most go north to the arctic feeding grounds, the occasional one has been known to stick around all summer to amuse and entertain picnickers. The whales also pass Long Beach in December on their return migration, but are far out to sea and rarely seen.

Had you been strolling on Long Beach at the turn of the century it is unlikely that you would have seen a gray whale. At that time they were being hunted relentlessly and the population was all but annihilated. International whaling protection was adopted in 1947 and since then the herd has increased from a few hundred to over 18,000. Currently the International Whaling Commission permits an annual catch of 180 gray whales by the native peoples of Alaska and Siberia.

Sea Lion Rocks is the name given to the cluster of barren, inhospitable rocks that stand about 1.5 km off the beach. (They are about 5 km north of the picnic table.) It is on these rocks that northern sea lions (Eumetopias jubata) choose to rest and sun themselves at various times of the year.

The northern sea lion is the largest of the seal group and larger than any land carnivore. A mature male can be up to 4 m (12 feet) in length and may weigh 1000 kg (2200 lbs).

By day the sea lions rest on the rocks, the males occasionally engaging in mock battles to establish territory and dominance. At night they fish and surf. The number of sea lions on the rocks varies from a peak in late spring to only a few by September.

Things to see and do

1. Watch for whales. Scan the ocean surface for a spout, a spray of tiny water droplets from the blowhole on top of the whale's head. Then use the binoculars for a better look.

2. Move up the beach and watch the sea lions.

Wickaninnish Beach

3. Frolic in the waves.

4. Examine the life of the inter-tidal zone. The park's Information Centre (open mid-March to mid-October) has a great pamphlet. Interpretive programs, including guided walks, are available during the summer months.

5. Check the park hiking trails. These are a number of interesting short (2-3 km) hiking trails. Again, check with the Information Centre for a hiker's guide.

6. This is a great place for the amateur or professional photographer.

7. Visit the displays, exhibits and films in Wickaninnish Centre, explaining the ecology of the open sea.

Things to eat

As well as salmon, other varieties of fish are very popular among the coastal native people. In the following menu halibut may be served instead of, or with, the salmon. Young thimbleberry or salmonberry shoots make a fine ending to this cook-out. The young shoots are found in the underbrush during the spring.

Caution: make sure you have a reliable plant book along for reference when gathering these plants, as there are many poisonous plants in the forest that can be picked by mistake. If you are not feeling adventurous, pack some fresh raspberries and whipped cream to serve as dessert.

MENU

Barbecued Salmon Steaks
or
Poached Halibut
Crisp Fresh Vegetables
Wild Berry Shoots and Sugar

Grill the salmon steaks to perfection and baste with herbed butter before serving with lemon wedges. Serve with a crisp, tossed green salad. To prepare the halibut dish, bring along your wok and have a meal-in-one. Serve the halibut with some fresh vegetables as a side dish.

Poached Halibut

halibut steaks, cut into chunks (bring enough for everyone)
a few onions, cut into slices
enough potatoes for everyone, cut into pieces
salt and pepper to taste
butter
milk

Rub the wok with butter, put the halibut chunks, onion slices, pieces of potato, and seasoning into the wok. Pour the milk over the fish mixture. If you are cooking this for a lot of people, adjust the milk so that you do not have an excess. The fish and vegetables will cook with a moderate amount of milk as the wok is covered during the cooking. Before covering the wok and setting it on the barbecue or fire grill, dot the mixture with butter. Cook for about an hour, checking frequently to ensure that the heat is not too high.

Wild Berry Shoots and Sugar

Pick wild thimbleberry or salmonberry shoots in the spring. Peel the tough outer skins off. Dip into sugar and munch away. It's just like eating candy, as the canes are sweet and succulent.

3 Cathedral Forest Port Alberni
A Pining Picnic

Douglas, David - botanist
Born at Scone near Perth, Scotland - 25 July 1799.

At 23 became a collector for North America for the Horticultural Society of London. He described nearly 200 new plant species, and introduced many species (245) to Europe on his return from North America. About 50 plant species and one genus are named for him including that sentinel of the Pacific coast, the most important tree in the North American lumber trade, the Douglas fir.

He died in Hawaii in 1835 when he accidentally fell into a pit that was used to capture wild bullocks and was trampled.

In the Forestry Building at the University of Alberta is a section of a Douglas fir that was about 900 years old when it was felled. From the counting back of the tree rings (which is called dendrochronology) it was determined that the tree germinated in the year 1083 A.D; it was cut down in 1981. Its diameter is 2.7 metres, or 8 3/4 feet. Marked on the section are labels indicating the size of the tree when the Magna Carta was signed, when Columbus discovered America, and when Canada became a nation. We can never pass this tree without reading the labels, and gazing in wonder. Thus an obvious picnic spot is in one of the remaining stands of these ancient giants — the beautiful and easily accessible grove of Cathedral Forest.

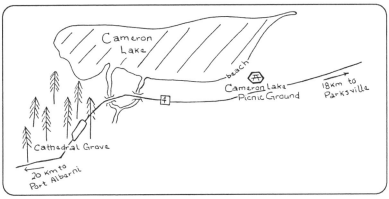

How to get there

Cathedral Grove, also know as MacMillan Provincial Park, is on Highway 4, 20 km (12 1/2 mi.) east of Port Alberni and 22 km (14 mi.) west of Parksville. You will find no picnic site in the Grove itself, so our choice of picnic site is at the Cameron Lake Picnic Ground, 4 km (2 1/2 mi.) to the east of the Grove.

The giant trees of British Columbia

The wonder of the forests in MacMillan Provincial Park are aptly described by the name of the woodland — Cathedral Forest. The magnificent trees tower thirty storeys above the ground and there is little

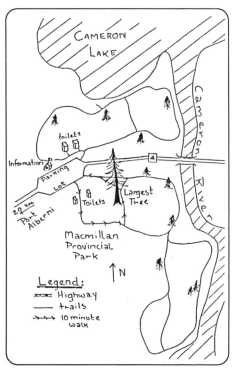

undergrowth between the enormous tree trunks, as the cascading branches spread so thickly that only a few beams of light manage to filter through the canopy to the ground.

A forest fire swept through this area in the late 1600s and so most of the trees are about 300 years old. There are a few that survived the fire and these, which have been dated back 800 years, are the giants of the forest.

The Douglas fir is the tallest of these giants, 75 m (245 ft.) tall and with a trunk circumference of 9 m (29 ft.). It would take six adults holding hands to encircle this tree.

The western red cedar is another of the giants. Although not as tall as the Douglas fir, the cedars more than compensate with their tremendous girth. The largest western red cedar is on Meares Island and it is 43 m (140 ft.) tall, and 19 m (62 ft.) in circumference. Also to be found in the Grove are western hemlocks, grand fir, and broadleaf maples. The broadleaf maples are the puniest trees in the forest by comparison, barely reaching heights of 30 m (98 ft.).

The great trees have been the mainstay of the B.C. forest industry but now their numbers are so diminished that a concerted conservation movement has arisen to protect them. The conservationists point out that it takes only 12 minutes with a chainsaw to fell a tree that took 800 years to grow. The lumbermen counter that the same tree will produce 40,000 board feet of lumber, sufficient to construct four family homes. Cathedral Forest was a gift to the Province of British Columbia from a lumber company.

Things to do

1. Allow lots of time to wander in the Grove. You can take a short, ten-minute walk, but the trees really do merit a longer pe-   riod of contemplation.

Cameron Lake Picnic Ground

2. Set sail on the mail ship, the Lady Rose. She leaves daily at 8 a.m. from the Argyle Street dock in Port Alberni and sails down the inlet to the Pacific. Monday, Wednesday and Friday (June 1 to Sept. 30) she sails to Ucluelet; Tuesday, Thursday and Saturday (year round) to Bamfield and the West Coast Trail. Bring a warm sweater, rain jacket, and wear sensible shoes. Phone (604) 723-8313 for information and reservations.

3. Visit the "Martin Mars" water bombers on Sproat Lake. Originally Second World War planes, these giant aircraft are now on active duty fighting forest fires. Tours can be arranged in the non-firefighting season. Sproat Lake is just west of Port Alberni on Hwy. 4.

4. Port Alberni claims to be the Salmon Capital of the World. Take a charter and go after the big ones. The Labour Day Salmon Festival has a first prize of $10,000.

Things to eat

The largest trees in the world are not in B.C. but are in California. The uncontested giant is the bristle cone pine, some of which date back 5,000 years. For that reason, and to please our publisher, Lone Pine Publishing, the picnic menu includes pineapples and pine nuts.

One cannot picnic near Port Alberni without having salmon, but we must also acknowledge the lumber company (MacMillan Park) with a Loggers' Casserole. The meal is rounded out with Lone Pine Salad, and Pineapples and Kirsch.

Smoked Salmon Soup

(Gigonassigan-abo)

This recipe is provided by Mrs. George Clutesi of the Seshelt Tribe at Port Alberni, and is found in *Indian Recipes*, by Bernard Assiniwi.

> 1 pound smoked salmon, sliced
> 32 ounces water
> 1/4 tsp. pepper
> 3/4 cup black mustard leaves

Break the salmon up into small pieces and place in a saucepan with water and pepper; simmer slowly, stirring occasionally, for 15 minutes.

Add the black mustard leaves and simmer another 5 minutes. (Note: black mustard, commonly known as just mustard, has bright yellow flowers in late spring. The young leaves are good as salad greens or potherbs, but must be collected early in the spring, because they become bitter as the plants mature.)

Reheat at the picnic site.

Logging Camp Casserole

(serves 4)

Saute in butter until tender:
> 500 ml fresh mushrooms, sliced

Trim the bones and fat from:
> 4 pork chops
> 6 lamb chops

Brown chops on both sides and place to one side.

Slice:
> 6 potatoes
> 2 onions

Arrange them in the bottom of a large greased casserole dish. Cover with the mushrooms, and sprinkle generously with flour.

Mix together:
> *5 ml salt*
> *2 ml dry mustard*
> *2 ml oregano*
> *5 ml thyme*
> *1 ml coarse ground pepper*
> *5 ml ground rosemary*

Sprinkle half of the spice mixture over the mushrooms.

Scald:
> *500 ml whole milk*

And pour over the casserole.

Prepare top layer of casserole by placing the chops carefully, and sprinkling with remaining spice mixture.

Bake covered for 1 hour in 180 °C (350 °F) oven. Remove cover and bake for additional 15 minutes.

Keep hot by packing casserole in newspaper in box for transport to picnic site. Serves 4 hungry loggers.

Lone Pine Salad

(serves 4)

The trick to a nice rice salad is making sure that the rice is not mushy. Use long grain basmuti or Patna rice. Before cooking soak it in boiling water and salt to remove the starchy dust, which often causes it to become sticky, and then rinse in a sieve under cold running water. Proceed to cook the rice as usual.

Mix together:
> *2 cups cooked, cooled rice*
> *1/4 cup finely chopped red pepper*
> *1/4 cup finely chopped green onions*
> *1/2 cup pine nuts*

Dress with:
> *1/2 cup plain yogurt*
> *1 Tbsp. lemon juice*
> *dash of cayenne*
> *1/4 tsp. white pepper*

Picnic Pineapple

(serves 4)

The day before the picnic:

Cut a fresh pineapple into chunks, pour over it 2 ounces of Kirsch, and refrigerate.

At the picnic site:

Mix the pineapple chunks with vanilla ice cream that has been allowed to soften, but not melt (the drive to the picnic site might just do this for you).

Serve with sugar cookies that you have cut with your Christmas Tree cutter.

To carry this picnic to its logical pinnacle, prepare the following beverage.

Pine Tea

Soak half a cup of chopped or broken young pine twigs and needles in boiling water. Let steep until cool enough to drink. Serve with lemon and/or sweetener.

Note: it doesn't matter if you cannot distinguish between pine, spruce, fir or juniper. They all make good tea.

4 Butchart Gardens Victoria

The Green Thumb Picnic

When Jenny Butchart moved to Victoria just after the turn of the century, she found that her own natural affinity for growing things combined well with the climate of the island to produce magical results. Within a few years her gardens were attracting hundreds of visitors, people who were welcome to sip their tea on the concrete benches provided by the cement factory of her husband, Robert. Robert died in 1943, followed by Jenny in 1950, but Jenny's garden remains a legendary place of peace and beauty.

How to get there

The Butchart Gardens are 21 km (13 mi.) north of downtown Victoria, and 20 km (12 1/2 mi.) south of the Vancouver-Victoria ferry terminal at Swartz Bay.

From Victoria, take Highway 17 North to the Brentwood-Butchart Gardens turnoff. Turn left onto Keating X Road, and drive 5.5 km (3 1/3 mi.) to the Gardens.

From the Vancouver-Victoria ferry, drive south on Highway 17 to the Airport-Brentwood turnoff. Turn right onto McTavish Road, and follow to Highway 17A South. Turn left here, and follow 9 km (5 1/2 mi.) to the junction of Benvenuto/Keating X Road. Turn right on Benvenuto, and drive 2 km (1 1/4 mi.) to the gardens.

The gardens are open daily at 9 a.m.; closing time varies from 11 p.m. in July

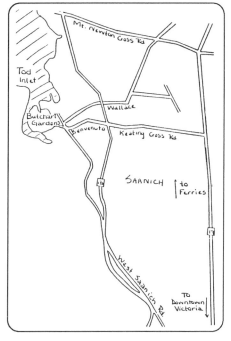

and August to earlier during other seasons. The gardens are at their most attractive between March and October.

You will find the picnic tables on the grass verges around the parking lot. Our favourite is the one next to the pond, by the flowers.

Jenny's legacy

Jenny Butchart was already in her middle years when she decided to turn the old quarry into a sunken

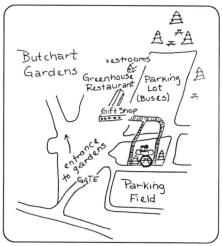

garden. Born and raised in Toronto, Jenny Foster Kennedy married Robert Pim Butchart of Owen Sound, a dry goods merchant. As time went on, Robert became interested in manufacturing Portland cement. The process required large quantities of limestone, and Robert knew of extensive limestone deposits on the west coast. In 1904 he built a factory at Tod Inlet, and the family established their home nearby. Although she had not gardened much before, Jenny planted a Japanese garden facing the cove. She learned about flowers from books, from neighbours, and from the employees of Robert's cement plant. By 1909 the limestone quarry nearest the house was exhausted, and abandoned. Its ugliness was a challenge to Jenny. She had tons of black earth brought in from neighbouring farms, creating a growing surface on the bottom of the quarry. She herself was lowered down the 50-foot walls into the quarry in a chair so that she could personally direct the development of the garden.

Soon the sunken garden was established, and this was followed by a formal Italian garden — and then by thousands of visitors, as word of Jenny's green thumb spread. The Butcharts travelled extensively, always returning to the estate with a few more flower cuttings and seeds. By the 1920s their estate, called Benvenuto (the Italian word for "welcome"), was a regular attraction to Victoria's visitors and residents alike. And often visitors would be met and guided through the gardens by a diminutive lady in a straw hat with an encyclopedic knowledge of the plants. Although she preferred to masquerade as an anonymous gardener, Jenny Butchart enjoyed showing people through her wonderful garden, secretly savouring their uninhibited pleasure in the landscape she had created.

Butchart Gardens

The gardens

The gardens cover approximately 50 acres of the 135-acre estate. Ian Ross, the present owner and administrator of the gardens, extends and enhances the work of his grandparents, Jenny and Robert Butchart. The gardens are open daily year round, with a special Christmas light display in December. The ornamental beds flower continuously from March to October as thousands of bedding plants and perennials bloom according to a carefully planned schedule. A botanical calendar brochure is available at the information booth, listing the special features of the garden by month, January through December.

Things to do

1. Bring your camera and practice your photography skills on the colour groupings of flowers as well as on close-ups of individual blossoms. Cameras are available on loan if you forget yours.

2. Visit the gardens at night, June through September. Hidden lights throughout the gardens create a magical atmosphere entirely different from the daytime.

3. Attend the *Just for Fun* revue on stage in the gardens on week-nights, or the puppet show on Sunday afternoons, in July and August.

4. Watch the fireworks display on Saturday evenings in July and August. Heavy traffic may force early closure of the admission gates, so plan to arrive early.

5. Buy some seeds packaged from the gardens, and enhance your own garden according to the enduring inspiration that is the legacy of a visit to the Butchart Gardens. Seeds and other gifts are available for sale in the Gift Store.

The rainy day option

Have tea in the gracious Dining Room Restaurant, in the home of Jenny and Robert Butchart. In true Victorian fashion, tea with crum-pets, scones and Jersey cream can be had any afternoon. Jenny used to serve tea to visitors until so many were coming that she was forced to limit herself to providing hot water for them to make their own tea.

The Floral Menu

Nasturtium Sandwiches
Marigold Cream Cheese on Melba Toast
Chamomile Tea
Geranium Custard

Nasturtium Sandwiches

Nasturtiums have fallen out of favour in recent years, but have long been a favourite in sandwiches and salads because of their delightfully pungent flavour, and their colour. They are also called Indian Cress.

Select the colours of your choice — nasturtiums come in every shade in the spectrum, from pale yellow to deep burgundy. You should probably bring these from your own garden, as the Butchart family frowns upon people picking theirs.

Use thinly sliced white bread (crusts removed, of course), and spread lightly with unsalted butter. Shred the flowers with your fingers and place on the bread; add a few of the tender seeds and several smaller leaves. Top the sandwiches, cut into dainty triangles and serve, garnished with more of the pretty flowers.

Marigold Cream Cheese

Pick the fresh petals of the marigold (any variety will do) and mix them into softened cream cheese until you like the colour. Spread on Melba Toast.

Geranium Custard

(Serves 4)

Aromatic geraniums are grown by both indoor and outdoor gardeners for their attractive scents. There are several varieties, and any will do for the following custard: rose, lemon, peppermint or apple geraniums.

We love to eat custard, but the hassle and the likelihood of lumps has daunted us for years — until one wonderful day a friend told us that custard can be made easily in the microwave, and failures are almost eliminated. So . . .

Beat together:
  3 eggs
  250 ml sugar
  5 ml vanilla
  1 ml salt

In a microwave casserole place 6 or so leaves from a scented geranium.

Scald 375 ml milk by microwaving in a glass measuring cup at High for 4 minutes. Gradually add the milk to the egg mixture, stirring all the while. Pour egg mixture over the leaves.

Cover with casserole lid, and microwave at Low for 10 - 13 minutes, rotating the casserole 1/4 turn every 3 minutes.

Serve chilled, garnished with geranium blossoms.

Chamomile Tea

Buy chamomile tea bags, available at most grocery stores and all health food stores, or grow your own chamomile, and dry the flower heads.

5 Fort Rodd Hill
Victoria / Esquimalt
A Naval Picnic

The coast artillery batteries at Fort Rodd Hill were built between 1895 and 1900 to protect Esquimalt Harbour. While Victoria Harbour was used by commercial shipping, Esquimalt has been used by the Navy ever since the first Royal Navy warship anchored here in 1848. The British staffed the Pacific coast defences until 1906, when they were turned over to Canadian troops. The fort continued to be an active military station until 1956, by which time more sophisticated weapons had made it obsolete. There is a picnic site with tables and other facilities near the parking lot: for a more private picnic take a blanket to a section of secluded beach where you can enjoy the spectacular view.

How to get there

From central Victoria head north on Douglas Street. Follow the Trans-Canada Highway (#1) out of the city for about 7 km (4 1/2 mi.), then follow the signs that lead you to Highway 1A. Take 1A to the first traffic light and turn left. There is a sign at the intersection pointing the direction to Fort Rodd Hill.

The facility is open from 10 a.m. to 5 p.m.

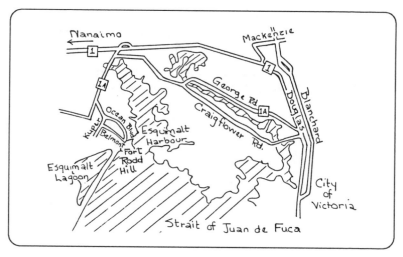

The Royal Victorian Submarine Navy

Fort Rodd Hill's batteries have never fired a shot in anger, but there was one time when they almost did.

It was July of 1914; the British Empire was about to go to war with Germany, and the Government of British Columbia was convinced that Admiral Von Spee and his China Squadron were about to bombard Vancouver and Victoria and then, in cooperation with German residents, invade the Pacific Coast. It seemed that there was little to stop the Germans. Vancouver had no defences; the only warship, the twenty-three-year-old HMCS Rainbow, was away on escort duty, and the Victoria and Esquimalt batteries had obsolete guns and hardly any ammunition.

This situation was discussed by the gentlemen in the Victoria Union Club on the evening of July 29, 1914. One of these gentlemen, a Mr. Paterson of Seattle, volunteered that his firm had just completed building two submarines for the Government of Chile. British Columbia Premier Richard McBride quickly determined to purchase the submarines. He located an ex-captain to conduct negotiations, and a retired Royal Navy officer to inspect the merchandise. He also requested that the commander-in-chief at Esquimalt advise them.

McBride knew that time was of the essence because as soon as the British Empire was formally at war, a neutral country like the United States could not sell them war machines. Thus on the night of August 4, 1914, he sent his rehabilitated team of Navy men to Seattle to collect the subs and move them to Trial Island, five miles outside Canadian waters. The payment, a Province of British Columbia cheque for $1,150,000 was delivered to the Seattle company by a civil servant the Chief Janitor of the Parliament Building.

On the morning of August 5 there was excitement and fear in the batteries. Two submarines had been sighted moving towards Esquimalt harbour. Fortunately, a hurried exchange of phone calls established that they were McBride's subs and not the Germans', and so the awesome firepower of the batteries remained untested.

Later that day a signal was received from the Admiralty instructing them to "Prepare to purchase submarines. Telegraph price," to which the gentlemen of Victoria replied, "Have purchased submarines." For three days, British Columbia had its own Navy, having paid for it with its own funds. On August 7, the federal government took over the subs and CC1 and CC2 joined the Canadian Navy.

Things to do

1. Tour the gun batteries, guardhouse, and barracks. The interpretive displays make this both interesting and enjoyable.

Early morning at Fort Rodd Hill

2. Visit Fisgard Lighthouse. The first permanent light on Canada's west coast, it was built in 1860. The H.M.S. Fisgard was a British ship of the line that did the surveying of the harbour in 1847. All the points and islands around the harbour are named after the officers of the Fisgard.

3. Frolic on the beach below the battery.

4. Visit Royal Roads Military College (Hatley Castle). Once the residence of Premier James Dunsmuir, Hatley Castle and the 700-acre grounds have been a military college since 1939. Exit from Fort Rodd Hill to Highway 1A, and turn left. You are now on the Sooke Road. Stay on this road. Royal Roads Entrance at 2050 Sooke Road is on the left (south). The grounds are open from 10 a.m. to 4 p.m. during the summer and admission is free. Sometimes there are guided tours; phone 380-4660 to enquire.

Things to eat

We insist that you eat submarine sandwiches on this picnic. You can pick them up in advance at any of the submarine sandwich shops in Victoria, or you could make your own at the picnic site from fresh buns and a variety of meat, cheese, tomato and onion slices. Purists will include fresh, dried or pickled chili peppers because, after all, the subs were actually made for Chile, although they never got there.

Our beverage pays tribute to the hearty British sailors who stood watch in the cold grey dawn. They drank lukewarm tea with far too much sugar and milk in it. Bring a Thermos full.

6 Laurel Point Victoria

A Class-Conscious Picnic

Much of Victoria's charm is created by the elegant and distinctly "olde world" buildings that surround the Inner Harbour. The principal buildings — the Parliament, the Empress Hotel, the CPR Terminal, and the Crystal Garden — were all designed by the same architect. His name was Francis Mawson Rattenbury: his buildings were Victorian and neoclassical, his life like a Gothic novel.

How to get there

Find a place to park near the Inner Harbour, preferably near Laurel Point. From there, wander through and around Rattenbury's buildings and after, while lunching on Laurel Point with a commanding view of the Inner Harbour, learn the gruesome details of Rattenbury's life.

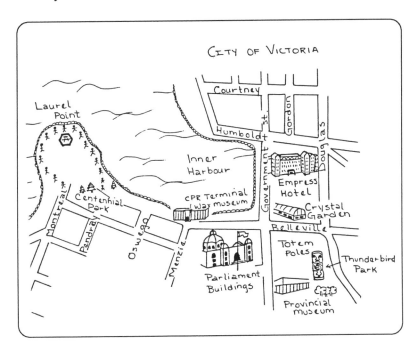

Tour the buildings

The Empress Hotel
It was in 1901 that the voters of Victoria decided to replace the bridge across James Bay with a causeway. This would permit the stinking tidal garbage dump on the mud flats at the end of the bay to be filled in. Because the area was mud to a depth of thirty to forty feet, the Victoria voters could envisage only a park on the reclaimed land. There was no apparent commercial potential because it was assumed that the mud could not support the weight of a major building.

However, the Canadian Pacific Railway had just purchased the Canadian Pacific Navigation Company and was intending to establish a modern, elegant, and expensive steamer service that would run between Victoria, Seattle, and Vancouver. As part of the service a large tourist hotel was required in Victoria. The reclaimed flats in the centre of town were an ideal showpiece site.

Rattenbury, the CPR architect, astounded Victoria by solving the mud problem. He sank timber piles to bedrock, and the Empress Hotel opened its doors in 1908. It was, as the architect intended, a dominating structure that would forever be the centerpiece of the Inner Harbour.

As was also intended, the Empress attracted the rich and famous, including the Prince of Wales, Queen Elizabeth, King George VI, Winston Churchill, and the King of Siam. It has also had its share of elderly long term residents, people so old that it was said in jest, "they read the obituaries in the morning to see if they were still alive."

The Parliament Buildings
Victoria began as a fur trading fort in 1843. In 1847 it became the Pacific headquarters of the Hudson's Bay Company and from this position evolved quite naturally to become the capital of the colony of British Columbia.

The rush to the mainland in the 1880s and '90s started to threaten Victoria's dominance of the province. In 1886 the City of Vancouver was incorporated, and by 1891 the federal census showed the population of Vancouver to be 13,709 — only 3,000 less than that of Victoria! In a move to permanently anchor the capital on the Island, in 1892 the government held an international competition to select a design for a new parliament building. The winner of the competition was Francis Rattenbury, a 25-year-old architect who had only that year come to Victoria from England. The competition specified a final cost of less than $500,000 . . . but the completed buildings cost almost one million dollars!

Although constructed primarily of native materials, the buildings contain a wealth of detail and decoration with gilt and marble

Empress Hotel from Laurel Point

finishes, oak panelling, luxurious carpets, stained glass and plasterwork.

The gilded statue on the top of the main dome is of Captain George Vancouver, and flanking the entrance are statues of Sir James Douglas, the Father of British Columbia, and Judge Mathew Begbie, the so-called hanging judge of the gold rush days.

The grounds and portions of the buildings are open to the public, and regular guided tours are available.

The Crystal Garden

Conceived by Rattenbury, and built by Percy James in 1925, the Crystal Garden was the city's social center. Here Victorians would swim in the giant salt water pool, dance among the palms, have banquets, flower shows, concerts, dog shows and, of course, afternoon tea. When the attraction of The Crystal faded, it was sold to the province for one dollar. The province has subsequently transformed it into a conservatory where, once again, in the tranquil setting, one can have a proper afternoon tea.

The CPR Steamship Terminal

The CPR Steamship Terminal, 468 Belleville Street, currently houses the Wax Museum. This building was completed by Rattenbury in 1924. Having the appearance of a Greek temple this building was commonly referred to as the "Temple to Neptune" (the god of the sea). If you look carefully you can see Neptune's bearded face staring down at you from atop the pillars.

And now:

The True Tale of Francis Mawson Rattenbury
A Gothic Tale of Love and Murder

It was an unknown and inexperienced twenty-five-year-old Francis Rattenbury who won the architectural competition to design the largest and most expensive building in the province — the Parliament Building. Brilliant and headstrong, the young architect withstood the pressures to economize and saw his commission through to a completion that was only 80% over budget (some things never change). Rattenbury's style can be seen in his response to the Chief Commissioner when it was suggested that, as a cost-cutting measure, the marble be omitted:

> The grandeur of the whole scheme would be absolutely ruined should the culminating feature, the Legislative Hall, be poor and commonplace, as it would be if the marble is omitted, for the whole character of the Hall depends entirely on the rich and massive marble columns and we cannot, in any adequate way, replace these with any cheaper imitation material.

The marble was installed and the building was completed by 1897.

Other commissions followed and soon Rattenbury buildings were appearing in Vancouver, Banff, Nelson and Nanaimo. At the height of his fame, in 1898, he married Florence Nunn. In her book, More English than the English, author Terry Reksten comments, "Short and stocky, with a prominent nose and pale blue `frog-like' eyes, Florrie had seemed an odd choice for a successful, handsome young architect, especially since she brought him neither wealth nor social standing. But for the first year of their marriage they seemed to be happy enough . . . ."

However, over time the marriage deteriorated and by the 1920s, they had ceased speaking to each other and were communicating only through their children. Then, in 1923, at age 56, Rattenbury met Alma Pakenham, a woman who, in Ms. Reksten's words was, "Thirty years his junior, beautiful, giddy, a gifted pianist and twice-married woman who smoked cigarettes in public."

Rattenbury divorced Florrie and married Alma. His actions so scandalized Victorian society that he was shunned at his club and excluded from the social set. It was a saddened couple that left Victoria in 1930 for retirement in England.

In retirement the age difference between Alma and Francis began to tell and in 1934, Alma began an affair with their 17-year-old chauffeur, George Stoner. Stoner killed Francis in his sleep to prevent him from discovering the affair.

Alma and Stoner were tried for the murder, but Alma was acquitted and Stoner was sentenced to hang. After the trial, however, Alma committed suicide. Stoner did not in fact hang, and was eventually released from prison.

So ended the tragic saga of Francis Mawson Rattenbury.

Things to eat

We have two menus here, in keeping with fine British Tradition. There is an Upper Class Tea, to be served with fine bone china and the good silver on pristine white linen. And then there is the Working Class Pub Lunch, eaten casually while quaffing ale. The choice is yours.

The Upper Crust Picnic

The upper classes would have watercress sandwiches — nothing else will do!

Watercress sandwiches are known more for their attendant prestige than for their substance. The object is not to get full, but to eat daintily in a restrained fashion. (You may have to make a quick stop at McDonald's after this one.)

The sandwiches are small, white, and precise. Thin slices of white bread without any trace of a crust (and no nutritional value whatsoever) are spread with the following filling — not too much of it. Remember: dainty, and garnished with more — you guessed it — watercress. (Garnishes are not to be eaten; they are purely decorative, and eating them is gauche.)

A note on shape: watercress sandwiches may be cut into "lady fingers" by halving each sandwich, and then cutting the pieces carefully lengthwise; the sandwiches may also be cut with a cookie cutter into simple shapes, such as circles or diamonds — do not use the more frivolous cutters with hearts and Santa Clauses. Arrange the sandwiches artfully on a silver platter. Sip Earl Grey tea with lemon (not sugar).

Watercress Sandwich Filling

50 ml softened cream cheese
50 ml softened butter (no oleomargarine, please!)
5 ml chives
salt and pepper to taste

Mix together. Make the sandwiches, placing a layer of fresh chopped watercress in the centre of each sandwich.

Dessert is English Trifle, and any time that we have had this in England, there were substantial quantities of it. We suspect that this is to make up for the tiny sandwiches. So make lots of trifle, but serve it delicately in crystal bowls, and be inconspicuous when you serve the third helping.

Trifle

Begin with the remains of a stale cake. Place in a bowl and drizzle with rum or sherry. (This is possible among the Upper Classes, because they never finish their cake, and have decanters of sherry everywhere.) Cover this soggy cake with 1/2 cup jam or sweetened fruit if available. (Fudge it with tinned fruit cocktail, if necessary.)

Make a trip to your provisioner, and purchase a tin of Bird's Custard. No other brand will do. Follow instructions to the letter, and when complete, pour the custard over the soggy cake. Cool and serve with a side pitcher of double cream.

Working Class Picnic

Standard pub fare — Melton Mowbray Pie — a hearty crusted meat pie, is served with Branston pickle and ale, and provides a substantial alternative for those who need energy to work for a living. Serve the pieces of pie on a napkin or paper plate, or just pass out chunks to each outstretched hand.

Melton Mowbray Pie

(Serves 4 - 6)

Have on hand pastry dough for 2 pie crusts (see Aunt Nell's Pie Crust).

Roll out pastry to cover the bottom and sides of a greased 20 x 10 x 7 cm (4 x 8 x 3 inch) loaf pan.

Mix together:
500 g pork shoulder, cubed
250 g ham, cubed
1 medium onion, chopped
3 ml sage
3 ml thyme
coarse black pepper to taste
1 ml salt
15 ml Worcestershire Sauce

Place half of this mixture in the loaf pan. Arrange 4-6 peeled, hard-boiled eggs down the middle, end to end. Cover with remaining meat mixture. Press down firmly. Top with pastry crust in which large round steam holes have been punched. Seal the edges.

Bake at 350 °F (190 °C) for 20 minutes, or until pastry is golden. Reduce heat to 250 °F (120 °C) and bake for 1 1/2 hours to cook the meat. Cool.

Soften 30 ml gelatin in cold water, and dissolve in 200 ml hot broth. Pour through a funnel into the steam holes. Cool again. Slice and serve cold with Branston pickle, which you buy at the nearest branch of Crabtree and Evelyn. Alternatively, you should find the Cross and Blackwell equivalent in most larger grocery stores.

SOUTHWESTERN BRITISH COLUMBIA

7 Gibsons The Sunshine Coast
A Beachcomber's Picnic

There is a certain magic in wandering along a beach and surveying the bounty delivered by the tide. Our particular pleasure is beach
glass, broken bits of coloured glass ground smooth by the sand and
the sea. Others find pleasure in rocks and driftwood, or in just
wandering barefoot along the beach while the water licks at one's
toes.

How to get there

A beautiful beach on which to picnic and beachcomb is in Chaster
Park on Bonniebrook Beach, just outside of Gibsons. Gibsons is
reached from Vancouver by taking the Horseshoe Bay Ferry to
Langdale, which is a five-minute drive from Gibsons.

You will enter Gibsons from the north on Marine Drive. At
Molly's Reach (the set of the TV Series, The Beachcombers) the road
doglegs to the right and you are now on Point Street. Turn right after
one block (at the post office), onto Winn Road, and then take the first
left on South Fletcher Road. As you travel south on this road the name
changes to Gower Point Road, then to Stewart, and then back to
Gower Point Road. If you stay on this road for five to ten minutes you
will soon be driving alongside a pleasant, and usually deserted,
beach. Park the car, select an appropriate piece of driftwood for your
back-rest, relax and enjoy the beach and the seagulls.

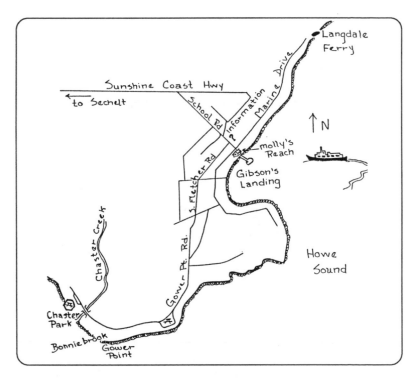

Sunshine and Salmon

The mainland coast north of Vancouver, from Langdale to Lund, is called the Sunshine Coast. It is so named because of its climate of warm summers and balmy winters, and because its annual precipitation of 900 mm is about 170 mm less than Vancouver's.

The first European visitor to these parts was Captain George Vancouver who, while mapping the Pacific coast for the British government, stopped here in June of 1792. The cairn on Gower Point marks the stopping place. It was Vancouver who named it Gower Point: after Admiral Sir Erasmus Gower, Knt. R.N., eldest son of Abel Gower of Glandoven, Pembrokeshire, and one of nineteen children. Erasmus had an illustrious naval career that spanned sixty years.

It was in May of 1886 that 58-year-old George William Gibson and his two grown sons sailed their homemade sloop, the Swamp Angel, from Vancouver into the small sheltered bay just inside Howe Sound. Gibson, a retired Navy lieutenant with a bent for farming was looking for a place with "enough ground to raise vegetables, keep a cow, some chickens and where there is good fishing...." Here in this beautiful bay he found it. He and his sons staked homestead claims on the land, started their market gardens, and the place became known as Gibson's Landing. The choice proved ideal; the land was fertile, there were natural springs in the area, the sea provided salmon, cod and herring, and the new city of Vancouver, just across Howe Sound, provided a market for all they could produce. His wife and family arrived on the first train west in 1887. Gibson lived to be 84 and watched his bay become a community. It was in 1947 that some local businessmen persuaded the post office to change the name from Gibson's Landing to Gibsons.

Salmon Rock, near the entrance of Gibson's Harbour, is one of British Columbia's finest salmon fishing areas. Chinook and coho salmon are present throughout the year, although the best times for fishing are between June and August.

The Sunshine Coast

Things to do

1. Walk along the beach searching for glass and other treasures.

2. Visit Molly's Reach, the set for the CBC TV show, The Beachcombers. If you are lucky enough to arrive when the cast is not filming you can look inside and sign the guest book.

3. Hike to the top of Soames Hill for a panoramic view of Howe Sound and Gibson's Harbour. The hike starts in a parking area, half way between Gibsons and the Langdale ferry terminal, on the west side of the highway. Follow the Old Woods Road to the base of the hill, and then climb up the stairs cut into the logs. Be careful, as the steps can be slippery.

4. Visit the Elphinstone Pioneer Museum which is just across from the post office. The museum has focussed its collection on the Sunshine Coast area and features the Charles Bedford Shell Collection with over 25,000 different shells.

Things to eat

Gibson was a market gardener, with a fishing sideline. Steamed shellfish with crusty bread, a fresh vegetable frittata and a fine white wine are appropriate fare for an afternoon at the beach.

Steamed Shellfish

Catch or buy enough clams and mussels for your picnickers, allowing at least 6 large clams and 4 or 5 mussels per person. If you are gathering them be careful, because although there are no poisonous shellfish, shellfish from polluted waters, or shellfish which have fed on poisonous substances, are indeed dangerous. Red tide or paralytic shellfish poisoning may occur on the West Coast during the summer months (May to October).

Clean shellfish thoroughly, place in a kettle, and add about an inch of water. Cover tightly and steam for 5 - 10 minutes, or until the shells have opened. Serve hot on the shells with melted butter and lemon wedges.

Garden Frittata

(Serves 6)

A frittata is an egg dish, easily made, and with endless variations. It is a staple Italian meal, and lends itself to the colour and flavours of a market garden selection. We often make this over a campfire on picnics. We use either a cast iron skillet with a lid (or use a plate), or what we call "the French Pot," a teflon-lined kettle with a tight-fitting lid which has a steam valve. These pots are made in France, but sold in most houseware departments—a bit pricey, but versatile. In any case, you need a slow fire so as not to burn the eggs, but to cook the vegetables. (The frittata can also be made in advance at home and served cold.)

Heat olive oil in the pan and add a couple of cloves of crushed garlic.

Chop all the vegetables that you plan to use. Sauté, in descending order of cooking time, i.e. the quickest last. Some suggested vegetables are: onions, zucchini, peppers of all colours, celery, broccoli, cauliflower, peas, asparagus, mushrooms.

Mix together:
6 eggs
freshly ground pepper
spices from Italy   — basil, oregano, rosemary and thyme   — fresh, if possible.

Pour over the still-crisp vegetables and stir once. Cover tightly. Cook over low heat for 10 - 15 minutes. To serve, place platter over the skillet and up-end. Serve in pie-shaped wedges.

8 Sasquatch Park Harrison Hot Springs
A Sasquatch Picnic

Sasquatch — from the Salish Indian word Saskehavas meaning mysterious hairy wild men.

The hills around Harrison Lake are Sasquatch Country. Dozens of sightings have been reported, although not one has ever been clearly photographed or tracked. However it is obvious that the provincial government takes this part of its constituency very seriously since it has designated an area for these creatures and made it a provincial park. We were not able to locate the appropriate statute and regulations but we assume that, within the park boundary, hunting, treeing, or otherwise molesting a Sasquatch is prohibited and those caught doing so will be prosecuted to the fullest extent of the law.

How to get there

The picnic is at the beach/picnic area in Sasquatch Provincial Park which is 6.5 km (4 mi.) beyond Harrison Hot Springs on Rockwell Drive. The way is well-signed and leaves Harrison Hot Springs from the west side. It then follows along the edge of Harrison

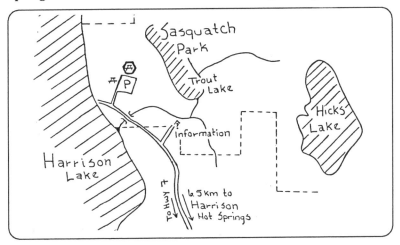

Lake until arriving at the park. From the parking lot one can see a large expanse of grass with picnic tables set a good distance apart. There are so many nice sites: no one is better than any other. Pick one with the view, and the shade, that suits you.

Harrison Hot Springs

The first Cariboo Trail involved travel by boat up the Fraser and the Harrison River to Port Douglas at the northern end of Harrison Lake, then overland to Lillooet, and on to Barkerville. This route was used from 1858 until 1863 when the Royal Engineers completed the Cariboo Waggon Road up the Fraser Canyon. The hot sulphur springs, long used by the Indians as a place to heal "body and spirit," were discovered by the miners one cold winter evening when one fell out of his canoe and discovered that the lake water was warm.

It seems that wherever a hot spring is found, entrepreneurs are quick to follow. The first resort hotel in British Columbia was the 40-room St. Alice Hotel, with its bath houses beside the spring. Fire destroyed the St. Alice in 1920 and in 1926 the present Harrison Hot Springs Hotel was constructed. The Hotel was an internationally famous resort in the 1950s and '60s but entered the '80s with fading grandeur. It was purchased in 1987 by Japanese interests, Itoman and Co. of Tokyo, and they are planning an extensive multimillion dollar restoration.

For the less affluent, there is a public hot pool in the middle of town — not as luxurious, but the hot water is the same.

The Legend of the Sasquatch

Archaeology and Louis Leakey to the contrary, the idea of a "missing link" between the human race and its purported ape ancestors has been immortalized in legends in various parts of the world. We have the Abominable Snowman of the Himalayas, and the Sasquatch of northwest British Columbia, among others. There are reports of Big Foot appearing now and then just south of the American border, but it is thought that this is just another Sasquatch — or a close relative.

The physical characteristics of the Sasquatch are as follows: very tall (perhaps twice the size of a man), extremely hairy, a large forehead sloping down to a flattened nose, and long, pendulous arms. His (or her) footprint is reported to be almost 45 cm long! This certainly fits the ideal image of a missing link, except for one thing: the height. All anthropoids except the gorilla, from which we are clearly not descended, are much smaller than most adult specimens of the human race.

The first references to the Sasquatch are in Indian legends. There were also sightings reported in the diaries of some of the first travellers in the remote mountain regions, and there have been reports of several contemporary sightings. There is even a short bit of film of the Sasquatch, although there is some dispute about its authenticity. It was purportedly taken by an amateur photographer in Washington during the 1960s, and it shows a hairy creature crossing a clearing.

Procedure for Sasquatch Sighting

It is important that you know exactly what to do, in case you actually see a Sasquatch. The following is a procedure designed by a professional anthropologist to maximize the data collected on any Sasquatch sighting.

Sasquatch Protocol
1. Make sure that you have your binoculars near to hand, already adjusted to your eyes, for quick confirmation of the sighting. If the Sasquatch is moving rapidly, it is best to skip this confirmation step and just take a picture or two.

2. Keep your camera (with a telephoto lens attached) with you at all times while you are in the area of the Sasquatch habitat. Make sure there is a fresh film in your camera. (Some of the best Sasquatch photos have been taken without film.) And do remember to take the lens cap off.

3. If at all possible, approach the Sasquatch, saying meaningless, but soothing things in a low voice as you draw near. We don't yet know whether or not the Sasquatch is violent. You will be serving science in either case: if you are killed, we will have evidence that the species is indeed violent; if you survive, we will have evidence to the contrary.

4. In preparation for a trip into Sasquatch country it is best to stop shaving for a week or so, so that your appearance more closely approximates that of an ape.

5. Keep dried meat — preferably some tasty beef jerky, in one pocket, and some carrot and celery sticks in another pocket while in Sasquatch country. If you can get close to the creature, offer first the meat, and then the vegetable. If he eats the meat we will know that he is carnivorous (or that he likes beef jerky); if he eats the vegetables only, he is undoubtedly herbivorous; if the Sasquatch eats everything,

he is omnivorous — and you should likely turn around and run away before he selects you as his next gustatory experiment.

6. Remember to write down everything that happens, and take the results to the nearest university anthropology department.

7. Although these sightings almost always take place when there are no witnesses, it is handy to have one along.

Things to do and see

1. Hunt the Sasquatch. See instructions above.

2. Swim, boat, and fish in Harrison Lake. If you do try fishing make sure you bring strong tackle. In addition to trout, smelt, and salmon, the lake is also home to 7-metre-long sturgeon. In 1935, a whale came to visit the lake, swimming upstream from the ocean.

3. Hike to the Springs. Behind the Hot Springs Building at the west end of town, the trail leads across the Miami River and on to the bubbling source. It is about a five-minute walk. For the more adventurous, stay on the trail as it climbs, and in about 30 minutes you will be at Sandy Cove.

4. Time your picnic for the last weekend of May or September and watch or participate in the Harrison Sand Sculpture Contests. Top prize is $2,000.

5. Visit the Agassiz-Harrison Museum which is a restored 1893 CPR Railway Station. The Museum is on the Agricultural Research Station property just north of Highway 7, in Agassiz. It is open from 10 a.m. until 4 p.m., seven days a week, from mid-May until Labour Day.

6. Visit the Kilby General Store Museum in Harrison Mills. It is a preserved and restored turn-of-the-century general store. To get to the store turn south on Highway 7 at the east end of Harrison River Bridge, approximately 16 km (10 mi.) west of Agassiz. Provincial historic park signs will guide you. Open from 10 a.m. until 4 p.m. from mid-May until Labour Day. There is no admission charge.

Things to Eat

Based upon your research as to the eating habits of a Sasquatch, the picnic menu should be made to match. If the Sasquatch is a vegetarian, then he is surviving in those hills on mushrooms and

---

Wild Mushrooms

An inexperienced mushroom picker should be extremely careful about eating mushrooms collected in the wild. Many edible mushrooms are deceptively similar in appearance to other poisonous species. Some are so closely related that specialists must use microscopic analysis to identify which are the edible species. It is recommended that one accompany a more experienced mushroom picker on a few expeditions before venturing out alone.

In the Rocky Mountains there are a number of poisonous species of mushrooms, and one source (*Buckskin Cookery*) suggests "watch the squirrels. Take what they take." The most commonly consumed and tasty, Rocky Mountain mushrooms are the common morel, the shaggy mane (Old Man's Beard), and the hydnum puffball at the early, pure white stages. You can carry with you the *Guide to Common Mushrooms of British Columbia,* by R.J. Bandoni and A.F. Szczawinski. This is Handbook No. 24 published by the British Columbia Provincial Museum in Victoria.

---

huckleberries, with the occasional pine nut salad thrown in. If he is carnivorous, then all manner of mammals from fat tender marmots to plentiful deer and succulent beaver could be his fare. Because we are uncertain, not yet having completed our research, we suggest the following menu.

Carrot and celery sticks (just in case)
Spinach and Mushroom Salad
Barbecued Beef Ribs
People Cookies
Bloody Marys

Spinach and Mushroom Salad

Wash and sort 1 pound fresh spinach leaves. Tear into a salad bowl. Add 1 1/2 cups sliced fresh mushrooms and 2 Tbsp. capers. Toss with the following dressing:

Whisk:
  1/3 cup vegetable or olive oil
  2 Tbsp. tarragon vinegar

Add:
  1 tsp. sugar
  1 tsp. Dijon mustard

Rena's Ribs

Allow 1 pound spareribs per person. Precook ribs by parboiling them for 4 minutes. Preheat oven to 500°F (260°C). Place the ribs on the rack of a covered roaster. Reduce heat to 350°F (190°C) and bake for 1 hour.

Prepare the sauce at home, too.

Mix together in a pot and simmer:
> *1 cup tomato ketchup*
> *1/4 cup cider vinegar*
> *1 tsp. dry mustard*
> *1 tsp. Worcestershire sauce*
> *1 tsp. paprika*
> *1 clove garlic, crushed*
> *1/2 cup brown sugar*

Bring your portable barbecue to this picnic: one with a lid.

Pour sauce over the cooked ribs, place in barbecue and cook for about 30 minutes with low heat: sauce will be bubbly.

People Cookies

Use your favourite gingerbread cookie recipe and a cookie cutter which turns out cookie men, women and children. If the Sasquatch turns out to be carnivorous, and wants to eat picnickers, you might be able to play for time by offering these.

Bloody Mary Mix

Do Sasquatches drink blood? Or pina coladas? We opt for the former, to be on the safe (?) side.

Fill each tall glass 3/4 full with tomato juice. Add:
> *dash Tabasco sauce*
> *2 shakes of Worcestershire sauce*
> *juice of 1/2 lemon*
> *pepper*
> *dash celery salt*

Some people have also been known to add a jigger of vodka or gin, but then they weren't picnicking in a provincial park. Besides, you should keep your wits about you, in case you do see a Sasquatch.

9 Othello Quintette Tunnels Hope

A Shakespearean Picnic

> Dost thou think,
> because thou art virtuous,
> there shall be no more cakes and ale?
>
> *Twelfth Night:* II, iii, 122

Rambo, Pierre Berton, Shakespeare, and Andrew McCulloch, together with a rugged gorge and some clever engineering combine to make the Othello Tunnels in the Coquihalla Canyon Recreation Area a spectacular site for a picnic.

How to get there

You can reach the tunnels either from the Town of Hope, or from the Coquihalla Highway.

From Wallace Street, the center of Hope, go south on Sixth Avenue to Kawkawa Lake Road. Go east on the Kawkawa Lake Road and across the Coquihalla River, staying to your right. As Kawkawa Lake Road comes to a fork above the lake, stay to the right side following Othello Road past the Westcoast Energy Inc. yard and

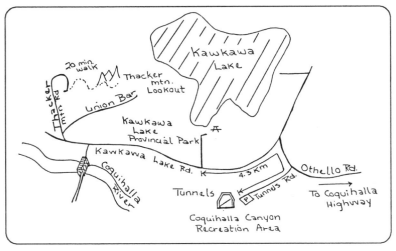

down to the bottom of a long hill. There, make a right turn at Tunnels Road, a well-maintained gravel road.

If you are on the Coquihalla Highway from Hope, the first exit puts you on the Othello Road heading west. Follow this road to Tunnels Road — it is marked by signs for the Coquihalla Recreation Area.

A parking lot, information shelter and pit toilets have been constructed several hundred metres from the first tunnel. Since the path is an abandoned railway grade, the walk is very easy. Our favourite picnic spot is just in front and off to the left of the first tunnel, although there are others along the trail.

Please note that the area is closed in winter, due to ice hazards.

A Canadian path through the cascades

In 1844 an American politician named Polk campaigned for the presidency with a policy that asserted the United States should include not only Oregon, but the entire Pacific coast up to the tip of the then Russian-owned Alaska panhandle. Polk wanted the boundary between British territory and the U.S. to be at the 54th parallel of latitude, and "Fifty-four forty or fight" was his election rally.ng cry. After he was elected he pressed his demands. As a result, in 1846 the British compromised by foregoing Oregon, and the boundary was set at the 49th parallel of latitude.

It would appear that the British negotiators had only a sketchy idea of the geography of the region. By setting the boundary at the 49th, and giving away the Columbia River valley, they effectively isolated the interior of B.C. from the lower Fraser valley and the administrative centre on Vancouver Island.

Between the Hudson's Bay Company's interior fur trading forts of Kamloops and Alexandra, and the supply fort of Langley, lay the formidable Coast and Cascade Mountains. The only passage was through the Fraser Canyon and this route was generally too hazardous and difficult for the HBC fur brigades.

In 1847 a young HBC clerk, Henry Newsham Peers, discovered a route up the Coquihalla River and Peers Creek, over the Hope Pass, and down the Similkameen River. In 1848 he was sent to establish Fort Hope and open this All-British route.

The Kettle Valley Railway

The mines of the boundary district at Greenwood, Rossland, and Trail were originally serviced by American railways and riverboats. In 1901 the Kettle Valley Railway (a spur line of the CPR), regarded by many as the most scenic railway route in the world, was incorporated by federal statute. When it was completed in 1916, it linked with other lines to form a continuous southern railway from the Crowsnest Pass in Alberta to Hope on the Fraser River.

Most of the construction, including the most difficult stretch of the railway, from Hope to Merritt, was undertaken by engineer and Shakespeare devotee, Andrew McCulloch (the man who also designed and built the spectacular spiral railway tunnels near Field). The problem with railway construction is that trains cannot climb steep hills; a four percent grade (rise of four feet in one hundred feet) is about as steep as a track can be. And immediately to the

Othello Tunnels

west of Hope, blocking the entrance to the valley, is a very steep hill (you may recall driving down it). The river passes through this hill in a narrow gorge. The question McCulloch faced was how to get the railway through this impossible terrain.

His answer was the Othello Tunnels which permitted the railway to crisscross the river, but still follow a relatively straight line through the gorge to the valley beyond. It remains to this day a spectacular engineering feat.

This portion of the line was closed by a washout in 1959, and officially abandoned in 1961. The Hope-Princeton Highway, completed in 1949, had already taken much of the railway's freight and passenger traffic anyway.

McCulloch mixed a love of engineering with a love of Shakespeare. With the job of chief engineer goes the right to name the creeks and sidings; the Othello tunnels are just a short distance from Lear siding, and those who drive the Coquihalla Highway will also encounter Juliet Creek.

The tunnels are called the Quintette Tunnels, but you will notice that there are only four tunnels, not five. The name "quintette" originated with the engineers, since the longest tunnel was approached simultaneously by construction crews from both ends, meeting in the middle. Thus there were five portals for four tunnels a quintette. For those who would like more detail about the construction of the tunnels, hunt up the book *McCullough's Wonder*, by Barry Sandon.

Things to do

1. The first, and most exciting, thing to do is to explore the tunnels. The two bridges have been restored by the Canadian Military Engineers, the Hope Chamber of Commerce and B.C. Parks; there are high guardrails, and the bridges are safe to walk on. The wooden arch on the trail is an example of the 1916 tunnel portal technology. The site is so spectacular it was used as the set for several scenes in the Rambo film First Blood, in Shoot to Kill with Sydney Poitier, and for the film based on Pierre Berton's book, The National Dream. Just beyond the far end of the last tunnel is where the Kettle Valley Railway roadbed meets the 1876 Hope-Nicola Valley Cattle Trail, a reminder that Hope is truly the gateway to the interior.

2. If you are here in September or October, check Kawkawa (Sucker) Creek. The chum salmon return to spawn in September, and the coho salmon return in late October. To get to the viewing area, cross the Coquihalla River on Kawkawa Lake Road, and turn onto the first road to your left after crossing the bridge. The parking lot is about 100 m farther on and the signs will guide you to the spawning area.

3. Swim and water ski in Kawkawa Lake.

4. The fur brigades, the gold seekers, the pioneers and the Indians are all represented in the Hope Museum. Reconstructed scenes depict common daily occurrences in the lives of residents of the area long ago, and perhaps not so long ago. These include a schoolroom, a blacksmith shop, a kitchen, a bedroom, and a gold ore concentrator. The museum is at 919 Water Street, and is open 8 a.m. to 8 p.m. during the summer. Admission by donation.

5. Early Saturday morning, January 9, 1965, 46 million cubic metres of earth, rock, and snow plunged down 2,000 metres into the Sumallo Creek valley, filling it to a depth of 61 metres and engulfing and killing four people. The slide site is 17.5 km (10.8 mi.) out of Hope on the Crowsnest Highway, also called the Hope-Princeton Highway (#3). There is a parking area and a viewpoint.

6. Popkum, an unincorporated community 25 minutes west of Hope, combines a beautiful waterfall, Bridal Veil Falls (15 minutes stroll), the spectacular Minter Gardens, Flintstone Park and the Trans-Canada Water Slides. There is truly something for everyone.

Things to eat

> I would give all my fame for a pot of ale,
> and safety.
>
> *Henry V*, III,ii,14.

The Shakespearian influence of the tunnels suggests something British, and so we offer a pub standard, The Plowman's Lunch. It consists of:

Generous wedges of cheddar or Colby cheese
Large pieces of bread, cut from a French baguette and split
European, unsalted butter
Pickled onions — the large kind
Branston pickle
(HP sauce can be substituted but it really isn't as nice)
A fine dark ale

Alternatively, a more substantial, while still British, pub offering:

BILL OF FARE

Pickled Eggs
Toad-in-the-Hole
Tinned Peas
A Pint of Bitter

Pickled Eggs

1 dozen eggs
3 cups white vinegar
2 cups water
2 Tbsp. salt
1 Tbsp. sugar
petals of three marigolds
2 Tbsp. mixed pickling spice

Hard-boil, cool and peel the eggs. Place in a crock or glass jar. Mix together the remaining ingredients in a pot, bring to a boil, reduce heat and simmer for 10 minutes. Pour over eggs, and refrigerate for at least 24 hours before serving.

Note: if marigold petals are not immediately at your disposal, 1/2 tsp. of turmeric can be substituted. This is for colour.

Toad-in-the-Hole

(Serves 4 - 6)

What do you say to a piece of beef and mustard?
William Shakespeare

At Characters Pub in Littlewick Green the secret process is to cut 1 1/2 pounds of steak into 1-inch cubes, place them in a deep dish and soak in a pint of Guinness (Youngs Brewery's Beamish is an acceptable substitute) for 2 days.

Spread the meat in the bottom of a greased casserole.

Make a batter of:
 1 cup flour
 2 eggs
 2 cups milk
 1/2 tsp. salt
and pour over the meat.

Bake in oven for 30 minutes at 350°F (175°C).

Keep warm in newspaper to transport to picnic site, or reheat in your barbecue oven. Not bad served cold, either.

Serve with English mustard.

Tinned Peas

Open tin, pour into a pot, and boil until the peas are almost mush. Serve without draining. (This is how we often encountered peas in Britain.)

10 Fort Langley Langley

A Provisioner's Picnic

It has been suggested at times, quite uncharitably we feel, that Canada is a country founded by a department store. However, it is at places like Fort Langley that the suggestion is reinforced. Here these palisades (15 foot hewn cedar logs) neither repelled attacks nor withstood sieges. The half-pounder cannon has not fired a shot in anger. No, this fort is known for its salted salmon, which it sold to the Sandwich (Hawaiian) Islanders; for wheat and butter, sold to the Russians, and for cranberries sold to the Americans. Such is the history of the fort that was the first European establishment in the Fraser Valley, and is called the birthplace of British Columbia.

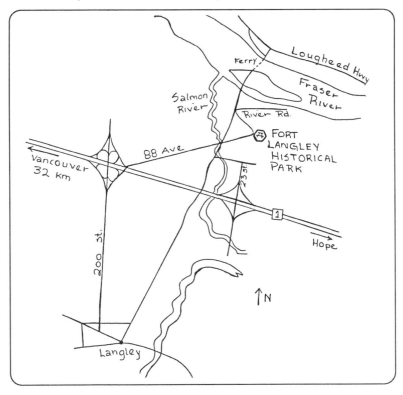

How to get there

Fort Langley is on the south bank of the Fraser River, about 40 kilometres (25 miles) upstream from Vancouver. It can be reached either by driving out the Trans-Canada Highway (Highway 1), or by driving out the Lougheed Highway (Highway 7), and crossing the Albion Ferry. We prefer the north bank approach but

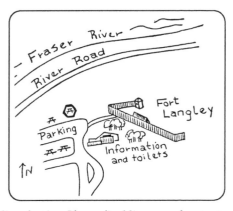

that is just because we like riding ferries. If you find line-ups frustrating, take the south route along the Trans-Canada. In either case, follow the signs to Fort Langley. The fort is open daily, June to September, from 10 a.m. to 6 p.m.

The fort in history

With the union of the North West and the Hudson's Bay Companies in 1821, the British Crown issued a new licence to the Hudson's Bay Company (HBC) giving it exclusive rights to trade west of the Rockies. Unfortunately, as was often the case in history, the American traders did not care to whom the British gave the licences. They continued to trade where they wanted and they were already doing a booming business in furs with the Indians along the Pacific Coast.

The HBC had just emerged from a long and unpleasant battle with the North West Company, and from that it had learned how to conduct trade wars. The basic strategy was to place oneself between the Indians and the competition, and offer better prices. For this they needed a fort at the mouth of the Fraser River, and after a preliminary reconnaissance in 1824, Fort Langley was established in 1827. The site was chosen as the farthest point inland that seagoing vessels of the day could navigate on the Fraser.

The strategy worked, and the HBC quickly cornered the local fur market from the American traders, and with its "Fur Brigades" extended its trading network to the forts in the interior. The company also developed farming in the rich soil around Langley, and traded with the Indians for salmon and cranberries. The salmon were preserved by salting and packing in barrels, which weighed up to 800 pounds. These were developed into major export items, and by 1854 Langley was exporting 2,000 barrels of salted salmon each year.

In 1839 the HBC agreed to lease the trading rights in the Alaska Panhandle from the Russian American (Fur) Company for an annual rent payable in otter skins and specified farm products. The farm products, wheat and butter, came from the company farm at Fort Langley.

1858 was the year Fort Langley peaked. Economic activity, fueled by the Fraser gold rush, was at an all-time high. This was the year when British Columbia was declared a Crown Colony. It was also the year that a steamship called the *Surprise* destroyed the fort's economic base.

Fort Langley was important because it was situated at the head of all inland navigation routes. This is where the goods were transferred between the ocean-going steamers and the Brigade canoes or flat-bottomed cargo *bateaux*: Fort Langley was the terminus. However, in 1858 the *Surprise*, an American side-wheeler with an Indian pilot, steamed right past Fort Langley and on up the Fraser another 78 miles to the HBC Fort Hope. Fort Langley was often bypassed thereafter, and it slowly declined in economic importance until, in 1896, it was abandoned by the HBC.

Fort Langley

Things to do and see

1. Step back in history and visit the Fort. Inside you will see demonstrations of barrel-making and blacksmithing, and displays of Hudson's Bay Company trade goods, and you will meet and talk to characters from the 1850s.

2. The Coast Salish Indians were here 12,000 years before the Europeans. Visit the Langley Centennial Museum and see the exhibits

of Native Indian culture and technology. The museum is on the corner of Mavis and King Streets, and is open from 10 a.m. until 5 p.m. Tuesday to Sunday. There is no admission charge.

3. On the way to Vancouver stop at Surrey and tour the St. Michel Winery. Tasting and tours are a regular feature from May through August. The Winery is at 15050-54A Avenue: phone 576-6741.

4. Visit the Historic Transportation Centre at 17790 Highway 10. The centre has over 100 cars, trucks, planes and motorcycles, and is open from Tuesday to Sunday. Phone 575-5191.

Things to eat

This is certainly a place for a hearty historic Hudson's Bay Post picnic, with salted salmon, bread fresh from the oven, and freshly churned butter.

However, salted salmon is hard to find, bread is hard to keep warm and the "best before" date in the supermarket implies that the butter was not churned yesterday. We suggest smoked salmon spread, bagels, and a soft cream cheese. This may seem somewhat derivative, but the thread is still there; to reassure the purists, bring along some dill pickles that have been aged in old barrels. For dessert, from the *British Columbia Heritage Cookbook*, we have Langley Cranberry Pie.

The appropriate libation for this site would be a tot of Hudson's Bay dark rum (available at your nearby government liquor store) but this is:

a. illegal (you cannot drink at a national historic site); and

b. sufficiently potent to destroy one's sense of taste.

The illegality is unfortunate because some of the products produced by St. Michel's Winery (see above) nicely complement the salmon and cheese, but we suggest some cool water with perhaps a few drops of lemon juice instead.

Smoked Salmon Spread

Place in the blender and blend:
250 g smoked salmon
juice of 1 lemon

Add in a stream:
125 ml melted butter

Mix and add:
125 ml plain yogurt
50 ml fresh dillweed

50 ml white vermouth
pepper to taste

Chill in covered container. Make this several days ahead, and keep it well-chilled.

Langley Cranberry Pie

Preheat oven to 450 °F (230 °C)

Prepare 2 pastry shells — see Aunt Nell's Pastry

Place in a bowl:
1 L fresh cranberries, washed and chopped
375 ml sugar
25 ml flour
50 ml cold water
1 ml salt
15 ml melted butter

Mix together well, place in pie shell, cover with lattice top.

Bake at 450 °F (230 °C) for 15 minutes. Reduce heat to 350 °F (180 °C) and continue baking for 30 minutes.

11 Cascade Falls
Mission

A Father - Daughter Picnic

In everyone's life there are some special places where magic, memories and majesty combine. Cascade Falls is one of John's, and the following is strictly his.

How to get there

Turn north off Highway 7 onto Sylvester Road immediately west of Dewdney. Don't worry about getting confused; there is only one road. After 3.7 km (2.3 mi.) veer to the right where the road forks to stay on Sylvester. Eleven km (7 mi.) after the first fork there is a Cascade Falls Regional Park sign and another road leading off to the right. Turn right again onto Ridgeview Drive and drive for 2 km (1 mi.) up onto the dike to the parking lot. The path starts on the right (east) side of the road.

Handicapped people can view the falls by driving up the forestry road to the first bend to a small parking area. A wheelchair access ramp allows easy access to the upper falls viewpoint.

Cascade Falls

John:
When I was nine years old my father was working for the Fraser

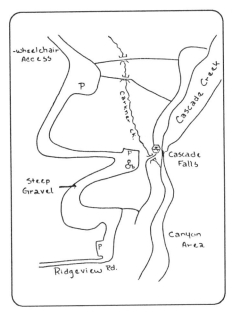

Valley Diking Board and so weekend outings were always up the Fraser to look at some dike, or dredge, or gravel pit. Sometimes the outings were interesting, with neat machinery to watch; sometimes they were just a boring drive. However, on one special occasion I was taken to a hunting lodge off in the mountains. The lodge wasn't particularly memorable, and a nine-year-old boy found little of interest in adult conversation, so I went exploring. A creek ran by the lodge and I started to follow it upstream. This led me into a lush rain-forest and a narrow canyon, and at the end of the canyon was the most beautiful waterfall I had ever seen.

This memory has remained with me and when we started working on this book, I wondered where the place was. I also wondered if a place that had been magic for a nine-year-old would still please a forty-eight-year old. And so, with my daughter Diana, we packed up the picnic basket, grasped our *B.C. Recreational Atlas* (which shows every deer trail and creek) and set off to rediscover my special spot. All I could remember was that it was on the north side of the Fraser Valley.

The task proved easier than we expected. First, there are not that many roads that lead north from the Fraser Valley, and second, someone else had realized what a special spot it was. A tiny sign on Highway 7 said "Cascade Falls" and that was sufficient to send us driving up the Sylvester Road. The falls were there and, except for the paths and the viewpoints being fenced, it was just as I remembered it and just as beautiful. We sat and picnicked beneath the trees, and gazed at the picture-perfect waterfall, and now it is a very special place for Diana, too.

Mission

The town, originally known as Mission City, takes its name from the St. Mary's Indian Mission founded by Father Fouquet, O.M.I. in 1861. The original site became part of the CPR right of way, and in 1865 the Reverend Father built a school, convent and church on the hillside overlooking the valley. It was the first and largest mission in the Pacific Northwest and remained a familiar landmark on the Fraser River for more than one hundred years. In 1960 a new educational institution was built for native children and in 1961 the St. Mary's Mission was officially closed. It was demolished in 1965 and the site was zoned for high-density housing. In 1980 the Mission Heritage Association began its drive to save the historical land; the site is now the Fraser River Heritage Park, run jointly with the Dewdney-Alouette Regional District. On the rock bluff to the north and east of Heritage Park is Westminster Abbey, a Benedictine Abbey established in 1953. It is definitely worth a visit: the stained glass walls and unique church design combine with spectacular views of the Fraser Valley to create an atmosphere of majesty and peace.

Things to see and do

1. Explore Cascade Falls. Paths have been built below, above and around the falls. You can enjoy this beautiful place without ever leaving the path, which is just as well as the forest is delicate.

2. Visit the Sto:lo Bigfoot Moccasin Factory on Highway 7 on the west edge of Mission, and learn of the 16 stages in the creation of a moccasin. Tours are available Monday to Friday during working hours.

3. Visit Westminster Abbey, the Benedictine Abbey in Mission. Tours are offered. Wander along the short path to the rock bluff for a spectacular view of the Fraser Valley.

4. Go to the Fraser River Heritage Park and tour the Old Mission Ruins, the Memorial Garden and the Pioneer Cemetery. The park is 3 km (2 mi.) east of Mission's core, north of Highway 7.

Things to eat

This is a nine-year-old's picnic. The following is a list of things suggested by the nine-year-olds we know.

Reese's Peanut Butter Cups
Cheesies
Salt and Vinegar potato chips
Peanut butter and banana sandwiches
A selection of soda pop
Oreo cookies
Smarties
Marshmallows

12 Capilano Canyon
North Vancouver

Two Sisters Picnic

Capilano is the hereditary name of every chief of the North Vancouver Indians. It was from her friend, Chief Joe Capilano, that the Indian poet, E. Pauline Johnson, learned many of her Vancouver legends. From the lookout at the top of Capilano Canyon, by the Cleveland Dam, one can see the twin peaks called "The Lions of Vancouver." The British called these mountains "the Lions" because of their resemblance to the Landseer Lions in Trafalgar Square. The Indians, however, know that the correct name, the one wrapped in legend, is the Two Sisters.

How to get there

Although the best view of the Two Sisters is from the park and picnic area beside the Cleveland Dam, the more desirable picnic site, and the one we choose, is near the fish hatchery. To reach the site, go north on Capilano Road. You can reach Capilano Road either by taking the Capilano Interchange Exit from the Upper Levels Highway, or from Marine Drive at the north end of the Lions Gate Bridge. Turn off Capilano Road and onto Capilano Park Road. The turn, as can be seen from the map, is an awkward left, from a major road to one not much more than a lane. Follow the signs directing you to the Fish Hatchery. The picnic area is just beyond the parking area, downstream from the hatchery.

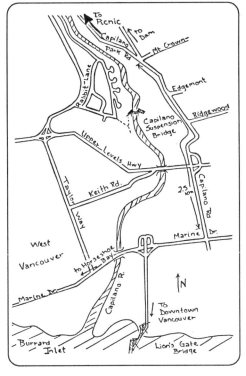

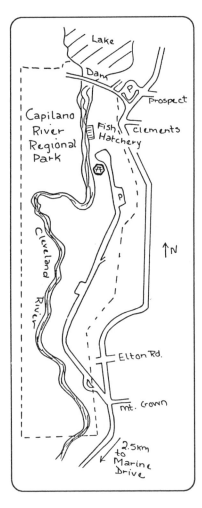

The Legend of the Two Sisters

Many thousands of years ago there lived in the area a great chief who was famous for his wisdom, his wealth, and his prowess in battle. At that time the Indians did not live in peace, but rather were engaged in a great war which had the tribes of what is now the Vancouver region constantly fighting with the Upper Coast Indians (who lived near the present site of Prince Rupert). Giant war canoes moved along the coast and the silence of the night was often broken with the cries of war parties. Hatred, vengeance, strife and horror seemed to fester everywhere on the surface of the earth.

A custom common at the time was to celebrate the passage of a daughter from childhood to womanhood. This was a time of great rejoicing and a girl's parents would hold a great potlatch in her honour. (See Ambleside Picnic for information on the potlatch.) This feast would last many days and, in the case of the daughter of a great chief, there would be guests from many tribes. During the festivities the girl would be exalted on a high seat, for among the Coast Indians womanhood and motherhood were the most honoured of all callings.

A certain great chief had beautiful twin daughters who were coming into womanhood, and he planned a feast such as the Coast had never seen. There were to be many days of rejoicing and people were invited from as far away as the Cariboo and the Island. The people would bring gifts to the girls, and would in turn receive gifts from the chief. Great would be the rejoicing and much honour would be accorded to the young women.

The war was going well for this chief; although there were no major decisive battles, he emerged victorious from all the skirmishes and raids. Confident of his superiority, he left the battle scene to plan his daughters' potlatch.

Seven days before the feast his daughters approached him with a request. Would he, for their sakes, invite the great northern tribe against whom they were fighting to the celebration? He could not, on this occasion, deny his daughters anything and so, on his command, fast war canoes paddled north: not in anger, with weapons, but bearing an invitation to the great feast.

The great northern tribes flocked down the coast to this Feast of the Great Peace. They brought game and fish, gold and white stone beads, baskets and blankets, and they brought their women and children. The hostile war songs ceased and in their place were dancing, the songs of women and the games of children. As a result, a Great Peace came to these two powerful tribes that had always been enemies.

The Great Spirit saw this and was pleased and said, "I will make these maidens immortal." In the cup of his hand he lifted the two maidens up and set them in a high place. A woman was honoured because of her ability to bear children, and these two had borne two mighty offspring — Peace and Brotherhood — each of which was now a great leader in the land.

Pauline Johnson remembers the words of Chief Joe Capilano when once they stood together gazing at the twin peaks:

And on the mountain crest the Chief's daughters can be seen wrapped in the suns, the snows, the stars of all seasons, for they have stood in this high place for thousands of years, and will stand for thousands of years to come, guarding the peace of the Pacific Coast and the quiet of Capilano Canyon.

Legends of Vancouver

Things to do

1. See the Two Sisters (The Lions). It is a short walk, or a longer car ride, to the upper park. You can have your photo (wedding photo, perhaps) taken under the strategically placed arch with the Two Sisters in the background.

2. Tour the Capilano Salmon Hatchery. The salmon population is currently only about one-half of what is was in 1900. The Salmonid Enhancement Program (SEP) is working to change that, and at the Capilano Hatchery over one million eggs are collected and hatched yearly. The hatchery has displays and guided tours, and admission is free. It is open from 8 a.m. until dark every day of the year.

3. Hike in the park. The 160 hectare park provides spectacular

Capilano Canyon

views and scenic terrain. An ideal walk is along the 7.5 km (5 mi.) Capilano Pacific Trail which extends from the Cleveland Dam downriver to Ambleside Park. Have someone drive the car down to the park to pick you up: only the super-fit or the slightly insane will want to walk back up the hill (the dam is about 150 metres, or 500 feet, above the ocean).

4. Take a ride to the top of the world. The Grouse Mountain Superskyride provides breathtaking views of the lower mainland. It is open Monday to Friday, 10 a.m. to 10 p.m., and Saturday and Sunday from 9 a.m. to 10 p.m. You reach the Skyride by travelling north up Capilano Road, which becomes Nancy Green Way: the ride is at the top of the road.

5. Not for the faint of heart, the Capilano Suspension Bridge is the longest and, at 230 feet (70 m), one of the highest pedestrian suspension bridges in the world. It is open summers from 8 a.m. until dark; winters from 9 a.m. until 5 p.m. There is an admission charge.

Things to eat

Although the coastal native people had access to fish, plants, berries, birds and other foods, these were not always in abundant supply because of local variations in temperature and elevation. In fact, there are many descriptions of groups suffering periods of actual or near starvation. Few, if any, foods—other than salmon—could be described as being staples. Nevertheless, native people enjoyed, as they do today, a varied diet of traditional foods depending on what was in season and available in their area.

MENU

Salmon Stir Fry
Pickles
Fresh Vegetables
Cranberry Upside-down Cake

A wok is indispensable at this picnic. For the stir fry dish, pack all the ingredients you need and prepare them in the wok when you get hungry. The following recipe makes a meal for one — multiply the ingredients for up to 4 persons and prepare in the wok at one time.

Salmon Stir Fry

2 Tbsp. oil
1 salmon steak cut into chunks
chopped green onion
1 Tbsp. soy sauce
a few sliced mushrooms
salt and pepper to taste

Heat oil in the wok; sear salmon chunks. Add the green onions with the soy sauce and toss gently. Cover with a lid or foil and cook for a few minutes. Add mushrooms and stir, cover and cook again for a few minutes. Season and serve hot with a platter of crisp, sliced, fresh vegetables and a variety of pickles.

Cranberry Upside-Down Cake

Fresh or frozen whole cranberries *3/4 cup white sugar*
2 Tbsp. lemon juice *1/2 cup milk*
1 Tbsp. butter *1 egg*
1/3 cup brown sugar *1 1/4 cups flour*
1/4 cup margarine *2 tsp. baking powder*
pinch salt

Melt butter in an 8-inch cake pan; add brown sugar and put a thick layer of cranberries over the butter and brown sugar in the pan bottom. For the cake mixture, cream margarine and sugar thoroughly. Add a well-beaten egg. Sift dry ingredients and add alternately with the milk. Pour the batter over the cranberries. Bake at 375 °F for about an hour. When cake is done, turn pan upside-down onto a plate.

13 Shannon Falls Squamish

A Sea Serpent Picnic

According to the Squamish Indian legend, Say-noth-kai, the two-headed sea serpent carved out Shannon Falls by wiggling on the mountain. The height of Shannon Falls, 335 metres (1,100 feet), gives you some idea of the size of the average Pacific Coast sea serpent.

How to get there

The Seaview Highway (Highway 99) is reached by taking the Upper Levels Highway (Highway 1) out of Vancouver and onto Horseshoe Bay. There are a few tense moments when you are sure that you will finish up on a ferry to the Sunshine Coast, and then, at the last minute, you encounter a slip-road off to the right (Highway 99) and you can begin to enjoy some of the most spectacular coastal scenery in British Columbia. Passengers, however, will enjoy it better than the driver for the highway, blasted out of the granite on the east side of Howe Sound, is narrow and curved. Forty km (25 mi.) beyond Horseshoe Bay you will come to Shannon Falls Provincial Park. If possible — that is, if the gate is open — try to get to the upper parking level. It makes for a shorter distance to haul the picnic basket. If the gate is closed, the walk is only a few hundred metres.

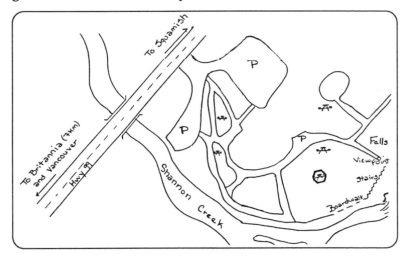

Sea Serpents and the Coast Indians

The Sea Serpent is a fearsome dragon-like creature who is the harbinger of evil. These mythological creatures never attained guardian-spirit status, and only occasionally do they appear on totem poles.

Sisiutl, the two-headed serpent of the Kwakiutl legend, is four feet in diameter and twenty feet long, and always causes death when encountered. Sisiutl often is allied with the Thunderbird, causing havoc and destruction, thunder and lightning.

Tsi-a-kish, another two-headed serpent, is so large that it swallows canoes and occupants. Death does not seem to be instant with Tsi-a-kish because in one myth, when the hero found the serpent and sang a certain song, the monster's stomach burst open and the hero's entire tribe, having been previously devoured, emerged unscathed.

Our favorite sea serpent story concerns the great serpent, Saltchuck Oluk, and is recounted by Pauline Johnson in her book, *Legends of Vancouver.*

It was during the great gold rush craze that Shak-shak, one of the Indian braves who had helped the white miners, returned to his tribe with much money and many gold nuggets. To the dismay of his village, he behaved toward this money just like a whiteman — with greed and avarice. He jeered and laughed at the suggestion of a potlatch; he loved to count and to gloat over his money.

Seeing this the Great Spirit was most distressed, and came out of the sky and said, "Shak-shak, you have made of yourself a loathsome thing; you will not listen to the cry of the hungry, to the call of the old and sick. You will not share your possessions. You have made yourself an outcast from your tribe and disobeyed the ancient laws of your people. Now I will make of you a thing loathed and hated by all men, both red and white. You will have two heads, for your greed has two mouths to bite. One bites the poor, and one bites your own evil heart — and the fangs in these mouths are poison, poison that kills the hungry, and poison that kills your own manhood. Your evil heart will beat in the very centre of your foul body, and he that pierces it will kill the disease of greed forever among his people."

The loathsome monster thus created was over a mile long and his huge ugly body blocked the Burrard Inlet Narrows and fouled the water. It could not move since it was the sacred totem of the white man's world, symbolizing greed and love of money. It was four years before the young Indian boy, Tenas Tyee, fighting with cleanliness and generosity as his weapons, managed to kill the monster of greed that had come among his people.

Things to do

1. Wander along the boardwalk to the Shannon Falls viewpoint. It is hard to sort out how people who measure waterfalls actually do it; we suspect that they count only free unimpeded vertical drop. The *Canadian Encyclopedia's* list of Canadian Waterfalls has Takakkaw Falls (near Field, B.C.) as the highest, with a drop of 380 m, and Niagara Falls in Ontario with a drop of 57 m. Nowhere does it list the Shannon, which from top to bottom falls 335 m. (The encyclopedia also neglects the Della Falls (444 m) near Port Alberni on Vancouver Island; and one of our B.C. references lists Takakkaw at 508 m.) As you will see, whether the water is free-fall or bouncing, 335 m (which is 1,100 feet) is a long way down and makes for a spectacular waterfall.

Shannon Falls

2. Don a hard hat and a raincoat, and tour the mine that was once the British Empire's largest supplier of copper. Over its 70 years of operation the Britannia Mines produced over 600 million kg of copper. Recently declared a National Historic Site, the mine offers guided underground tours on electric trains. There are continuous displays over 365 m (1,200 ft.) of operational mining equipment. The mine is open Wednesday to Sunday, May to September. Call toll-free from Vancouver, 688-8735, for information. Britannia Beach is 7 km (4.5 mi.) south of Shannon Falls on Highway 99.

3. If you are an experienced rock climber you may consider climbing the Stawamus Chief Mountain, the 762 m (2,500 ft.) mountain that overlooks the town of Squamish and resembles the head of an Indian. Otherwise, like us, you may enjoy just looking at it.

4. Squamish, 3 km (2 mi.) beyond Shannon Falls on Highway 99, was a logging town where giant logs were dumped into the sea for towing to the mills. It takes its name from that of the local Indian tribe. In 1909 developers, in an attempt to attract customers, changed the name to Newport. The name was never popular and so, when the Pacific Great Eastern Railway held a contest to select a name for the town, the old name of Squamish won. Visit the Squamish Valley Museum on 2nd Avenue. It is open daily Wednesday to Sunday.

5. Go swimming at Murrin Park, just near Britannia Beach.

For something a little different:

There is a tour which takes you from Vancouver up Howe Sound by boat — the *M.V. Britannia* — to Squamish, providing a tour of Shannon Falls, and then brings you back to Vancouver on the Royal Hudson, an authentic steam-engine train. Departures are at 9 a.m. daily throughout the summer. Phone 681-8687 for ticket reservations and free hotel pick-up.

Things to eat

A sea serpent picnic suggests something squiggly and possibly multi-limbed. Bernard Assiniwi's book, *Indian Recipes*, has one for Nibina-midass, a Kwakiutl word meaning "many legs in deep frying oil," or octopus. This is accompanied by Pickled Shrimp, Squiggly Salad, and completed by Sea Serpent Slice (which to the uninitiated may resemble jelly roll). Perhaps you'll also want to include devilled eggs.

Nibina-Midass (Fried Octopus)

(Serves 4)

Place
   3 small octopuses
(totalling 1 1/2 pounds) in a large saucepan of boiling water for 15 to 25 minutes.

Drain and plunge into cold water. With a rough brush take off the purple skin. Cut off legs and chop them in small, rounded pieces; discard the heads.

Mix together in the corn flour
   1 1/2 tsp. sea salt
   3 wild duck eggs or 10 turtle eggs or 3 hen eggs, beaten
Make a uniform mixture. Dip the octopus leg pieces in this mixture.

Heat
> 1 1/2 cups oil in a frying pan

Fry octopus together with 10 diced wild onions.

Pickled Shrimp

(Serves 4)

Cook, clean and de-vein 500 g shrimp.

Prepare brine:
> 250 ml vinegar
> 125 ml water or shrimp stock
> 5 ml salt
> 1 ml sugar
> 5 ml pickling spice
> 1 clove garlic

Combine in a pot, bring to a boil, and pour over the shrimp in a sterilized jar. Seal, chill before serving.

Squiggly Pasta Salad

(4 to 6 servings)

Prepare ahead and bring along to the picnic:

> 4 cups broccoli florets
> 1 cup baby peas
> 12 stalks asparagus, diagonally
> 　　sliced (optional)
> 1 cup diagonally sliced celery
> 2 cups diagonally sliced zucchini
> 2 Tbsp. vegetable oil
> 12 cherry tomatoes, cut in half
> 2 tsp. minced garlic
> 1/2 cup pine nuts
>
> 1/4 cup chopped parsley
> Salt and pepper
> 1/3 cup butter
> 1 cup whipping cream
> 1/2 cup grated Parmesan cheese
> 2 Tbsp. dried basil or 1/3 cup
> 　　fresh, finely chopped
> 10 large mushrooms, quartered
> 1 lb. squiggly corkscrew pasta
> 　　(rotini)

Blanch broccoli, peas and asparagus, if using, in boiling salted water until just crisp, about 1 to 2 minutes. Rinse under cold water and drain. Set aside with celery and zucchini.

Heat oil in skillet. Sauté tomatoes, garlic, pine nuts and parsley for a few seconds. Season with salt and pepper to taste. Remove from heat. In large heavy casserole, melt butter. Stir in cream, parmesan cheese, basil and mushrooms. Heat through, stirring occasionally.

In large pot of boiling salted water, cook rotini until tender but firm, following package instructions; drain well. Add pasta to cheese-cream mixture in casserole. Toss to coat. Add tomato mixture and vegetables, toss lightly, taste and adjust the seasoning, and keep chilled until you are ready to serve.

Sea Serpent Slice

Heat oven to 375 °F.

Grease sides of a 15x10x1-inch jelly roll pan. Line bottom with waxed paper.

Beat until thick and fluffy:
  3 eggs

Gradually add:
  1 cup sugar
beating well after each addition

Sift together into egg mixture:
  1 cup all-purpose flour
  1 tsp. baking powder
  1/4 tsp. salt.

Beat until smooth, and pour into jelly roll pan.

Bake for 12 -14 minutes or until top is golden brown, and cake springs back to the touch in the centre.

Sift icing sugar over the top of the cake, and turn out on clean dish towel. Roll cake and towel up together loosely from narrow end, and let stand on cake rack until cool. Unroll gently, and remove towel. Spread cake with filling of your choice — jam is usually ours — and roll it up evenly again. Serve in thick slices.

14 Granville Island
Vancouver

A Market Picnic

Granville Island was:
A fishing place for the Indians; a sandbar in False Creek; the industrial heart of Vancouver; a dirty polluted eyesore; and Canada's most exciting experiment in urban revitalization by the federal government.

Granville Island is:
A market comparable to Boston's Faneuil Hall; the site of the Emily Carr College of Art and Design; a place of absolute confusion where cars and pedestrians compete for available space; a village that mixes industrial, commercial, educational, residential, cultural, and recreational land uses together in a tiny area, and a fascinating place to spend a Saturday morning. It's also a great place to have a picnic.

How to get there

Getting there can be more than half the fun, if you are imaginative and out for an adventure. You can:
— Cruise across False Creek on the public mini-ferries from the Aquatic Centre on Beach Ave., the Marina at Vanier Park, Stamps Landing, or the B.C. Complex;
— Catch an Island-bound bus, #50 from Gastown or #51 from Broadway. Phone 261-5100 for schedules and routes;
— Arrive by boat and tie up at the public dock in front of the Market;
— Come by car. From downtown cross the Granville Street Bridge, take the West Fourth Avenue exit ramp, then follow the signs. From the south come along Fir, or Fourth Avenue, and again, follow the signs. Driving on Granville Island can lead to total confusion and consternation. It was once an industrial area where trucks, pedestrians, forklifts, and railway sidings all shared the same space. Revitalized, the Island tries to maintain that ambience. If you can find a space, parking is free on the street for three hours. There are several pay parking areas in addition, tucked into warehouses.
Summer hours are 9 a.m. to 6 p.m., seven days a week; in the winter many of the stores and markets are closed on Mondays.

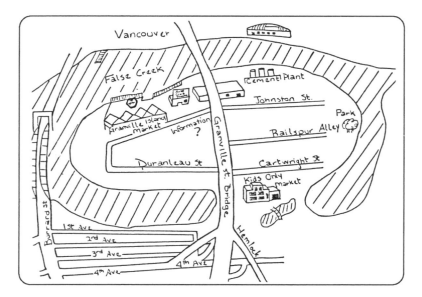

The island in False Creek

Vancouver is a port city, drawing her strength and diversity from both land and sea, and nowhere is this more obvious than on the converted sandbar in the tidal inlet called False Creek.

Long before the loggers and the railway, the Squamish Indians used the sandbar to catch fish. The bar was twenty acres or so at low tide, but at high tide it was submerged. The Indians would construct brush fences that would guide the flounders and smelt into fish corrals where they were trapped when the tide went out.

In 1886 the Canadian Pacific Railway chose Granville as the western terminus of the trans-Canada railroad. They renamed it Vancouver, and the boom was on. The population in 1886 was about 1000 and most of the area was woodland. By 1896 it was 20,000 people; the woodland had given way to houses, streets and warehouses, and there was an increasing need for industrial land.

After some questionable dealing by the provincial government to gain title to the land from the Indians, with continuous controversy among Ottawa, the Province, the City and the CPR as to which authority owned the land in and around False Creek, work started in 1913 to transform the sandbar into an island. A wooden bulkhead was erected around the bar, and over one million cubic yards of sea mud was dredged from the bottom of False Creek and poured into the walls. The result was that in 1916 Vancouver acquired an additional thirty-six acres of prime industrial land in the heart of the city with direct access to the sea and the railway.

Industries were quick to recognize the potential of the new land

and by 1923 there wasn't a vacant site left on the island. There were sawmills and foundries, machine shops and factories, coal companies and roofing firms, and the two major wire rope manufacturers which supplied the province's rapidly developing mining and forestry industries. One rope made in the Wrights' Canadian Rope Factory on Granville Island for the Coalmont Colleries was eight miles long.

The industrial attitude in the first half of this century was not oriented toward pollution control or industrial safety. The plants on Granville Island were unheated and uninsulated industrial buildings. There were no guards on the machinery, no protective glasses for the welders or earplugs for the riveters, and the factories' effluent was dumped directly into False Creek. Thus, although the Island industries represented money and employment to much of Vancouver, they were also a dirty, smelly, noisy eyesore in the middle of the city. Often there was pressure from the populace to remove the industry and to fill False Creek. In the 1960s the Island was considered a seedy blight that must be removed. Plants were burning down and the area began to grow derelict.

Entrepreneurs led the way for Island redevelopment. Bill Harvey and Mitch Taylor bought the old Monsanto Chemical Distillery and converted it into useful and attractive space. It is now the Creek House Project that houses Mulvaney's Restaurant. The municipal and the federal governments picked up on the theme, allowing and encouraging redevelopment that revitalized the district while preserving the Island's industrial history. Thus the structural and spacial integrity of the historic buildings remains undisturbed; renovated buildings still look like factories and warehouses; traffic and people compete for street space; benches, bollards and transformers stand next to one another.

Things to do and see

1. Walk, look and enjoy the incredible diversity. Even non-shoppers will appreciate the colour and variety of the market and the shops.

2. Find a spot to sit, and people-watch. Although some 6 million tourists visit the island each year, it is the people who live and work on the Island and the adjacent neighbourhoods that are its lifeblood. Most of the business comes from people who live within 3 miles of the Island.

3. Rent a boat and tour False Creek. Hourly rentals of power boats are available from the dock in front of the Bridges Restaurant.

Public Dock, Granville Island

4. Watch the free entertainment in the market courtyard.

5. Take the ferry to Vanier Park and the Maritime Museum to see the restored two-masted ketch, St. Roch, which was the first Canadian ship to traverse the Arctic through the Northwest Passage.

Things to eat

This is the place to pick up your picnic in the market, and eat it sitting on a bench by the public dock. But when faced with such an incredible selection, how do you choose?

Our first thought was to get a pile of the world-renowned Golden Mantel Oysters; then we saw the fresh-boiled lobster, then the succulent pickled asparagus. Then the smell from the bakery hit us. Finally, we determined that the suitable feast for the day would be sushi: this because sushi takes a lot of work and skill to prepare, and because it must be eaten while still very fresh. It seemed logical to buy it freshly-made by a talented artist just 20 metres from the picnic spot.

If you have never tried sushi, go cautiously, as raw fish on sticky rice is not everyone's cup of saki! Here is a partial list from which to sample sushi:

Yellow Tail (Hamachi)	Sea Urchin (Uni)
Abalone (Awabi)	Scallop (Hotategai)
Salmon (Shake)	Tuna (Toru)

To eat sushi you can use chop sticks, or you can pick up a bite-sized piece in your fingers, dip it quickly in a side-dish of soy sauce, turn it rice side up and fish side down, (so as not to lose the rice), and place the entire piece in your mouth at once. The visual beauty of each piece should be appreciated, as well as the flavour and texture. Don't rush — if you are really hungry, fill up on some rice before you begin the sushi, so that you will be free to savour each bite.

There are other things available at a sushi bar which are fun to try. Some of our favorites are:

Kappamaki (cucumber and rice wrapped in seaweed)

Norimaki (dried gourd shavings and rice wrapped in seaweed)

Negitoro (tuna and green onion in rice, wrapped in seaweed)

Gari (pickled ginger — a nice taste for cleansing your palate between different sushi samples)

You may wonder what the difference is between sushi and sashimi. Sushi is raw fish served over cold rice with a touch of mustard between the layers. Sashimi is raw fish or meat without the rice. It may be served on a bed of rice, but the rice is not an integral part of the item, as it is with sushi.

Note: in case you are wondering how they get the rice to stick together and stay in place in the sushi, you might like to read the following recipe from *The Complete Book of Japanese Cooking,* by Elizabeth Lambert Ortiz with Mitsuko Endo:

Sushi Rice

(Serves 6)

1 1/8 lb. rice	*4 Tbsp. rice vinegar*
3-inch square of kombu (kelp)	*1 Tbsp. sugar*
2 1/2 cups water	*2 tsp. salt*

Thoroughly wash the rice in several changes of water until the water runs clear, and drain in a sieve for at least 1 hour. Clean the seaweed with a damp cloth and cut with kitchen shears into a half-inch fringe. Bury the seaweed in the rice. Add the water, cover, and bring to a boil over high heat, removing the seaweed just before the water boils. Reduce the heat to moderate and cook for 5 - 6 minutes, then reduce the heat to very low and cook for 15 minutes. Raise the heat to high for 10 seconds, and then let the rice stand off the heat for 10 minutes.

In a small saucepan, combine the rice vinegar, sugar and salt. Heat through, stirring to mix. Turn the rice out into a large, shallow dish, preferably wooden. Pour the vinegar mixture, little by little, over the rice, mixing it with a shamoji (wooden spatula) or a fork, fanning it vigorously to make it glisten.

And now you know why we feel that take-out sushi is economical, both time and energy-wise.

15 Spanish Banks Vancouver
A Spanish Picnic

According to the European rules of conquest and discovery, and because of a Greek named Apostolos Valerianos, British Columbia should be Spanish. Jericho Beach Park on the Spanish Banks is therefore a logical place for a Spanish Picnic.

How to get there

To reach the Spanish Banks from downtown, cross either the Granville or Burrard Bridges and head west on West 4th Avenue. An abrupt curve to the right will indicate that West 4th has become North West Marine Drive. The road reaches almost to the water, and then turns sharply left. Park the car and select a suitable picnic table, one with a view of the bounding main.

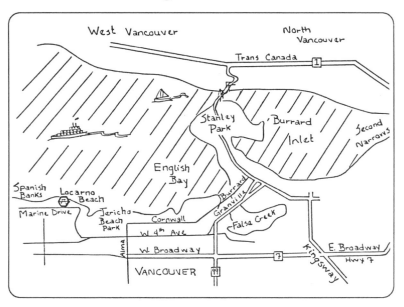

Spanish exploration and conquest

In 1592, the Spanish Viceroy of Mexico sent a ship piloted by Juan de Fuca, whose real name was Apostolos Valerianos, northward on a voyage of discovery. De Fuca followed the coast and at about latitude 47 degrees found a broad inlet that tended to the east. He sailed up the inlet for more than 20 days and found many islands and a broad sea. This he reported, but no one believed him.

In 1774 the *Santiago*, under the command of Juan Josef Perez Hernandez, sailed north as far as the Queen Charlotte Islands and then came south to anchor in Nootka Sound on Vancouver Island to trade with the Indians. The following year Juan Francisco de la Bodega y Quadra sailed the tiny thirty-six foot *Sonora* up to Alaska and took possession at 57 degrees, 20 minutes north latitude. Neither found the fabled inland sea of Juan de Fuca's report.

In July 1778, Captain William Barkley of the fur trading ship Imperial *Eagle* recognized the inlet and named it the Strait of Juan de Fuca; the Spaniard's discovery was finally acknowledged.

In 1778, Captain Cook came up to coast for the British. He missed Juan de Fuca's Strait, but did anchor at Nootka Sound and trade there.

It was Captain George Vancouver who in 1792, entered the Strait of Juan de Fuca for the British and charted the coast; that is, all except a stretch around Point Grey. This he avoided because the Spanish vessels, the *Sutil* and the *Mexicana*, were lying there at anchor. Thus the banks are shown on the Spanish charts, but not on George Vancouver's. This was the reason the officers of the Hudson's Bay Company called this strip of land the Spanish Banks.

Things to see and do

1. Frolic in the sea. Lifeguards are on duty from 11:30 a.m. to 9:00 p.m.

2. Count the 16,000 different plants in the University of British Columbia (UBC) Botanical Garden. The 55-acre garden which includes a medicinal garden, an Asian garden, and a rose garden, is on the UBC Campus at 16th Avenue and South West Marine Drive.

3. See the world's finest collection of Northwest Coast Indian art including the famous totem poles. Just go west from the beach to 6393 N.W. Marine Drive on the UBC campus. The Museum of Anthropology is open Tuesday through Sunday: admission free Tuesday, $2.50 Wednesday through Sunday.

Things to eat

The Spanish picnic has certain basics. There must be a glass or bowl of cold gazpacho soup, there must be olives, and there must be a paella. Other frills, like barbecued salmon, cucumber, tomato and octopus salad, or greasy sugar-dipped churros are optional, but always enjoyable.

MENU

a small glass of chilled fino sherry
a glass of gazpacho
a paella cooked at the table
fresh fruit
sangria

There are many different kinds of gazpacho, the cold vegetable soup favoured by Spaniards. Our favourite recipe comes from southern Spain, and includes bread crumbs. This can be made a day or two before, as chilling only increases the flavour of this wonderful soup. It is usually prepared with a hand grinder — we tend to use the blender, although it produces a more finely textured soup.

Gazpacho

(serves 8)

3/4 kg tomatoes
1 cucumber, peeled and chopped
1 green pepper, chopped
100 g dry bread crumbs
1 clove garlic, peeled
1 medium onion, chopped
2 Tbsp vinegar
1 1/2 tsp olive oil
1 L of water
salt

Reserve 1 tomato for garnish. Scald the rest of the tomatoes in boiling water for 1 minute, then remove skins and slice into quarters. Saute the green pepper, cucumber and onion until soft. Sprinkle the bread crumbs with the vinegar and let stand for a few minutes. In a blender or food chopper grind all the vegetables. Add the bread crumbs and the garlic, with a little of the water. Slowly add the oil, stirring well, and then the rest of the water. Chill well, and serve cold.

Paella

(serves 10)

Spanish are consummate picnickers, and the paella is a uniquely Spanish dish. It has a rice base, but the ingredients vary according to the region, and the pocketbook of the cook. Inland you will likely have chicken or pork in your paella, and by the sea, fish. Our recipe is Andalucian, taught to us by a Madrilena who learned it from her Basque parents. Paella is usually prepared over an open fire, but the grill of your portable barbecue works just as well.

1 1/2 kg rice
saffron
2 medium onions, chopped
4 cloves garlic, chopped
2 green peppers, cut into
small pieces
2 large red peppers, cut
into small pieces
1 tin tomatoes
1 tin peas
1/2 kg shrimp, unshelled
1 kg baby clams
1 kg mussels
5 chicken stock cubes
1 chicken, chopped into
pieces
oil
white wine

Put the saffron to soak in 1/2 cup water.

Maria Isabel Orribaren-Martin, teaching us to make paella over an open fire

Build the fire up and let it burn until you have a good bed of coals. Scrub the clams and mussels and soak in cold water for 1 hour. Remove the heads from the shrimp and wash in cold water.

Smooth the coals out and place the paella pan directly on them (if you don't have a paella pan, 2 large shallow frying pans will do. A wok won't — not enough bottom area). In the pan saute the chicken pieces with the garlic in oil until they are brown, and set them aside. Saute the chopped onions and peppers, and set aside.

In a separate pot boil the clams and shrimps until the clams open.

Add more oil to the paella pan and add the rice to the oil. Saute the rice until it is transparent, 2 - 3 minutes. Take the pan off the fire. Add to the rice the chicken, tomatoes, peppers, onions, clams, shrimp, 5 chicken stock cubes, the saffron liquid, and more liquid (roughly twice the volume of the rice). The liquid that was used to boil the clams is good, but so is water, and so is dry white wine, or chicken stock — or any combination of the above. Rake the coals down so that there is a level place for the pan; return the pan to the fire, and let simmer for 20 minutes. Resist the temptation to stir or cover, but do add more liquid if it seems to be boiling off too quickly.

In a separate pot boil the mussels until they open.

When the paella is cooked (liquid gone), remove it from the fire. Cover with a cloth and let stand for 5 minutes. Split the mussel shells, and arrange mussels on the half-shell as garnish just before serving.

Sangria

(Makes one serving)

In a tall glass, dissolve:
    2 cubes of sugar in *1 oz. brandy*

Add
    1 slice of orange
    1 slice of lemon
    2 maraschino cherries
    1 oz. of Grand Marnier
Crush the fruit slightly with a long-handled spoon

Add
    3 oz. Spanish red wine
    a handful of crushed ice

Fill the glass to the top with soda water.

Serve garnished with fresh fruit slices.

16 Stanley Park Vancouver
A Poet's Picnic

On March 10, 1913, flags flew at half mast throughout Vancouver and offices were closed. The Indian Princess Poet, E. Pauline Johnson, had died and, by special and unique dispensation, was buried in Stanley Park beneath the trees where she loved to wander. Thanks to her, we know the magic and the legends that pervade the trees and the rocks of this special island in the city.

How to get there

The picnic site is at a place called Lumberman's Arch, so named because of the gigantic fir that forms a great gateway. Because of the one-way road system in Stanley Park, there is only one way to get

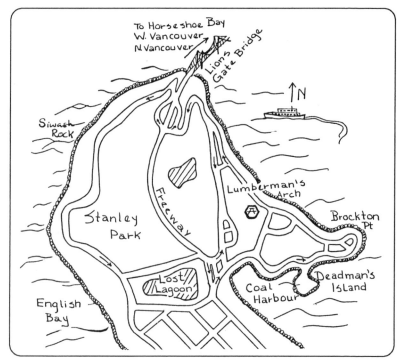

there. Starting from downtown Vancouver, approach the park on Georgia Street, staying in the far right lane. Just where the buildings end there will be signs directing you into the park — and once in the park the signs will point the way to Lumberman's Arch.

Stanley Park

Stanley Park is unique among municipal parks in that it is a natural forest reserve. Even more unusual was the action of the first Vancouver City Council in 1886: in its first resolution, and as its first official action, the council moved to preserve for future generations this tidal island of natural forest. This action was taken at a time when Vancouver was still surrounded by forest! Then, one had to travel through the heavily timbered West End Forest to get to Stanley Park.

Stanley Park was originally a tidal island that was reached by way of a wooden bridge, although now the land is filled in. The large lagoon, called Lost Lagoon, was so named by Pauline Johnson who, while canoeing in Coal Harbour, found herself stranded in the Lagoon when the tide went out.

One of the early residents of the island was an Indian known as Supple-Jack. He had a cow and, because of the help and friendliness he showed to the Royal Engineers, they presented him with a bull. The resulting herd allowed Jack to become the main milk supplier to the Hastings Sawmill Company for many years. When Supple-Jack died the cattle were left to run and became

Stanley Park

known as "the wild cattle of Stanley Park."

Tekahionwake — Emily Pauline Johnson

Pauline Johnson was born on the Six-Nations Reservation at Brantford, Ontario in 1861. Daughter of a Mohawk Chieftain and an English woman, she was Indian by law, by temperament, by upbringing and by choice. The name Johnson was her Mohawk grandfather's christening name but she preferred her Indian name, Tekahionwake. Between 1892 and 1910 she travelled on the lecture tour circuit in Canada, the U.S. and England; dressed as an Indian princess, she always included a reading of her poetry which celebrated both Canada and her Indian heritage. In 1909 she settled in Vancouver where she renewed her friendship with Chief Joe Capilano of the Squamish Tribe. It was Chief Joe who told her the legends of Stanley Park which she published in 1911 in a collection entitled, *Legends of Vancouver*. Two of the legends are paraphrased below.

E. Pauline Johnson

The Siwash Rock

Half-way between Ferguson Point and Prospect Point, slightly detached from the shore, stands an erect sentinel of grey stone, the Siwash Rock. The legend goes that a brave, handsome, strong young Indian chief and his wife were going to have a baby. According to custom, when an Indian father first sees his child he must be perfectly clean, so clean that a wild animal will not scent his proximity. Only in this way can a father guarantee that his child will have a spotless life.

When his wife's time was near, the chief started swimming in the narrows. Hour after hour he swam, with each passing stroke making him more clean and better prepared to greet his child. While he was swimming, there came a great canoe with four giants in it — these were the messengers of the great god Sagalie Tyee. They ordered the chief out of the way so they could pass through the narrows unhindered. The young chief refused, telling them that being a responsible father and doing the right thing for his child was more important to him than obeying the gods.

Because he placed his child's future before all things, the Sagalie Tyee commanded that he should live forever as an example for his tribe. He swam toward shore, and when his feet touched the line where the land and water meet, he was turned into a pillar of stone, an indestructible monument to one man's fidelity to a generation yet unborn — and a celebration of Fatherhood.

So that he would not be alone, the wife and baby were also transformed into rocks and, if one searches in the woods behind the

Siwash Rock, you will find a large rock with a small one beside it. These are the shy bride-wife from the north with her hour-old baby beside her.

The Lure in the Centre of the Park

Deep in the woods beyond the cathedral trees, where the bush is the most dense, resides a spirit that has no name. No Indian will guide you into this area, and even animals avoid this place. Anyone who comes within the aura of the spirit can never leave. Will-power is dwarfed, intelligence blighted, and your feet will refuse to lead you out by a straight path. Your feet will forever circle about the Lure and, should death release you, your spirit will continue to circle and will never enter the Happy Hunting Ground.

The Lure was once a human spirit, a soul depraved, a witch woman who went up and down the coast casting her eye on innocent people and bringing them untold evils and diseases. She carried "bad medicine" which weakened the warriors' arms in battle, caused deformities, poisoned minds and engendered madness. The Sagalie Tyee could not stop this woman, but he did turn her into a stone — a stone so evil that no moss will grow on it.

Then, to balance her evil he chose from the nations the kindliest, most benevolent people whose hearts were filled with love for their fellow beings, and transformed them into a stately group of "Cathedral Trees."

In time the good has predominated over the evil. The beauty and tranquility of the great trees exists almost throughout the park. Only in one spot, where the bush is dense and dark, do the forces of evil still dwell.

Things to do

1. Walk on the Sea Wall. It is a great experience to walk under the Lion's Gate Bridge, and along the edge of the ocean. It is easy walking, but Stanley Park is big. From the Lumberman's Arch to the Lion's Gate Bridge is probably 3 km (2 mi.), and it is another 3 km to the Siwash Rock.

2. For the kids, there are pony rides, a children's zoo, and a miniature train at the Arch.

3. For the whole family there is the incredible Vancouver Aquarium. South American crocodiles, Amazon piranhas, toothy sharks and killer whales: the aquarium has them all. The Aquarium is open every day of the year. Phone 682-1118 for hours and show times.

4. Monkeys, otters, seals, reptiles, exotic birds, and polar bears are all waiting for you at the Stanley Park Zoo. Free admission, open daily 8 a.m. to dusk.

5. Wander in the park. The trails will take you past Beaver Lake, monumental trees, and rose gardens. Take your time.

Things to eat

The Poet's Picnic —
> A Book of Verses underneath the Bough,
> A Jug of Wine, a Loaf of Bread — and Thou
> Beside me singing in the Wilderness —
> Oh, Wilderness were Paradise enow!
> *The Rubaiyat of Omar Khayyam*

As well as the obvious loaf of bread (fresh) and the jug of wine (Okanagan), we suggest a menu of divers colour, texture and form, with a gentle, but apparent rhythm.

Cold Baked Salmon
Little Tree Salad
Poetry in Motion
and
Chocolate Mousse

Baked Salmon

(Serves 6 - 8)

Preheat oven to 325 °F.

Scale, remove the entrails, and clean the salmon. Stuff with your favourite bread crumb or rice stuffing.

Place on thick foil, dot with butter and arrange thin slices of lemon on the salmon. Wrap the foil, and seal. Bake for 30 minutes, or until a thermometer inserted in the thickest part of the flesh, just behind the gills, reads 145 °F.

Cool, and keep chilled until the picnic. Serve with lemon wedges, parsley, and mayonnaise.

Little Tree Salad (Cauliflower Vinaigrette)

(Serves 4 - 6)

> Poems are made by fools like me
> But only God can make a tree.

> Joyce Kilmer

1 head cauliflower	25 ml green relish
200 ml salad oil	5 ml sugar
100 ml white vinegar	5 ml salt
1 large tomato, chopped	5 ml paprika
2 green olives, chopped	2 ml pepper

Separate the cauliflower into flowerettes. Steam in a little water for 10 minutes; cauliflower should be crisp but tender. Drain and place in bowl. Combine remaining ingredients and pour over the cauliflower. Chill.

Poetry in Motion — A Tossed Vegetable Salad

(Serves 6)

Up from the meadows rich with corn,
Clear in the cool September morn

Barbara Frietchie

2 tins whole kernel corn, drained
2 avocadoes, peeled and diced
6 hard-boiled eggs, diced
2 Tbsp. chopped onion

Prepare a dressing as follows:
1 cup mayonnaise
1 Tbsp. lemon juice
1/2 tsp. chili powder
1/4 tsp. ground cumin

Pour over the salad and toss just before serving.

Chocolate Mousse

(Serves 4)

All bitter things conduce to sweet,
As this example shows;
Without the little spirochete
We'd have no chocolate to eat!

Richard Purdy Wilbur

4 eggs
150 g fine chocolate
150 g butter

Melt the butter and chocolate in a bain Marie (top of a double boiler), stirring constantly. When it forms a cream, remove it from the heat. Now add the four egg yolks, keeping them separate from the whites. Beat the whites until they stand in stiff peaks, and fold into the chocolate cream. Pour the mixture into a serving bowl. Top with whipped cream with a touch of brandy folded in, and garnish with grated chocolate. Serve very cold.

17 Cypress Provincial Park
West Vancouver
A Greek Picnic

Situated between the Pacific Ocean and the Coast Mountains, Vancouver can rightly claim to have one of the most magnificent city settings in the world. A short drive to a lookout in the North Shore Mountains provides a place to pause and admire the view. This picnic is designed to provide a view, an orientation, and an opportunity to appreciate this beautiful city.

How to get there

The picnic is at the Highview Lookout at the entrance to Cypress Provincial Park. The park access road joins the Upper Levels Highway (Routes 1 and 99) in West Vancouver, 12 km (7 1/2 mi.) from downtown via the Lion's Gate Bridge. The Highview Lookout is at the second hairpin turn on the road.

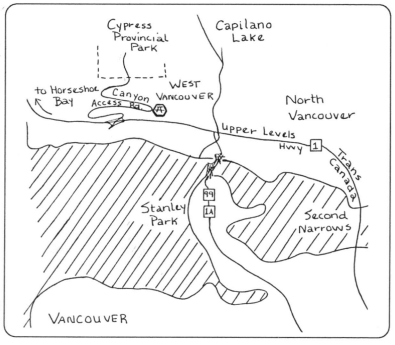

Things to do and see

There are only two things to do at this site. One is to picnic and the second is to admire the view. The notes following are intended to make the view more interesting.

The body of water immediately below you is called the Strait of Georgia, named in 1792 after — you guessed it — King George III. The Spanish, who were there a year earlier, had named it "Gran Canal de Nuestra Senora del Rosario la Marinera." Countless Canadian mapmakers and school children are grateful that the British name triumphed.

The Lions Gate Bridge spans the First Narrows of Burrard Inlet from Stanley Park to West Vancouver. It was completed in 1939, and the main span is 477 m (1550 ft.). At the time of its construction it was billed as the longest bridge in the British Empire; now, however, it is a lowly twentieth among the bridges of North America. It has sometimes been referred to as a bridge that beer built, since the financing came primarily from a north shore development company whose principal stockholder was the Guinness family.

Stanley Park, originally known as Coal Peninsula, was initially a military reserve where fortifications were to be erected to defend the Harbour. In 1886, the Vancouver City council, in an incredible burst of good sense and foresight, petitioned the federal government to lease them the land for a park. The lease was granted in perpetuity for a fee of $1.00 per year. Then, in an effort to curry favour, the council chose to name their park after the Governor-General of Canada, Lord Stanley of Preston. It remains to be seen whether Stanley will be best remembered for this park, or for the Stanley Cup of hockey.

The large point directly to the south is Point Grey. The vast wooded area on the point is called the Endowment Lands of the University of British Columbia.

Things to eat

As you gaze at the Olympian panorama at your feet, we will enjoy a Greek picnic. This may be stretching it just a bit, but we have to squeeze in a Greek picnic somewhere, because we love Greek food. So here it is.

MENU

**Pita Bread
Houmus
Greek Salad
Lamb Kabobs
Baklava**

Houmus

(Serves 6 - 8)

*1 tin cooked garbanzo beans
1/3 cup lemon juice
2 - 3 large cloves of garlic
1/3 cup tahini
1 tsp. sea salt
2 Tbsp. olive oil*

Do not drain the beans. Empty can into blender along with other ingredients and blend until smooth. Chill for 2 hours before serving. Garnish with parsley.

Lamb Shishkabobs

Buy 1/2 pound lamb per person. Cut lamb into 1-inch cubes and soak in marinade in refrigerator overnight.

Prepare the following marinade:
*3/4 cup dry red wine
1/4 cup lemon juice
3 Tbsp. olive oil
1 tsp. salt
fresh ground pepper
2 garlic cloves, minced
1 onion, minced
1 bay leaf
2 Tbsp. oregano*

At the picnic thread the lamb onto skewers, alternating with chunks of green pepper, cherry tomatoes, and mushroom caps.

Broil on your portable barbecue, turning as needed. Baste with the marinade several times during broiling.

Greek Salad

(Serves 6 - 8)

Mix together in a bowl:
  1 head romaine lettuce
  1/2 Spanish onion, thinly sliced and separated into rings
  1 green pepper cut into small triangles
  4 tomatoes, quartered
  1 cucumber, peeled and cut into chunks
  1/2 pound feta cheese, crumbled

And dress with:
  2 cloves garlic, minced
  1 Tbsp. wine vinegar
  1/4 tsp. salt
  1/2 cup olive oil
  pinch of tarragon
  dash of black pepper

Toss the salad and sprinkle liberally with calamata olives — the black ones.

Baklava and pita bread can be purchased at the Greek bakery, or at most large grocery stores. Check the frozen foods.

The appropriate beverage is retsina wine. Drink it if you like it — we don't.

P.S. West Vancouver has several good Greek take-out restaurants; you could pick up the entire picnic on the way.

18 Ambleside Park West Vancouver
A Potlatch Picnic

Potlatch:

A large gathering and party to celebrate some event at which the host presents costly gifts to the guests. Practised by all of the West Coast Indians until the whites outlawed it in 1884. Practiced by many in secret until it again became legal.

How to get there

Ambleside Park is on Burrard Inlet at the mouth of the Capilano River, just southwest of the Park Royal Shopping Plaza. To reach the picnic site proceed west on Marine Drive over the Capilano River, past the Park Royal shopping enter, and turn left (south) on 13th Street. Follow this road over the tracks, turn left at the T-intersection, and continue on to the parking area and picnic tables.

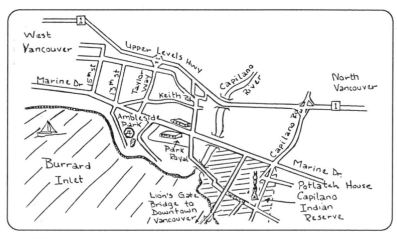

The Potlatch

For 67 years this important religious and social ceremony was outlawed by the Canadian government in an effort to assimilate the Coast Indians into mainstream Canadian life. The government misunderstood the economic function of the potlatch, seeing it only as a flamboyant destruction of goods. It can be assumed that the officials

Potlatch House in Ambleside Park

were affronted at the very idea of giving away material wealth — blankets, metal ornaments, and even money. The religious and economic significance of the tradition escaped them. Missionaries were also shocked by the apparent idolatry as well as the display and redistribution of wealth. The combined power of the church and the government effectively outlawed potlatch ceremonies in 1884. By the 1920s traditional potlatch goods were being confiscated by government officials. The potlatch prohibition was not removed from the Federal Indian Act until 1951. Nevertheless the potlatch has remained a central institution in the lives of the Coastal Indians.

The economic implications of the ceremony are far-reaching, as the sponsor or host of the potlatch must provide elaborate gifts for all who attend. Effectively, this accomplishes a redistribution of wealth within the community, and ensures that food and material goods are available to everyone. Rather than hoarding goods to gain wealth, goods were given away and sometimes destroyed during a potlatch ceremony. The consequent redistribution of wealth was actually an adaptive strategy for the community. Families with fewer resources could, by attending a potlatch, gain access to the goods that they needed. It was expected that they would reciprocate when their fortunes were reversed.

The potlatch ceremony continues to serve many other purposes. One of these is social, in that it brings together a large group of people to mark an important occasion, such as a birth, naming, coming of age, marriage, or death. These potlatches are public acknowledgments of life passages, and often carry with them the implication of a passing on of hereditary rights or position within the family or tribe. Potlatches may also be held by an individual to save face, or to compensate a family or tribe for a breach in the host's conduct. In the past competitive potlatches were also held, in which each host tried to outdo the other in the value and number of gifts, and thus gain prestige in the eyes of the community.

Probably the most important purpose of the potlatch is the religious significance of the masks, the dance and the ceremonial communications with the spirit world. Many of these spirits are represented as family crests on the totem poles just outside the potlatch lodge.

This type of ceremony is common to several tribal societies in different parts of the world, always where the material goods required for survival are plentiful and varied.

Things to see and do

1. When we last picnicked there, the water immediately off the mouth of the river was thick with small sport-fishing boats. Because of the low water levels, the Cleveland Dam (see Capilano Canyon Picnic) was severely restricting the flow of water down the Capilano River at that time. This meant that the salmon, wanting to move up the river to spawn, were forced to wait around the mouth in the waters of Burrard Inlet. It's something like the bank on payday when half the tellers have gone for lunch. Anyway, it is on these waiting salmon that the fishers descend. Apparently, the frustrated fish readily take to the bait.

2. See the potlatch house. The current extent of the Capilano Indian Reserve is from the Capilano River to Capilano Road, and from the Inlet to Marine Drive. It is the area spanned by the north approach of the Lion's Gate Bridge. At the corner of Capilano Road and Welch (see map) the tribe has constructed its potlatch house.

3. Promenade along the seawall to Dundarave Park: a short, pleasant stroll of about 3 kilometres.

4. Play Pitch and Putt golf at the Ambleside links.

Things to eat

Ideally at a Potlatch Picnic everyone would receive a large and luxurious gift from the host. However, since most people are not ingrained with the reciprocal behavior of the Sunset Tribes, this could be a self-deprivation strategy. Here we suggest a return to the original idea of picnics wherein everyone brings something to the feast. This may require a little organization, because if left to chance you might end up with 13 variants on potato salad, and no high protein goodies. If however, portions of the proposed feast are assigned, then a true bacchanale, or at least its Squamish equivalent, can result.

Many wonderful dishes were prepared for the potlatch feast. Salmon was always accompanied with various vegetable dishes, birds' eggs, berries, and eulachon oil (the oil rendered from candle fish).

MENU

Smoked Salmon with Capers and Lemon
Egg and Bacon Pie
Spinach and Watercress Salad
Cake with Strawberry Sauce

Serve slices of smoked salmon with mounds of capers and lemon wedges on a platter. Wedges of egg and bacon pie are set out with the salad that has been tossed with your favourite dressing. End the meal with slices of angelfood cake covered with strawberry sauce.

Egg and Bacon Pie

(serves 6-8)

1 pound bacon rashers, diced
8 - 12 eggs
enough of your favourite pastry for a 2-crust, 8 - 9 inch pie
salt and pepper to taste
a bit of grated nutmeg (optional)
milk

Partially cook the bacon pieces and then drain. Roll out pastry and use half for the bottom crust. Beat eggs with a few Tbsp. of milk and the spices until well mixed and frothy. Sprinkle half of the bacon over the bottom of the pie. Add the beaten eggs and sprinkle the rest of the bacon over the top. Prepare a pastry top and cover the pie, making a hole in the centre for a vent. Brush the crust with milk and bake at 425 °F for 20-25 minutes, or until the pastry is golden and the eggs are set. Serve cold slices of pie with green salad.

Cake with Strawberry Sauce

Serve slices of angelfood cake with dollops of this delicious cold sauce.

1 qt. fresh strawberries, washed and stemmed
(or 1 pkg. frozen berries)
1/4 cup honey
2 Tbsp. sugar
2/3 cup water

If using frozen berries, partially thaw and save berry liquid. Place honey, sugar, and water (or berry liquid from thawed berries, with water) to make 2/3 cup in a sauce pan. Boil for about 5 minutes. Reduce heat and drop in fresh or thawed berries. Simmer for 5 minutes. Let the sauce cool to room temperature. Pack into a container and refrigerate until needed. At your picnic serve sauce over slices of cake.

19 Emory Creek
Yale
A Chinese Picnic

Emory was one of the first miners to stake a claim on the creek. In 1858 over 25,000 gold seekers poured up the Fraser, working the bars in an attempt to strike it rich. It is recorded that 500 men spent the winter of 1858-59 camped at Emory's Bar. They mined the bars and moved on.

The construction of the Canadian Pacific Railway by 10,000 Chinese navvies brought a short life to Emory Bar, but the railroad and the people all moved on.

The Dominion Provincial Mining Training Project, located at Emory's Bar in the 1930s Depression, was an attempt to teach unemployed men how to be prospectors and to encourage them to pan for gold.

The township is now a campground, and a great picnic spot.

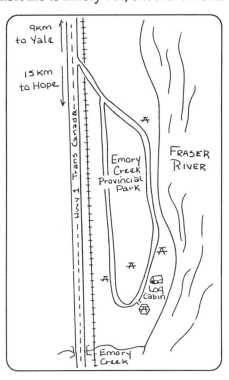

How to get there

Emory Creek Provincial Park is located on the site of Emory City, 6 km (4 mi.) south of Yale on Trans-Canada Highway No. 1. Our favorite picnic spot is Number 17, beside the log cabin and the river; but any of the riverside tables will do.

The Chinese and British Columbia

In Emory Park there is a historic-interest plaque that mentions the Chinese who built the Cariboo Waggon Road and the Railway.

There is another at Yale, and still another at Craigellachie, belated recognition to a courageous group of pioneers without whom the transcontinental railway might never have been completed.

The first Chinese came in with the miners from California in the 1850s. They were often forced to follow behind the white miners, but with patience and industry they gleaned the gold that others had failed to find. They also became the house-boys, the laundrymen, the cooks, the maids and shopkeepers for the British at Victoria. By the 1880s, B.C. had a white population of about 35,000, and an oriental population of several thousand.

Then came the railway. American contractor Andrew Onderdonk was granted a contract to build a railroad from Emory Bar at the mouth of the Fraser Canyon to Kamloops in the interior, 203 km (127 mi.) in all. The contract would employ over 10,000 labourers and it was understood that arranging this was the responsibility of the contractor. Onderdonk had acquired the contracts by buying them from the lower bidders; thus he was undertaking the contracts for two million dollars less than his original tendered price. He had considered a number of factors: that the wages in B.C. were less than the Americans were offering for similar work; that there was a construction boom in the States; and that the B.C. labour pool was very small. Also, in the construction of the Central Pacific in California, the Chinese had proven themselves to be the best and most adaptable railroad labourers. Although Onderdonk hired all the B.C. labourers — whites and Indians — that would work for him, there were just not enough people to do the work. The choice was clear. Over the complaints of the Victoria-based Anti-Chinese League and the cries of an alarmed and bigoted white citizenry, and despite laws that forbade the employment of Chinese on public works, he brought in shiploads of Chinese coolies. It was, as Prime Minister John A. MacDonald told Parliament in 1882, ". . . simply a question of alternatives: either you must have this labour, or you can't have the railway." In 1882 alone, Onderdonk imported about 6,000 Chinese.

By 1885 there were over 17,000 Chinese immigrants in B.C. However, with the completion of the railroad, many of the Chinese workers had not made enough money to return to China. They had been paid one dollar a day, but after deductions for shelter, food and clothes, and the winter lay-off, it was difficult for them to save more than 40 dollars a year. The first year's saving went to repay the agent for the passage over, and many did not save the additional 300 dollars necessary to buy a farm back in China. So they stayed on in Canada and looked for work. Many dug cave homes in the hills by Emory Creek and sifted the sands of the Fraser for gold that the first miners might have missed. They later moved on to other jobs, and other places.

The new city of Vancouver acquired a Chinatown, vegetable

gardens grew in the Fraser Valley, and the Chinese-Canadians became an essential and vibrant part of the British Columbia community.

Things to do and see

1. Pan for gold at the edge of the Fraser. A gold pan can be acquired at many of the tourist or rock hound shops and it is still possible for an amateur to get some flecks of gold dust in the bottom of a pan — not the fortunes the early miners found, but enough to make the afternoon fun.

2. In 1886 Emory City had two hotels, nine saloons, a brewery, a sawmill, a newspaper, and a number of houses and business establishments. Search through the campground for signs of this lost city.

3. Read the Yale — Fraser Canyon picnic, since the site is only 10 kilometres down the road, and the histories are closely related.

Things to eat

An Emory Park picnic must be a Chinese Feast. One can stop off at a Chinese restaurant and get the combination plate to go, or if one is feeling adventurous, here are some dishes to attempt at the picnic table. Bring a wok.

```
MENU
```

Hot and Sour Soup
Bean Sprout Salad
Green Onion Cake
Fried Rice
Sweet and Sour Fish
Tinned Lichee Nuts

Hot and Sour Soup

(Serves 4)

Soak for 1/2 hour
   4 dried Chinese mushrooms

Heat a wok, and add
   1 Tbsp. cooking oil
   1/3 pound chicken, cut into narrow strips and soaked in beaten egg
      white

Log Cabin at Emory Creek

> *the soaked mushrooms*
> *1/2 cup bamboo shoots*
> *1/2 tsp. chili oil (ah kee)*

Stir for 1 minute.

Add:
> *5 cups chicken broth*
> *2 Tbsp. rice vinegar*
> *2 Tbsp. corn starch mixed with 4 Tbsp. hot water*
> *1 Tbsp. soy sauce*

Let thicken.

Remove the wok from the heat.

Beat 2 eggs lightly. Add them to the mixture in a thin stream. Sprinkle with 2 Tbsp. chopped scallions, and serve.

Sweet and Sour Fish

(Serves 4)

> *1 pound fish fillets*

Combine the following in a jar at home:
> *1/2 cup lemon juice*
> *1/2 tsp. salt*
> *1/4 cup salad oil*
> *1/4 tsp. black pepper*

2 Tbsp. minced onion
1 tsp. dry mustard
2 Tbsp. brown sugar
1 tsp. soy sauce
1/2 tsp. powdered ginger

At the picnic, wrap the fish in serving sized packages, basted with the sauce. Bake in the barbecue oven about 20 minutes, depending on the heat of the coals.

Green Onion Cakes

(Serves 4)

These delicious cakes are well worth the trouble to prepare, and can be made well in advance and even frozen, and warmed up in the frying pan at the picnic. They are best served hot.

1 1/3 cup presifted flour
1/2 cup warm water
4 stalks green onions, chopped
1/2 cup fresh onion, finely minced
shortening
1/2 tsp. chili powder
1/4 tsp. salt
dash white pepper

Mix chopped green onions and minced onion together

Mix flour with water and knead the dough for 5 minutes

Separate into 8 to 10 parts and roll each into a flat 4-inch circle. Spread a thin layer of shortening on each, and sprinkle with spices and 1 Tbsp. of the onion mixture. Roll up jelly roll style, then coil it around in a snail fashion, tucking ends under. Roll out again to a 4-inch circle.

Store, chilled, with layers of waxed paper between the cakes, until you reach the picnic site.

Cook in a hot frying pan in oil, until golden brown on both sides.

20 Fraser Canyon Yale

A Fraser Canyon Picnic

There is a certain magic in the canyon around Yale. Every rock, every hillside, every whirlpool has its story. Here Simon Fraser rested after coming through the canyon; here the Hudson's Bay brigades stopped; here the B.C. Gold Rush began; here the miners fought the Indians; here the steamers discharged their cargo so that Barnard's Express (BX) could carry it up the Cariboo Waggon Road to Barkerville; here the Salish Indians catch the salmon from the Fraser just as they and their ancestors have done for 9000 years; and here we will picnic.

There are three special spots right around Yale and selecting the best depends upon your mood and the particular part of history that interests you.

1. The intersection of Front Street and Albert Street in the centre of Yale was where the offices of BX were located. One can picnic on the river bank across the street and listen to ghostly echoes of men and stage-coaches.

2. Immediately outside Yale is an abandoned stretch of the old Fraser Canyon Highway that ends on top of a railway tunnel, directly beside Lady Franklin Rock. Over a century of transport technology is compressed into that little spot. One can also picnic here watching cars above, the river below, and trains literally underfoot. However, it is an abandoned roadway and in some places it looks it.

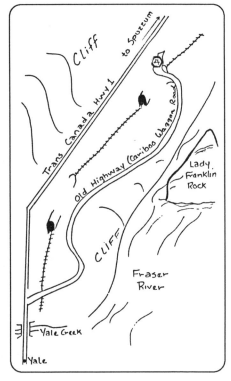

3. The most attractive spot, with picnic tables, interpretive displays, old trails and an abandoned suspension bridge, is 20 kilometres north of Yale at Alexandra Bridge in the Provincial Park, and this is our recommended spot.

How to get there

The first picnic spot is in the centre of Yale, on the waterfront by Front and Albert Streets. To get there go north one half a block from the Tourist Info Centre, turn right at the traffic light and drive west two blocks. You can't go any farther since the river is in front of you.

The second site, beside Lady Franklin Rock, is immediately north of Yale. To reach it leave Yale on Highway 1 heading north. Turn right immediately after crossing the creek. You will cross the tracks and wind along parallel to the new Highway. You are now on the old 1926 Fraser Canyon Highway and if you follow it along for a few kilometres, over the bumps and through the ruts, you will come to the end — opposite Lady Franklin Rock, and immediately over the portal of a railway tunnel.

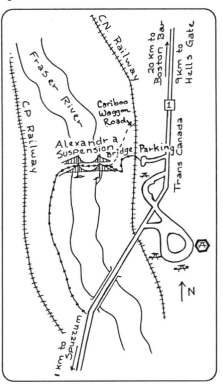

The third picnic spot, at Alexandra Bridge Provincial Park Picnic Ground, is on Highway 1, directly east of Alexandra Bridge, about 20 km (12 1/2 mi.) north of Yale. There are picnic tables on both the east and west sides of the highway. The ones on the west side are exposed to the traffic dirt and noise, but are next to the displays and the bridge trail. We prefer the ones on the east side, where we can picnic in peace, and we intend to drive part way down the bridge trail anyway.

History

As for the road by land we could scarcely make our way with even only guns. I have been for a long period in the Rocky Mountains but have never seen anything like this country. It is so wild that I cannot find words to describe our situation at times. We had to pass where no human beings would venture; yet in those places there is a regular footpath impressed or rather indented upon the very rocks by frequent travelling. Besides this, steps which are formed like a ladder or the shrouds of a ship by poles hanging to one another and crossed at certain distances with twigs, the whole suspended from the top to the foot of deep precipices, furnished a safe and convenient passage to the natives; but we, who had not the advantage of their education and experience, were often in imminent danger when obliged to follow their example.

Thus wrote Simon Fraser in his journal, describing his first passage through the Fraser Canyon in June of 1808.

Such was the canyon that was to frustrate, and challenge, the B.C. pioneers. The river, which at Hell's Gate is 30 m wide, 60 m deep, and travels at 7.5 m/second (17 m.p.h.) was a formidable foe; to get through the canyon required spectacular, and at times almost superhuman, feats of engineering.

Lady Franklin Rock

It is Lady Franklin Rock that makes Yale the gateway to the canyon. This huge black boulder, situated in the centre of the Fraser River, is so large that it blocked the steamboats from any further travel upstream. Thus the level spot by the river, originally a fur

Lady Franklin Rock

trading post called The Falls, became the head of navigation for the Fraser and the location of the town of Yale.

The naming of the rock has little to do with B.C. or its early exploration. It was actually a result of the Europeans not realizing how large Canada was, during their search for the fabled Northwest Passage.

In 1845, Arctic explorer Sir John Franklin set out from England to find the Northwest Passage to the Orient. We now know that his ships got trapped in the ice, that the explorers and crew went mad with lead poisoning from the tinned food, and that they wandered out onto the ice to starve to death; this within a few days' walk of an established Eskimo settlement. But in 1847 the fate of the Franklin Expedition was a major cause célèbre in England and thirty-nine relief expeditions were sent out to search for him. All failed. In 1859 it was learned that Franklin had perished in the Arctic.

After receiving confirmation of his death, Lady Franklin, then sixty-eight and frail, set out with her niece Sophia Cracroft, to see this continent that had claimed her husband. In March of 1861 she journeyed up the Fraser by canoe. The niece's diary has the following entry:

> On reaching the narrowest part of the canyon we beheld (suspended from the rafters of a salmon drying shed) a long pole stretching over the stream, on which was hung a white banner with the words "Lady Franklin Pass" printed in large letters. The Indians stopped their paddling and we were told that this name was bestowed by the inhabitants of Yale in honor of my aunt's visit.

Lady Franklin stopped for a while in Yale. At that time the little church of St. John the Divine was nearing completion, and so she put the members of her expedition to work at building the pews and choir stall.

Barnard's Express, the "BX"

It was here, at Yale, that the famous Cariboo Waggon Road, built in 1861 by the Royal Engineers, began. From here the Trail wound 400 miles up the Fraser to the goldfields of Barkerville. And it was here, at the corner of Albert and Front Street, that the freight was taken off the steamboats and loaded onto the famous stagecoaches of the Barnard's Express. The size of the operations can be appreciated by considering the following item from the New Westminster *British Columbian,* in December 14, 1864:

> . . . it only remains to give a few figures, in order to afford the

reader an idea of the present magnitude of the institution and the success with which it has met under the able management of Mr. Barnard and Messrs. Dietz and Nelson. The number of miles travelled during the present year is 110,600.

Number of men employed, exclusive of agents whose time is not entirely devoted to Express, 38. Number of horses employed in the Express service, 160. Number of Expresses dispatched from the head office in New Westminster during the year, 450. Total amount of treasure and valuables, exclusive of merchandise passing through the Express during the present year, $4,619,000.

Alexandra Bridge

Just north of Spuzzum there is no place for a road or a trail on the west bank, so the river must be crossed. Here in 1861, at the site of the old trail ferry, Joseph Trutch undertook to build a bridge.

It had a span of 100 m (300 ft.) and was the first suspension bridge built in the colony. Because cables of the required length were too much to pack in over the mule trail, Trutch packed in shorter lengths and spun the cables at the site. So well did he perform this task that over its lifetime, not a single cable ever snapped.

The structure looked flimsy, however, with cables anchored in rock, stretched over wooden towers and curving out over the racing river. A wooden plank deck was suspended from the cables.

In 1863 the bridge was completed. Trutch tested it with a four-horse team drawing a load of three tons. The deflection of the deck under this load was less than one quarter of an inch. It was a major achievement, for although the Indians and the earlier pioneers had crossed the torrent with fords and ferries, this was the first time man had bridged the Fraser.

The bridge cost $45,000 to build, a tremendous cost for a tiny colony to bear. However, a toll was charged of $7.50 per ton, and the cost was quickly recouped.

The bridge and Cariboo Waggon Road were the main pathway into the interior until the Canadian Pacific Railway was constructed in the 1880s. The construction of the CPR caused great damage, with the numerous cuts and fills blocking and diverting the road. The great flood of 1894 washed away much of the trestle work and part of the bridge, and so the road was abandoned. From then until 1926 the railway was the only way through the canyon.

It was Henry Ford's revolution that would next affect the canyon. The increasing use of the automobile in the 1920s brought with it a clamor for roads. In 1926, the first Fraser Canyon Highway was built. A new Alexandra Suspension bridge was constructed on the same site as the earlier one, using the same abutments. This bridge served until 1962 when the current highway, with its high bridge, was opened. The 1926 bridge has been declared a historic site and can be reached by travelling down the road just to the north of the exhibit site. There is space to park your car beside the railway tracks, and it is only a few hundred metres to the bridge. Alternatively, it is only a five minute walk to the bridge from the picnic spot on the west side of the road (see map).

Things to see and do

1. Regardless of where you decide to picnic, you must visit the other two sites. If you stand very still at the edge of the river, or by the BX office, you can still hear the ghostly noises of the steamboats, the packers, and the horses. When you visit Lady Franklin Rock, and the Alexandra Bridge, take your camera.

2. The Yale Museum, 31179 Douglas Street, has an interesting display of Indian artifacts and railway memorabilia. Stay and see their slide show on the history of the region. The museum is open daily, June to September.

3. Beside the museum is the little wooden church of St. John the Divine, the oldest church on the B.C. mainland standing on its original site. The actual date of construction is lost but it is believed to be sometime about 1860, the construction done or aided by the Royal Engineers who were building the Cariboo Waggon Road.

4. One of B.C.'s oldest cemeteries is located on the Trans-Canada Highway about 1 mi. (1.6 km) south of Yale. Some headboards date back to 1863. Try to find the headboard of Edward (Ned) Stout, one of the best known of the Cariboo Gold Rush miners. During the Indian wars of 1858 Stout was hit with seven arrows. He lived only because the Indians had run out of the rattlesnake poison that they usually put on their arrow tips. Stout survived and went on to Barkerville to make his fortune. He died in Yale in 1924 at the age of 99.

5. Delve into antiquity at the suspension bridge. Pictures from the 1860s show several white houses and a small orchard at the east end of the bridge. If you search you can still find a few fruit trees along with a lilac tree, traces of a pioneer garden. Also, try to find the 1863 Waggon Road — remember the 1863 bridge was 20 feet lower than the 1926 one.

Things to eat

If you look, while by or on the bridge, you can see the Indians' gill-nets sticking out from the shore. Some of the Indians still prepare fish in the manner witnessed by Simon Fraser in 1808. The head is removed and the fish cleaned, and the backbone is split from the flesh down to the tail. The fish is spread flat and slit into strips and dried. Sharpened twigs are threaded through the fish to keep it flat, and the fish is hung in the sun for three weeks to dry.

We can't wait three weeks for our fish to dry and so we will resort to barbecuing it. The menu we are proposing includes Sourdough Buns and Lady Franklin Coleslaw to go with the Barbecued Salmon followed by Toll House Cookies, in honour of the toll booth on the old bridge.

Sourdough Bread

Refer to the sourdough recipe in the Prospector's Picnic at Cranbrook for the recipe for sourdough starter.

To make the bread begin the night before by placing 1/2 cup starter in a mixing bowl. Add:

2 cups warm water
2 cups flour

Cover with a cloth and set in a warm place overnight.

In the morning set aside 1/2 for starter for the next time. Into the remaining sponge sift:

4 cups flour
2 Tbsp. sugar
1 tsp. salt

Add:

2 Tbsp. oil

And mix well. Add enough additional flour to make a soft dough, and knead for 10-15 minutes.

Place in a greased bread pan, cover, and set aside in a warm place to rise. This should take about 2 hours.

Place in 375 °F oven and bake for 50-60 minutes.

Barbecued Salmon

There are 2 traditional ways to barbecue salmon. One employs a vertical spit, and the other employs a spit and a reflecting oven. The fish is mounted the same way in both cases.

Vertical Spit
Cut the fish alongside the backbone, open and lay flat. Lay 6 little sticks

across the meat, pinioning each end slightly in the meat. Split one end of a small pole and slide the fish and sticks down the split, head end first. Tie the split pole together above and below the fish. Push the other end of the pole into the sand in such a way that the fish is positioned above the hot coals of the campfire. Cook 1 side for 20 minutes, then rotate the pole and cook the other side.

Reflector Oven
The cooking can be made more efficient by constructing a log reflecting panel as follows: cut 6 green logs of equal diameter (about 4-6 inches) and about 4 feet in length. Construct a rack by placing 2 poles the same distance apart as the diameter of your logs. Place another 2 poles in the same fashion about 3 feet away, in such a way that sliding the 6 logs between them will result in a wall about a foot away from the fire. This log wall will reflect the heat back onto the salmon.

Alternatively, turn a large flat rock on its side by the edge of the fire, to serve as a reflector. Place the fish, mounted as above, between the fire and the reflecting surface.

Lady Franklin Coleslaw

(Serves 8 - 10)

Combine in a bowl:
  1 medium head of cabbage, thinly sliced
  4 carrots, grated
  1 medium onion, finely chopped

Make a dressing of:
  250 ml white vinegar
  175 ml vegetable oil
  250 ml sugar
  10 ml dry mustard
  5 ml salt

Place in a sauce pan and heat, stirring occasionally, until the mixture boils. Pour the hot dressing over the vegetables, mix thoroughly and chill overnight.

Toll House Cookies

(makes 100 cookies)

  1 cup butter
  3/4 cup brown sugar
  3/4 cup white sugar
  2 eggs, beaten
  1 tsp. soda

1 tsp. hot water
2 1/4 cups flour
1 tsp. salt
1 cup chopped nuts
2 packages semi-sweet chocolate morsels (chips)
1 tsp. vanilla

Cream the butter, add white sugar and brown sugar and beaten eggs.

Dissolve soda in hot water. Add alternately with flour sifted with salt. Add chopped nuts, chocolate morsels and vanilla.

Drop by half-teaspoonfuls onto greased cookie sheet. Bake at 375 °F for 10-12 minutes.

OKANAGAN - SIMILKAMEEN

21 Keremeos Creek
Keremeos
A Grist Mill Picnic

In 1877, Barrington Price built a small water-powered grist mill on the banks of Keremeos Creek. Recent efforts of the BC Government have restored the mill and farm and created a superb spot for a picnic.

How to get there

Keremeos is on Highway 3, 30 mi. (48 km) southwest of Princeton, and 32 mi. (51 km) from the United States border crossing at Oroville, Washington.

From the centre of Keremeos, leave the town heading north on Highway 3A to Kaleden. Just at the edge of town you will cross the Keremeos Creek. Immediately after crossing the creek turn left (west) on Upper Bench Road. The Grist Mill is just a short distance along on the right. Watch for signs to the parking lot. The picnic site is on the lawn west of the mill, about 50 metres' walk from the parking lot.

History

In 1860 the Hudson's Bay Company closed down Fort Okanagan in what had become American territory and transferred its staff and stock to a new post in Canada at what is today Cawston. Here in 1861 the HBC conducted wheat trials and demonstrated that the area was suitable for farming.

This first post, however, was off the route that the miners were taking from Washington to the gold fields of the Fraser, and so the post was moved to yet another location just southeast of the present town of Keremeos.

Keremeos is an Indian word meaning, "wind channel in the mountains," which is appropriate since the trees in the valley show the result of the wind sweeping eastward along the Similkameen River.

Although the HBC Post closed in 1872, the early experiments at farming proved a success and settlers were attracted to the region. One of these settlers was a wealthy Englishman named Barrington Price. Price reasoned that there was sufficient grain grown in the area to justify the establishment of a mill and so in 1877, with mill machinery imported from England, he built a grist mill on the banks of Keremeos Creek.

This mill, run by John Coulthard after 1885, produced flour from wheat grown in the valley and served both the neighbouring ranches and the villages of Cawston and Olalla until the turn of the century. Now, over a century later, the mill still stands and the waters of Keremeos Creek still turn the big water wheel. When restored it will be the only operating water-powered grist mill in B.C.

Things to do and see

1. Tour the mill and the general store. Here there are hands-on models of how to clean and grind grain. The interpretive staff are hard at work restoring the original mill equipment to working order.

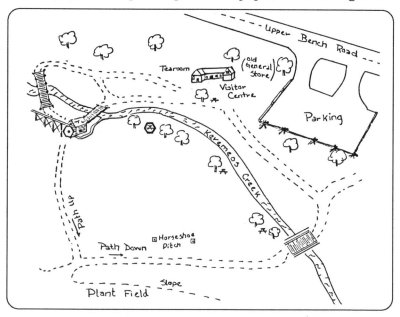

The Grist Mill at Keremeos

2. Almost as interesting as the mill itself is the historic wheat field where the staff are growing wheat varieties of the 1880s and 1890s.

3. Keremeos has two museums and both are worth a visit. Pioneer artifacts and machinery are in the Keremeos Museum on the corner of Sixth Ave. and Sixth St., whereas Indian tools and dance costumes are in the Similkameen Valley Museum on Main Street.

4. Listen to the stars at the Dominion Radio Astrophysical Observatory near Kaleden. Drive north on Highway 3A toward Kaleden. The road to the Observatory is on the right about 13 km (8 mi.) from Keremeos. The Observatory is open for tours in the summer; call ahead (479-5321) to get times.

5. Swim in the Similkameen River beside the historic covered bridge. Five km (3 mi.) west of Keremeos on Highway 3, turn south on the Ashnola River Road. About 150 metres from the highway the road passes through the Red Bridge. The bridge was built in 1907 as part of an American spur railway line that went from the mines at Princeton and Hedley to Washington State.

6. Hike, fish, camp, and enjoy Cathedral Provincial Park. Only 30 km (19 mi.) southwest of Keremeos, Cathedral Park is a 33,000 hectare wilderness of azure lakes, alpine meadows, and jagged peaks in the Okanagan Mountain Range. To reach the park, go to the Red Bridge (see item 5 above) and then continue on gravel-surfaced Ashnola River Road 21 km (13 mi.) to the Cathedral Lakes base camp,

or past it to the public parking lot. If you have made reservations with the Cathedral Lakes Resort (phone 604-499-5848) a 4-wheel drive taxi will pick you up at the base camp and spirit you into the park. Alternatively, from the public parking place there are some 32 km (20 mi.) of hiking trails.

7. Sample the wines at the St. Laslo Vineyard Estate.

Things to eat

A picnic at Keremeos, the Fruit Stand Capital of the World, must contain fresh fruit and vegetables. Thus, before the picnic one must first consult the Fruit Season Timetable to see what will be available.

Fruit Season Time Table	
Peaches	July to September
Pears	August 10 to October 30
Apples	August through October
Tomatoes	August 15 til frost
Corn	July 15 til frost

Since this is a Grist Mill Picnic, there must also be some grain. People have been eating wheat for at least 4000 years. Archaeologists have identified wheat kernels in the tombs of the Indus valley, dating from 2500 B.C. Today we only really encounter wheat in its derivative forms, usually as flour. Bulgur (parboiled cracked wheat) is one of the few ways that we still deal directly with a wheat kernel, albeit cracked and boiled. Bazargan, an ancient Syrian dish, makes a fine picnic salad. The rest of our menu for the Grist Mill Picnic includes a selection of fresh fruits and cheeses, roast corn (another grain!), and everything topped off by a peach cobbler for desert.

Bazargan

(Serves 8)

Soak in fresh cold water for 20 minutes and wash:
  1/2 k bulgur wheat
Drain through a fine sieve and set aside.

Saute in olive oil until soft
  2 large onions (finely chopped).

Combine onions and bulgur with:
  150 ml olive oil

225 g tomato paste
25 ml oregano
5 g chopped parsley
115 g walnuts, chopped
juice of 2 lemons
10 ml cumin
10 ml ground coriander
5 ml allspice
2 ml pepper
dash cayenne
salt to taste

Mix in large bowl, cover and refrigerate overnight. Serve garnished with slices of lemon.

Roast Corn

For this you require a hibachi or portable barbecue, since fires are not permitted at this picnic site.

Select as many choice ears of corn as you think you will need, and then a few more. Ensure that they were freshly picked. Resist the force of habit — do not shuck the corn! Seal each ear in tin foil. There is enough moisture within each cob to steam it. Place ears on the grill at low heat for about 15 minutes, turning one-third rotation every five minutes.

Peach Cobbler

Preheat oven to 425°F.

Grease a deep 8-inch pie pan, and cover the bottom with 4 or 5 peaches, peeled and sliced. Sprinkle the fruit with 1/2 cup sugar, a dash of nutmeg, and the juice and grated rind of 1 lemon. Dust with flour, and then drizzle 4 Tbsp. melted butter over the fruit.

Prepare the batter as follows:

Sift together:
1 cup all-purpose flour
1/2 cup sugar
1 tsp. baking powder
1/4 tsp. salt

Beat 2 egg yolks, and add 1 Tbsp. melted butter and 1/4 cup milk; stir liquids together.

Add wet ingredients to dry ingredients, blend together until smooth, and pour over the peaches.

Bake for 30 minutes.

Take to the picnic and serve in bowls, with a pitcher of fresh cream.

22 The Pocket Desert Osoyoos
A Desert Picnic

Osoyoos — the name comes from the Indian word soo-yoos which means the narrow point where the lakes come together — is the most southerly town in the Okanagan, and usually the hottest. Often referred to as the "Spanish Capital of Canada" because of its architecture and climate, the town is notable for having the warmest fresh water lake in the country, and for the constant background hum created by hundreds of air conditioners. Although Osoyoos was one of the first places in the Okanagan to be visited by a white man (David Stuart in 1811 is the first recorded visitor), it was the last to be developed. The sand spit which crosses the lake created a natural path across the valley and so it was used by the Indians for several centuries. With the coming of the Europeans it became a path for the fur traders. It was across the sand spit that the gold seekers passed along the Dewdney Trail, but it remained just a passing spot, for the valley was a desert and could not support human settlement. It wasn't until the early 1900s that the climate and irrigation combined to reveal the region's potential as a soft fruit producer. Now peaches, cherries, apricots, apples, prunes, pears, cantaloupes, grapes and watermelons grow in this area, which promises "the earliest fruit in Canada."

In the midst of the orchards and vineyards exists a Pocket Desert, a small natural preserve of what was — and would be still — were it not for the irrigation. It is British Columbia's only desert, and it is here that we have our picnic.

Desert Picnic, Osoyoos

How to get there

The Pocket Desert is reached by driving north from Osoyoos on Highway 97 for 7.5 km (5 mi.). Turn right (east) on Road 22, cross the bridge, drive past the abandoned farm buildings, follow the paved road off to the left, and then turn right and climb up the hill until it ends in the gravel parking area. In order not to disturb the reserve, and also because we do not want to share our picnic with the rattlesnakes and scorpions, it is here in the parking area at the edge of the reserve that we locate our picnic (see photo). Since the site is on land belonging to the Osoyoos Indian Band, you must ask permission before entering.

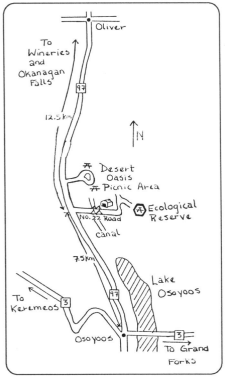

The desert is on a rise and it provides excellent views of the south Okanagan Valley with its startling contrasts between the irrigated green vineyards and the scorched hills.

The Pocket Desert

The desert, which originally stretched as far north as Oliver, is the northern tip of the American Great Basin Desert which extends south as far as Mexico. The 100 hectare Federal Ecological Reserve is a recent effort to save this unique habitat from the encroachment of irrigation schemes and development. It is one of the more unusual geological regions in Canada and contains some rare and unusual plants and animals. Plants like prickly pear cactus, antelope bush, sage, rabbitbrush, and all manner of marmots, toads, turtles, scorpions and lizards all inhabit the sand dunes of the desert. Watch for turkey vultures, the Great Basin spadefoot toads, the timid northern Pacific rattlesnake, the black-headed grosbeak, northern orioles, Lewis woodpeckers, American redstart, chukar partridge, and the smallest bird in Canada, the calliope hummingbird. Signs also indicate the program underway to re-establish the burrowing owl.

Things to do and see

1. Walk in the desert; an unusual experience for those of us who have never seen one before. Leave only footprints; take only pictures.

2. The warm waters of Osoyoos Lake are inviting. The swimming is great, the water-skiing fun and for the adventurous there is para-sailing.

3. Tour the wineries and taste the wines. There are three wineries located right by the pocket desert and all offer tours and tasting. Watch for the signs along the road.

4. Tour the authentic working windmill.

5. Visit the banana farm and see bananas, kiwi fruit, sugar cane and fig trees growing.

6. Visit the Osoyoos Museum where the exhibits include a history of local orchard irrigation.

7. Visit the Oliver Heritage Society Museum, 106 West 6th Ave., Oliver, which contains exhibits of the Pocket Desert's flora and fauna, as well as historical exhibits of the area's mining history.

Things to eat

Since the desert has stretched north from Mexico over the millennia, this location calls out for a Mexican picnic. We suggest this menu:

appetizers — taco chips and guacamole
do-it-yourself tacos with refried bean filling
a fresh fruit salad
made from the fruit you bought at the fruit stand
Margueritas
are an appropriate libation.

Guacamole

Scoop the insides of
   3 medium avocados
into the blender, along with:
   1 medium tomato, cubed   *1/2 tsp. salt*
   1 small onion, sliced   *dash of Tabasco sauce*
   2 Tbsp. lemon juice

Blend all ingredients at medium speed until smooth. Keep chilled.

Refried Beans (Frijoles Refritos)

(serves 6)

Buy taco shells at your supermarket. Make the following filling at home before the picnic, and then reheat the filling just before serving, thus creating re-refried beans.

2 cans kidney beans
1/2 cup lard or bacon dripping
1 cup chopped onion
1 clove garlic, minced
1/2 cup tomato sauce or cooked tomatoes
1 tsp. chili powder
salt and pepper

Use a potato masher to mash the beans together with 1/2 of the lard. Heat the remaining lard in a large skillet. Add the onions and garlic to the skillet and cook until the onion is soft (about 5 minutes). Add the mashed beans and cook at low heat until all the fat is absorbed by the beans (about 1/2 to 1 hour). Stir in tomato sauce, chili powder, salt and pepper.

Tacos

Prepare the garnishes at home and keep chilled in separate plastic bags or containers, as follows:

chopped tomatoes
chopped onions
shredded lettuce
grated Monterey Jack cheese
chopped jalapeno peppers
chopped, pitted black olives

Bring along a bottle of salsa, with the right level of "hotness" for your crowd. (We bring two, a mild and a picante!) At the picnic site, reheat the refried beans in a cast-iron frying pan with a little lard. Spread the pocket of each taco shell with a generous portion of the hot bean mixture, and then let the picnickers garnish as they please from your selection.

Fruit Salad

This is made at the picnic site from fruits bought from the fruit stands en route. Remember to bring a sharp paring knife, a cutting board and a large enough bowl, as well as serving bowls and spoons.

Grandpa Mike's Margueritas

Start this at home. Into a blender of cracked ice, for each serving pour the following:

1 ounce Tequila
1 ounce lemon juice
a few drops Rose's Lime Cordial
1/2 ounce Triple Sec
a little bit of egg white (Note: 1 white is enough for 6 drinks)

Buzz, and pour into a Thermos for transport to the picnic site. Once there, prepare the glasses by rubbing lemon around rim and dipping in saucer of kosher (or coarse) salt. Shake the Marguerita mixture well and pour into the glasses through a strainer.

23 Jade Beach
Vernon

A Picnic at the Lake

Vernon is situated at the confluence of four valleys — the Pleasant, the Coldstream, the Mission, and the Priest, branching out to the north, east, south and west respectively. The valleys acquired their names, as often happens, by convention.

The grass was up to his cattles' bellies in 1867 as Cornelius O'Keefe drove his herd through the pleasant valley on the way from Oregon to the mining camps of the Cariboo . . . they called this Pleasant Valley. On a hot day in July 1877 someone noticed that the water in the creek registered only a temperature of 48.5 degrees Farenheit . . . they called this river the Coldstream. The edge of Kalamalka Lake provided the main route to the Mission at Kelowna . . . this became Mission Valley. In the 1840s two Jesuit priests built a cabin at the north end of Okanagan Lake . . . they called this place Priests' Valley.

Jade Beach, Vernon

How to get there

Our choice of picnic site is Jade Beach in Kalamalka Provincial Park. To reach the park from Vernon, drive south on Kalamalka Lake Road and take the left fork at Kal Beach. Turn right on Postill Drive which will lead you to Kidstone Road. Follow Kidstone Road to the end which will be a parking lot in Kalamalka Park. The distance from the parking lot to the site is about 200 m downhill. The trail to the beach is paved for wheelchair use but is quite steep. The beach is a secluded gem, sheltered from the heat and the crowds of the Okanagan in tourist season.

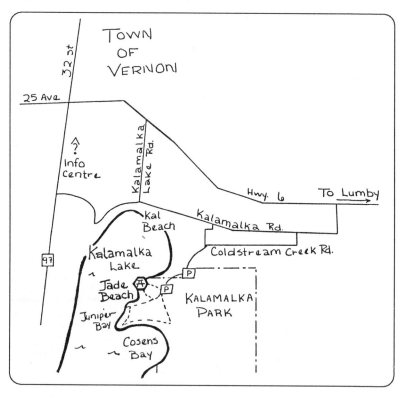

Kalamalka

The Indian name for this lake is Chelootsoos, which means "long lake cut-in-the-middle." Kalamalka was a wise old Indian that lived at the head of the lake.

Kay Cronin in her book, *Cross in the Wilderness*, relates the following story about Chief Kalamalka. It seems that the chief had accepted the teachings of the good fathers and had decided that he really wanted to become a Christian. However, whenever he asked Father Le Jacq to baptize him the father refused. The problem, explained the father, was that Kalamalka had four wives and Christians were only permitted one. Kalamalka truly wanted to be a Christian, but he was loyal to his wives because, as he explained to Father Le Jacq, one was the mother of his eldest son, another was lame with the terrible frostbite, and so on. So sincere, persistent and loyal was Kalamalka that the father even appealed to the bishop on his behalf, only to hear his own ruling repeated — Christians only have one wife.

Returning sadly from the bishop, Father Le Jacq received from Kalamalka the surprising tidings that he had only one wife, and further, that she was none of the four, but rather a new young wife that the four had selected to take over the tasks while they went into retirement. And so, from that day forth, Kalamalka had only one wife, but supported all five women as would be expected of a good Christian gentleman.

Rattlesnakes

Rattlesnake is the common name for any one of 31 species of snakes occurring from southern Canada to South America. Only 3 are found in Canada, and only the western rattlesnake can be found in the dry regions of Saskatchewan, Alberta and British Columbia. The western rattler is distinguishable by its flat, broad, triangular head, its scaly body, and specifically, by the rattling sound it makes as it moves. The rattler is located at the tip of the snake's tail; it is a cavity filled with unmolted, modified scales from the tail. The rattling sound warns predators of the snake's approach. The sound is very distinct, and if you hear it as you scramble over rocks searching for a picnic spot, watch where you put your feet. Rattlesnakes have a venomous bite which affects the nerves and blood tissues of the victim. The venom, delivered through fangs, causes death to the customary prey of the snakes: usually rodents, small mammals and birds. The western rattler rarely strikes a human unless it is threatened or stepped on. A bite will cause swelling, muscle paralysis and tissue destruction. Only 2% of bites result in death in Canada. Nevertheless, if someone on your picnic is bitten, immobilize the affected part of the body immediately, and transport the person to medical attention as soon as possible for an anti-venom shot.

Things to see and do

1. Wander in the park. The lake environment and open grassland provide an ideal nesting and feeding habitat for a variety of birds and other wildlife. In spring and summer you will be treated to a spectacular wildflower display. Be careful, however, as the signs at the parking lot point out, this is prime rattlesnake country.

2. Cornelius O'Keefe was a young man of Irish descent from the province of Quebec who came out west to make his fortune. He tried mining, and then road building, and then hit upon raising cattle to feed the miners in the Cariboo. Starting with 162 acres, he soon expanded to 15,000 acres and his ranch became one of the first cattle empires in the area. The ranch soon looked like a village, with its own general store, post office, flour mill, sawmill, blacksmith's shop, and church.

The ranch is still operated by O'Keefe's youngest son, Tierney. Some of the buildings and the church have been restored and can be toured. You will find the ranch on Highway 97, north of Vernon 6 km (3.5 mi.) past the turnoff to Highway 97A.

3. Soak in the Cedar Hot Springs. There are four pools ranging from hot (32° Celsius) to very hot (42° Celsius). Also one can get "Clearly Canadian" brand mineral water (bottled right there at the springs) in any of four natural fruit flavors. The Springs are about eight km (5 mi.) east of Highway 97 on the Silver Star Road. Call 542-5477 for information and reservations.

4. Watch the "Lake of One Thousand Colours" from the Kalamalka Lake Viewpoint, south of Vernon on Highway 97. Legend has it that the mysterious "Kalooey" bears of the Kalamalka swish their tails in the turquoise waters and leave behind brilliant pools of emerald green.

5. Tour Okanagan Spring Brewery, a cottage brewery which offers tours every Friday afternoon, phone 542-2337.

Things to eat

This is ranching and orchard country. The Coldstream Ranch at one time had 2000 cattle and 80 horses, plus poultry and hogs. In 1917 the region shipped 800 boxcars of apples and 200 boxcars of of miscellaneous fruit.

The menu for this picnic is cold sliced ham and scalloped potatoes, 3-bean salad, apricot cake for dessert, and to drink, "Clearly Canadian Mineral Water," of course.

You can bring the cold sliced ham from last Sunday's joint, or buy some from the deli. The scalloped potatoes are made at home and transported hot, insulated with newspapers, to the picnic site. Make the 3-bean salad the day before — it tastes so much better after 24 hours of chilling.

Scalloped Potatoes

(6 servings)

Preheat oven to 160 °C (325 °F)
4 L new potatoes, thinly sliced
1 medium onion finely chopped
35 ml flour
30 ml butter
500 ml milk
5 ml salt
pepper to taste
300 ml grated cheese

In the bottom of a greased glass casserole place 1/2 of the sliced potatoes. Sprinkle with half of the onions, flour and butter. Add the remaining potatoes and repeat the process. Heat the milk, and add the salt and pepper. Pour over the potato mixture, and bake for 2 hours. Sprinkle the cheese over the mixture for the last half hour of baking.

Three-Bean Salad

(Serves 8 - 10)

Combine:
1 tin cut waxed beans
1 tin French-style green beans
1 tin kidney beans
1 tin sliced mushrooms
250 ml thinly chopped onions
125 ml thinly chopped green pepper
1 tin pimento, chopped

Prepare a dressing as follows:
125 ml salad oil
125 ml red wine vinegar
200 ml sugar
salt and pepper to taste

Shake well, pour over the beans, and chill overnight.

KOOTENAY COUNTRY

24 Zuckerberg Island Castlegar
A Doukhobor Picnic

This picnic features hearty, traditional, Russian Doukhobor food on a peaceful island in the river. The island is now a memorial to Alexander Feodorovitch Zuckerburg, who spent his life working to help the Doukhobor people to retain their own culture within Canadian society.

How to get there

Castlegar is situated at the confluence of the Kootenay and the Columbia Rivers, at the southern end of the Arrow Lakes. It is on the southern Trans-Canada Highway (No. 3) halfway between Nelson and Trail. It is 622 km (390 mi.) from Vancouver. When you enter Castlegar you are on Highway 22 (Columbia Ave). Go toward the downtown area. Turn right at the RCMP station on the corner of 9th Street, then right again on 7th Ave. The side road to the left leads to the parking area by the bridge. You get to the island either by crossing the 473-foot suspension bridge or, if you don't like bridges, by walking along the path over the causeway, to the left. Our favourite picnic spot is on the other side of the island, about 100 metres walk (see map). From it you can see both the Kootenay and Columbia Rivers.

The Doukhobors

The Doukhobors are a sect of Russian Christians who came to Canada in 1898. In many respects they are similar to the Quakers, and

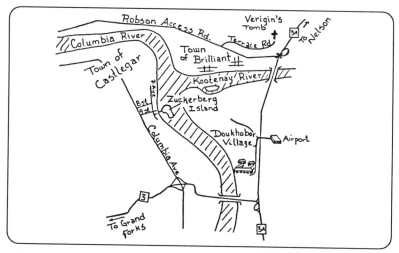

it was Tolstoy and the Quakers who were instrumental in getting them out of Russia and bringing them to Canada. They believe in pacifism and that God dwells in man, not in a church; this brought persecution from both the Orthodox Russian Church and the Czarist state. They would not do anything that they felt would conflict with the word of God. The Commandment, "thou shall not kill" instructed them to be strict vegetarians, and neither to join nor support any army. They could not pledge their allegiance to a secular government, since they could then be required to do something against the commandments of their God. Since they were illiterate, instead of a Bible they orally transmitted psalms and hymns, which they call the "Living Book."

They first settled in Saskatchewan where, under the Homestead

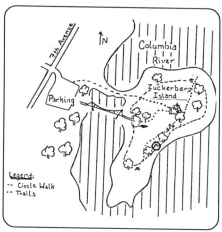

Act, each family was granted 160 acres. Initially they were allowed to practise their communal lifestyle and received concessions with regard to education and military service. Then in 1905, the Canadian government chose to interpret the Dominion Lands Act strictly; there is a condition whereby an oath of allegiance to the government is a condition of taking title to the property. Most of the Doukhobors would not sign and so the

The Chapel House

land that they had cleared and broken was taken away and given to other homesteaders.

Their leader, Peter Verigin, bought land in British Columbia around Grand Forks and Castlegar and moved 6,000 of his people there from Saskatchewan. They founded the City of Brilliant at the confluence of the Kootenay and Columbia Rivers, and there started a brick plant, a jam plant and a lumber mill. However, conflict with the authorities soon arose over the question of education of their children. The government said the children must go to school, but the Doukhobors felt that all their children needed only to understand the Living Book in order to live a Christian life. A tiny splinter group, the radical Sons of Freedom, aggravated the dispute by burning some public schools. The government's response was to send in the police, and to forcibly remove the children from the settlements to school.

During the 1930s the effects of the Depression, the actions of the fanatics, internal financial mismanagement within the community, unsympathetic practices of the financial institutions, and repressive policies of the government combined to destroy what had been the largest and most complex communal living experiment in North America. In 1939 the government and the banks foreclosed and the Doukhobors lost their land and their factories. Over 4 million dollars of assets were seized because of less than half a million dollars debt.

Descendants of the original group now number about 30,000. Many have repurchased the land and still live in the Kootenay region, and many are active in retaining the Doukhobor culture, including

Kekuli Pit House

the belief in pacifism and the use of the Russian language.

Alexander Feodorovitch Zuckerburg

Zuckerburg was a Russian civil engineer and high school teacher who emigrated to Canada with his family in 1921. In 1931, at the request of Peter Verigin, he came to Castlegar to teach the Doukhobor children. He settled on the island in the Columbia River, first building the tiny log house and later the Chapel House. He was loved and admired by many, especially by the Doukhobors. He died in 1961, and is buried with his wife on his island, which is now a public park bearing his name.

Things to do

1. Tour the island. For 3,500 years the island has served as a winter base for the Lakes Band of the Interior Salishan people.

See the reconstructed Salishan pit house (Kekuli), a winter lodge which was sunk about 6 feet into the ground, and was about 25 to 30 feet in diameter. Bows and bark were placed over the wooden frame, and then the entire structure was covered with earth, leaving only the hole in the top, which served as both entrance and smoke hole. The Salish, also known as the Shuswap Indians, had migrated from the coast generations before. They were hunters and fishermen, retaining many of the coastal customs, one of which was the winter lodge. In summer they had adopted the more easterly custom of living in tipis.

Also tour Zuckerburg's log hut and Chapel House; and pay a

Poison Ivy

This infamous plant, also referred to by its scientific name, Toxicodendron rydbergii Tradicans, is in appearance much like many other plants found along the trails and in the parks of B.C. Zuckerburg Island has a sign indicating a large patch of poison ivy near the lower picnic area. Note the three-part compound leaves, and the two types of stalk formations: the low, brush form and the long stalks of up to 15 metres. It is not only the fibres along the stalk and leaves of the poison ivy that cause the reaction which brings this plant its fame. These plants also secrete an oily juice which can be picked up simply by brushing by the plant. The result of contact is usually dermatitis. Reactions may be slightly delayed, but usually consist of an itchy, oozy rash of blisters.

If you wash with strong soap such as Fels Naptha immediately after contact with the ivy plant, the infection may possibly be avoided. Otherwise, mild cases of dermatitis are treated with ointments which are sold over the counter in drug stores. If the case is more serious, a physician should be consulted.

visit to the graves.

2. Visit the Doukhobor village. Just off Highway 3 by the Castlegar airport, it is a reconstruction of an original Doukhobor communal village.

3. Visit the tomb of Peter (Lordly) Verigin, the leader who brought the Doukhobor people to this valley. He died in 1924 in a train explosion — the cause was never determined, but some believe that it was a bomb planted by the small splinter sect of Doukhobors, The Sons of Freedom. To get to the tomb take Highway 3A, the Nelson turnoff; immediately after crossing the Kootenay River, take the right turnoff for Robson and Brilliant. The first road to the right leading up the hill (there is a sign) leads to Peter Verigin's tomb, which commands a fine view of the valley. It is about 800 m (1/2 mi.) up the road. The tomb and gardens are maintained by the volunteer labor of the young people of Brilliant.

4. Visit the Doukhobor Museum in Grand Forks. It is an original old communal house which contains photos and memorabilia.

5. Visit the museum in Nelson which also has many interesting displays and exhibits from the Doukhobor settlements.

Things to eat

A Doukhobor picnic must feature Doukhobor food. However, as is often the case, there is the easy way and the hard way. The easy way is to drive 16 km (10 mi.) along Highway 3A toward Nelson. On Highway 6, 500 feet past the intersection with 3A, is Rose's Restaurant. Rose will gladly fix you a feast of borscht, pyrahi, perogi, varenniki and nalesniki to go. If the group is large enough, Rose will even arrange to cater — and she serves Doukhobor food at its finest. If you intend to get the take-out food, bring along a Thermos and some insulated containers so the food will still be hot when you get to the picnic. If you want to try cooking your own food, we found the following recipes in a cookbook we bought in Castlegar called *Doukhobor Favorites*.

Borscht

(12 servings)

by Anne Hadikin

3 quarts water
8 med. potatoes
1 cup butter
1 cup grated carrots
1 med. beet
1 cup chopped onions
2 Tbsp. dill
6 cup shredded cabbage
1 1/2 Tbsp. salt
1 cup sweet cream
1/2 cup chopped carrots
4 cups canned tomatoes
1/2 cup chopped green pepper

Pour 4 cups canned tomatoes into a pan and mash. Add 2 Tbsp. butter and boil until thick. Place 1/3 cup butter, 3/4 cup chopped onions, and 1/2 cup very finely-grated carrots into a frying pan and fry, but do not brown.

In a separate frying pan, place 3 cups shredded cabbage and 1/3 cup butter and fry until tender. Boil 3 quarts of water in a large pot. Add 1 1/2 tsp. salt, 1/2 cup sweet cream, 1/2 cup chopped ca rrots and 6 medium sized potatoes (quartered to make approximately 2 cups) and 1 medium beet, halved. Boil until potatoes are tender.

Remove potatoes and mash with 2 Tbsp. butter. Add 1/2 cup sweet cream, set aside.

Place 1 1/2 cup diced potatoes and 3 cup shredded cabbage into potato stock and boil until tender. Pour the mashed potatoes slowly back into the stock water. Add fried onions, carrots, cabbage and tomato sauce. Add

1/2 2cup chopped green pepper and 2 Tbsp. dill. Bring to a boil, but do not boil. Turn off heat.

Remove and discard beet. Season to taste with black pepper and 1/4 cup onion greens or white onions.

Pyrahi

(Makes about 200 pyrahi)

by Lucy Wasilenkoff

12 eggs
1 lb. butter
3 cups milk
2 Tbsp. salt
1/2 cup sugar
2 cups sour cream
4 Tbsp. instant yeast
about 13 cups flour

Scald milk and melt butter. Cool slightly and pour over beaten eggs. Add sugar and salt; beat. Add sour cream and mix well. Add about 5 cups of flour and the yeast. Mix well. Add the rest of the flour and knead well. Let rise until doubled in bulk. Punch down and let rise again.

Form into balls about 1 1/2 inches in diameter. Roll out and fill with filling. Let rise on baking pan before baking. Bake at 400 °F for 15 minutes.

Pyrahi Fillings

1. Boil potatoes until tender. Mash fine and add salt to taste. Cool slightly and add one beaten egg. Use one heaping tablespoonful for each pyrahi.

2. Peel beets and grate fine. Place into a saucepan with a little butter and cook until tender, stirring so that they do not burn. Add salt and a little sugar to taste.

3. Boil pumpkin. Season and fry as the beets (above).

4. Fry sauerkraut in butter and use as above.

5. Cook Italian or kidney beans until soft. Mash and add a little salt and sugar. Add 1 beaten egg to each cupful and use as others.

6. Boil peas until tender. Drain and mash. Salt and butter to season. Add 1 tsp. sugar to each cupful. Use as the others.

7. Use cottage cheese, to which you add salt and egg. Add one egg to each cup of cottage cheese.

25 Kootenay Lake
Kaslo

A Steamboat Picnic

Once this village was a busy city. Here, at one time, the *S.S. Moyie* proudly carried supplies and passengers through the B.C. waterways. Now the village, by-passed by rail and highway, is a community of artists, fishermen, and people who like picking huckleberries. It is, to us, among the most beautiful places on earth.

How to get there

The Village of Kaslo is located on an alluvial fan of the Kaslo River on the west side of Kootenay Lake, on Highway 31. As you enter from the highway, after crossing the Kaslo River bridge, drive straight through town until you come to the junction of 4th and Front Streets. Turn left, and drive west 1 block to 5th Street. Turn right, and immediately right again at the war memorial on Water Street. You will see the picnic table, overlooking the

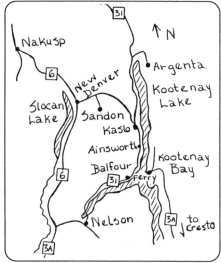

lake, which has what *Maclean's* magazine has called the most beautiful view in Canada. (They were looking from the bar window, which is right behind you). The picnic site is on a rise overlooking the old CPR slip, used in former days for loading railway cars onto the ferry. It is just west of the grand old lady of the lake herself, the *S.S. Moyie*, now dry-docked permanently on the beach.

The S.S. Moyie

The aura of the time of the big boats lingers in this valley. There are still lots of people around who rode the boats or even worked on them. The *Moyie* was earning her keep out on the water until 1957; along with her regular freight and passenger duties she carried

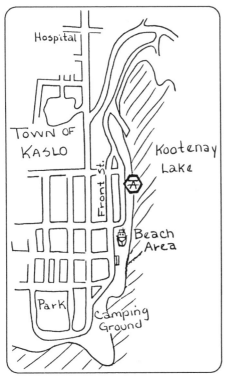

frequent picnic excursions to the various beaches around the lake.

The CPR commissioned the *S.S. Moyie* and ten other shallow-draft river steamers in 1898. It was the time of the Klondike Gold Rush, and the federal government wanted desperately to create an all-Canadian river-rail route to the Klondike. The *Moyie* was originally slated for a section of this route in Northern B.C., along the Stikine River. The all-Canadian route was soon found to be unrealistic, and the *Moyie* was deployed on Kootenay Lake. When she was serving as a passenger ship, she was licensed to carry 400 people, or 250 in combination with a freight load. In the beginning her daily task was to make the round trip from Kootenay Landing, at the southeast tip of Kootenay Lake where the Crowsnest Railway ended, to Nelson and the terminal of the Kettle Valley Railway—and return. The *Moyie* was the link between the two railways for passengers and freight. The steamer provided a very pleasant ambience, with comfortable sleeping accommodation, and excellent service in the lounges and dining saloon.

As the years passed the need for the steam barges faded, replaced by cars and trains. As most of the other boats were quietly retired, the *Moyie* continued to circle the big lake, often providing the only outside link to isolated shore settlements. Service was especially good for residents in the more remote parts of the lake—a phone call to the local CPR office would bring the *Moyie* to your beach the next morning! The *Moyie* was also the collecting service for the fruit production at the various landings, bringing it to larger centres for shipment elsewhere.

By the 1950s the gracious old lady was starting to fade; the CPR no longer maintained the ship as well as before, as she wasn't paying her way. Service in the dining saloon slipped, and then vanished altogether. Towards the end, she spent the weekdays as a rail barge out of Proctor, but on the weekends she recaptured past glory as a

Sunday School Picnic on S.S. Moyie, *1912*

freight and passenger boat, serving the people of the valley for weekend outings and picnics.

On April 27, 1957, she was officially retired. She came to Kaslo to settle, welcomed by hundreds of old friends as she arrived at the dock for the last time.

Kaslo

Indians passed through, and occasionally camped at Kaslo centuries ago, but they rarely stayed long in the Selkirks because of the inhospitable mountains — there were easier places to fish and hunt. Arrowheads and other traces of habitation have been found along the beaches. When the CPR was changing from the narrow gauge of the K & S to standard rail, an Indian skeleton was discovered. But it took the promise of resources of a new sort to bring people in to stay: silver, and trees. Some of the first men to arrive have become legendary, like Jacques Kasleau, after whom the settlement was named, and "Lardo Jack" MacDonald.

They dug all over the mountains, establishing mines on the edges of cliffs in the rocky face of the mountain, or deep in pits below the surface. If you look carefully as you drive along the highway, you will see traces of dozens of mining roads leading up, always up, to someone's dream of riches. And some of the dreams came true, if only for awhile. Some of the prospectors became local legends — most of them made lots of money, but died poor. Many of the towns and cities no longer exist — you have to know where to look to find the remains of Zincton and Whitewater. And nothing remains of Scottie Mitchell's famous hotel up by Bear Lake.

A sawmill appeared at Kaslo and mines proliferated, and by 1893 the town had 2 newspapers, 14 barber shops, and all the amenities of a booming financial centre. Kaslo became a city in 1893. And then the disasters began. The financial institutions in Spokane failed in the depression of 1893, taking the Kaslo banks with them. In February, 1894, fire struck, wiping out all the buildings on the lower half of Front Street, the heart of the business district. Only a few months later a hurricane destroyed most of the remaining buildings on the lower end of the peninsula. And then came flood, with water levels 33 feet above the high lake level. (It was with mixed emotions that the Kaslo citizenry watched the town's brothel, with some of the ladies sitting on the roof, float out into the lake.)

Kaslo would have faded into memory along with the other ghost towns of the Kootenay if it hadn't been for logging, and the fact that the town has always been a supply centre. By 1896 the determined citizens had rebuilt the town and altered the course of the Kaslo River, the source of the flood, forever, protecting the town with substantial dikes on the south side. Although the sawmill is closed now, logging and forestry still provide most of the jobs these days.

Huckleberries

Huckleberries are what everyone has in common in Kaslo — artists, old timers, loggers — everyone loves huckleberries. Everyone also has a favourite huckleberry patch but if you ask where, the answer will be vague: all the best huckleberry patches are family secrets. The first huckleberries may be spotted by a man driving his logging truck along a mountain road on a late July afternoon. When the news reaches town the word spreads quickly, and people drop what they are doing, grab their berry buckets, and rush to the mountain trails with a special determination in their eyes.

If you want to pick huckleberries, come to the valley in mid-August. Since no-one else is likely to tell you where to look, we'll share one of our huckleberry patches with you. Follow A Avenue up the hill to Upper Kaslo, and turn left onto Highway 31A to New Denver. Drive 33 km (20 mi.) until you come to the parking/picnic area at Fish Lake on Highway 31A. Park and walk back across Goat Creek.

As you climb slowly up the bank on the north side of the road you will notice that the hillside is covered with the low, reddish-leafed huckleberry bushes. One bush will lead to another, and another. Soon you will be able to spot the big, fat, reddish berries. They look like reddened blueberries, but there is a big difference — ask anybody in Kaslo! Take a bucket along, or eat them as you go. Watch also for tiny wild strawberries, and there might be some raspberries left, too.

Other things to do

1. Go for a swim in Kootenay Lake. There is a raft for diving and sunning, and a fine sand beach. This beach is a good source of beach glass, if you are a collector.

2. Tour the *S.S. Moyie*. The boat was bought by the town of Kaslo for $1.00 when the CPR retired it. The Kootenay Lake Historical Society has lovingly maintained it, and has raised several hundred thousand dollars for its preservation. The excellent museum displays items from the time of the steamboats, and the engine room is of particular interest to those who want to know how things work. Discover both ends of the communication system from the bridge to the engine room. The museum is open April 15th to October 15th, 10 a.m. to 4:30 p.m. daily.

3. Explore the Woodbury Mining Museum, 16 km (10 mi.) south on Highway 31. The tour takes you into a mine that was driven directly into the mountain, and provides insight into the work of a miner at the turn of the century. Tours leave on demand from June to September, and last about half an hour.

4. Visit Ainsworth Hot Springs, 21 km (13 mi) south of Kaslo on Highway 31. The horseshoe caves, part of the pool complex, should not be missed. This natural sauna has been bringing people to this spot for well over one hundred years.

5. Go fishing. Trout and Kokanee salmon abound here. You can fish off the point, or rent a skiff on the beach. Fishing in the Kaslo River is prohibited, however, as it is a protected spawning area.

6. Take a walk around the village to see some of the old homes. Don't miss the Langham, built in 1893, on the corner of B Avenue and 5th Street. It is now a community centre and art gallery, but it has had many lives. At one time it was a home to some of the Japanese people who were interned here during World War II. A block east on B Avenue is the gracious old Village Hall, built in 1898. It houses the village library as well. The gracefully curving stairways at the entrance are an excellent reminder of Victorian architecture.

7. Ride the longest free ferry in the world, across Kootenay Lake, from Balfour to Kootenay Bay (or vice versa). The ride takes about forty minutes, and the views up and down the lake are splendid.

Things to eat

This picnic begins at Rudolph's Bakery on Front Street, moves along to Andy's Meat Market across the street, and then adjourns to the picnic table behind the Mariner Inn Hotel, overlooking the lake. For dessert, walk past the war memorial to the Mountain King and have a sundae.

The following are a few Kaslo huckleberry recipes, courtesy of the Butler family.

Huckleberry Syrup

4 cups huckleberry juice (about 7 cups berries)
2 cups sugar
2 cups white karo

To make juice:

Place 6 to 8 cups huckleberries in a large kettle; crush with potato masher. Add 1/2 cup water. Heat mixture, mashing fruit as it cooks. Quickly bring to a full rolling boil, stirring constantly. Pour mixture into damp jelly bag; let drip. When cool enough to handle, squeeze out remaining juice by force. Discard pulp.

To make syrup:

Measure 4 cups juice into kettle, stir in sugar and karo. Bring to full rolling boil. Remove from heat, skim if necessary. Immediately pour into clean hot jars. Adjust lids; process in boiling water bath 10 minutes for pints or quarts. Yield: 4 pints.

Note: When you open the jar, if you discover that syrup has jelled, stir vigorously or place jar in pan of warm water and heat until jell disappears.

Delicious on ice cream!

Grandma Butler's Huckleberry Pudding

(Serves 4)

In a medium-sized casserole, spread a thick layer of huckleberries (3-4 cups). Add 1 cup sugar and place in oven while it is heating. In a bowl cream 1/4 cup sugar and 1/4 cup margarine. Add 1 egg and beat well with a drop of vanilla and 1/4 cup cold water. Stir a pinch of salt and 1 tsp. baking powder into 3/4 cup of flour and add to creamed mixture. The batter should be thin. Beat well and spread over the warmed huckleberries. Bake 3/4 hour at 375 °F. Serve warm with a dollop of ice cream.

26 Sandon New Denver

A Ghost Town Picnic

This was the first city in the Interior to have electricity. Two railway lines served the valley, and the town had 3 newspapers and 24 hotels. Hard to believe, isn't it? Almost all of this has vanished in the last 80 years from with the effects of time, forest, flood, fire, and the Great Depression. There are enough traces of the past here, however, to fuel the imagination! It began with the claim of a retired circus performer, Eli Carpenter (you'll note that the stream is called Carpenter Creek) and the three ring circus which followed his discovery.

How to get there

Sandon is just 8 km (5 mi.) off Highway 31A, between New Denver and Kaslo. Watch for the turnoff at what used to be the town of Three Forks (another ghost town), so named for the meeting of the Carpenter, Kane and Seaton Creeks. Select a spot along the creek in Sandon, perhaps facing the few remaining buildings, and enjoy your

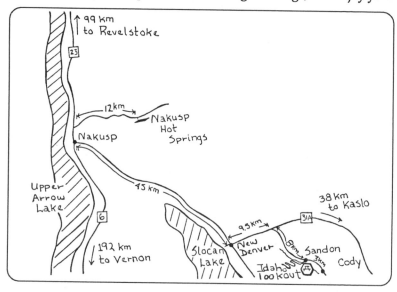

picnic. It is somehow appropriate that there are no amenities; after all, the time for formality in Sandon is long past!

The Story of Sandon

In 1891 Eli Carpenter — who had left his job in an American circus to make his fortune prospecting in the north — and his partner, John Seaton, wandered into an unmapped valley. Near the top of Payne Mountain, 1700 feet up, they happened upon an extremely rich outcrop of silver. Carpenter rushed off to the nearest assay office in Ainsworth to have the ore tested. He took too long in getting the results back to Seaton, and Seaton began to worry. Finally Carpenter returned and reported that the ore was worthless.

Later, while Seaton was drowning his disappointment in the local saloon, he heard that Carpenter, who should have been equally despondent, was, on the contrary, quietly lining up John Sandon and a few others for a return trip to the valley. Seaton quickly recruited four Irishmen (two Hennesseys, McGuigan and Flint) got there ahead of Carpenter's group, and staked the claim of the Noble Five. The mine was successful for many years.

This was the beginning of the rush to The Silvery Slocan, and by 1898 the mining camp of Sandon (another prospector immortalized) had become an incorporated city, with narrow streets winding up the steep hillsides, and the most astonishing main street in the West. Because of the lack of room in this valley in which to build a city, even the creek had to do double duty. It was boarded over and became the main street, as well as serving as the city's water supply.

Sandon suffered the usual calamities which threaten mountain communities. There was a fire in 1900, and some say the town never fully recovered. Others say that the rebuilt town looked better than ever before, despite the fact that it was done in record time! You may wish to have a look at the old photos in the museum and judge for yourself.

Sandon continued to exist for some decades, its community spirit briefly recaptured when hundreds of Japanese families were interned here during World War Two. Once again gardens grew, and children played in the creek.

But one day in the spring of 1955, Carpenter Creek became a raging torrent, and carried away most of the remaining buildings. Three or four buildings representative of the Silvery Slocan era of Sandon still stand. There are boards from others, and you can imagine how Carpenter Creek must have looked when it was a boardwalk, with horses tied up here and there outside the saloons.

The K & S at Payne's Bluff

The K & S Railway

There was nothing peaceful about life in Sandon ninety years ago. Within months of the Noble Five claim, dozens of mines peppered the mountains for miles. There was a critical need for a railway to carry the galena (ore in which silver is found) down to Kaslo and onto the steamers which would take it to the railhead at Nelson, and then to the smelter at Trail.

The construction of the Kaslo and Slocan Railway was begun in 1892, but because of the rough terrain, it took until 1895 to complete it. It operated until 1909, with William Rostron Whittaker (grandfather to John Whittaker) as one of the locomotive engineers.

The Canadian Pacific Railway came into Sandon from New Denver on the other end of the valley, much to the chagrin of the K & S shareholders. In fact, the normally friendly rivalry got a little carried away one night when the K & S boys put a rope around the CPR depot, attached it to one of their engines, and hauled it into the middle of Carpenter Creek. The CPR can perhaps be forgiven if, a few years later, its directors declined a request from the K & S to bail it out of debt!

In 1909 the Cody/Sandon end of the K & S was forced to close down. Maintenance costs were overbalancing profits, owing to frequent avalanches and washouts on the line up to Payne Bluff, the narrow little ledge 1700 feet above the valley. Here the famous photograph of the K & S was taken. The silver deposits were quickly exhausted, and the ever-fickle miners began to move on. The forest fire of 1910 virtually closed the rest of the railway operation; tracks were melted and twisted beyond repair. Parts of the route were later purchased and incorporated into a line connecting Kaslo and Nakusp, and the CPR continued to operate its branch line into Sandon for a few years longer. But soon the trains stopped coming into the Sandon valley altogether.

Things to do

1. Spend some time in the Sandon Museum. It is in an old house near the City Hall — these are two of the few remaining buildings. There is a fine collection of memorabilia from the heyday of Sandon, plus fascinating information on mining history in the region. It is open from 9 a.m. to 6 p.m. daily, July 1 to October 1.

2. Take a tea break in the Tin Cup Cafe, at the west end of the valley. The cafe is in an old house which used to stand on the hill above, until a few years ago when it slid down.

3. Drive or walk on up the valley 3 kilometres to another ghost town: Cody. Cody never really got off the ground as a town, although it did house the head office of the Noble Five Mine for some years. The concentrator, hotel, several houses and a warehouse are still standing. If you walk along the trail to the south, past one of the old houses, you will come across the interesting remains of the town's water system. The old barrel stave water pipes are still in place, and still carrying water down the hill. They have, however, sprung a few leaks!

4. This road is not for the faint of heart, nor for the weary car! But, for one of the most accessible and spectacular mountain-top views around, fill your car with gas and drive it up the gravel switchbacks to Idaho Lookout parking lot, far above Sandon. You will see the beginning of the road on the southwest end of the valley, just past the museum. (We have taken a Ford station wagon, and a Pontiac sedan, up this with no trouble at all.) The road up takes about half an hour, and it is advisable to go up before noon, and come down in the afternoon. That way you will be going with the flow, which is helpful as passing can, in some places, be challenging. The road is a single lane with an abrupt drop on one side and a rock wall on the other, and when you meet another car one of you must back up to the nearest widening in the road. From the parking lot there is an excellent trail

Giardiasis

Commonly known as "beaver fever," giardiasis is an intestinal infection which causes fatigue, abdominal cramps and nausea. Giardiasis occurs all over the world, transmitted in unsanitary conditions, and is often transmitted through water sources. In Canada, as the nickname for the disease implies, the beaver is among the animal carriers of the disease. The excreta of these animals contaminates water in the streams and rivers; the parasite is carried through the water systems, and humans pick it up from the water farther downstream from the site of contamination. The disease is very contagious, and can be spread by unsuspecting persons before the symptoms even occur.

Avoidance of giardiasis is not difficult if you take the necessary precautions. Find out about drinking water before you drink. Local health authorities and parks staff can confirm whether the parasite is present in the local water. When in doubt, boil all drinking water at 100°C (212°F) for five minutes to kill the parasite.

along the crest of the valley, and a breath-taking ridge leads to the forestry lookout at the top (elevation 7,480 feet). It is called Idaho Lookout after the Idaho Mine. The meadows by the trail are almost vertical in some places, and the colour and variety of the flowers are splendid. We have taken kids and spry grandparents on this hike. It is truly spectacular!

4. Recently the Valhalla Society developed — or rather, redeveloped — another hiking trail, this one not hair-raising at all. It begins on the south side of the valley, just before the Tin Cup Cafe, and proceeds along the old K & S railbed. The Kaslo and Slocan was a narrow gauge railway; even so the surveyors and builders had many problems laying the track to get into this valley. If you walk along the gentle grade for a while you will end up at Payne Bluff, where the archival photo of the K & S engine was taken in 1896. The Sandon-McGuigan portion of the line, including the spur to Cody, was closed down in 1909. Watch for huckleberries along this trail if you are walking in August.

Things to eat

Hearty miners' food is what is needed here, stuff that sticks to your ribs so that you can climb the high mountains to the mine with a heavy pack on your back. The menu, therefore, consists of chili con carne, fresh buns (the Kaslo bakery is only 50 kilometres away), cold onions in vinegar, cold vegetables with a dip (celery, carrots, cucumbers, turnips), and apple pie for dessert.

Chili Con Carne

(Serves 6)

45 ml olive oil	5 ml tomato paste
250 ml chopped onion	500 g ground beef
1 clove crushed garlic	1 tin whole tomatoes
125 ml chopped green pepper	1 tin kidney beans
45 ml finely chopped chili pepper	5 ml salt
250 ml chopped celery	1 ml pepper
10 ml chili powder	

Heat the oil in a frying pan. Add onions, garlic, peppers and celery, and fry until soft. Add chili powder and tomato paste and cook for an additional 2 minutes. Add ground beef, and cook until brown. Add tomatoes, kidney beans and seasonings, and stir until boiling. Reduce heat and simmer for one hour, stirring occasionally.

Onions in Vinegar

Select a jar that seals tightly to prevent leakage during transport. Fill the jar with thinly sliced onions. Mix together 1 cup vinegar — malt or cider are best — and 1 cup of water. Add one teaspoon honey, 1/2 tsp. salt and a dash of pepper. Shake, pour over onions and chill until serving time.

Vegetables in Dips

For exotic dips refer to guacamole recipe in the Osoyoos picnic, and houmus recipe in the West Vancouver Cypress Park picnic. Alternatively we suggest a herb mayonnaise.

Herb Mayonnaise

To make the base mayonnaise —

Mix together in a blender at medium speed
    1 egg
    50 ml lemon juice
    2 ml salt
    1/4 ml dry mustard
for about 70 seconds.

Then add 250 ml olive oil in a slow, steady stream through the opening in the top of the blender cap, while the blender is running. Ingredients will emulsify while the oil is being added. If, however, the ingredients fail to emulsify, pour mixture into cup, rinse out blender with hot water, put a new egg and lemon juice into it, and repeat the process, using the mixture in place of the oil, and this time pouring in a slow, steady stream.

Blend in with a spatula:
1 clove of garlic, crushed
85 ml minced green herbs (parsley, chives, basil, marjoram, thyme)

Let stand in refrigerator overnight so that spice flavours permeate.

This is a dangerous food for picnics, since it has real eggs in it, so keep well chilled until serving.

Aunt Nell's Pie Crust

4 cups flour
1 lb. lard
butter the size of an egg
4 Tbsp. sugar
salt
1 Tbsp. vinegar
water

Sift the flour and mix together the dry ingredients. Cut in lard with a pastry cutter until the mixture has the consistency of corn. Place the butter in a measuring cup, add the vinegar, and fill cup to 3/4 full with water. Add to first mixture. Mix well. Store in refrigerator until needed (can also be frozen). Makes 4 pie crusts.

Apple Pie

Preheat oven to 450°F

Mix together
3 cups diced apples
2/3 cups sugar
1 Tbsp. flour
1/2 tsp. cinnamon or nutmeg

Place mixture in
1 unbaked 9" pie crust

Score the top crust to permit steam to escape and place on the pie; fasten securely at the edges. Bake in a hot, 450°F, oven for 10 minutes; then reduce heat to 350°F and continue baking for 30 minutes or until the crust is nicely browned. Set aside to cool, then refrigerate.

Serve cold with a sharp old cheddar cheese.

ROCKY MOUNTAINS

27 Columbia Lake
Canal Flats

A Transportation Picnic

The magic of this plain is that here two mighty river systems, the Columbia and the Kootenay, are just a few feet apart. People have tried to modify this accident of nature to suit their own purposes, as they sought new ways to move people and goods across the difficult terrain. Transportation is therefore the theme for this unusual picnic. As you cross the bridge you have the Columbia River on the east side of the road, and water from the Kootenay system on the west. The canal was a few feet south of the bridge, and residual water from the Kootenay is now separated from the Columbia by the road bed.

How to get there

Canal Flats is at the south end of Columbia Lake, on Highway 93/95. We offer a choice of two picnic sites here: one for the purist who wants to be near the old canal site, and one for people who have kids in the car, and want them to have a place to swim and play.

The Purist Picnic Site

As you drive south on the highway and come down to the flats, you cross a bridge. Just past the bridge is a sharp turn to the left (east) on a gravel road. (If you reach the historic sign you have gone too far — the road is between the sign and the beginning of the bridge.) This road leads down to the level of the lake below. You will need a portable picnic table or a blanket, as there are no facilities whatsoever, but there is a great view of the end of the Columbia and the marshes from which the canal was begun. You are just below the highway viaduct, not far from the railway tracks, and near the site of an ancient Indian canoe portage between the river systems: a veritable picnic of modes of transportation!

The Beach Picnic

Drive straight south on 93/95, and turn east on Burns Road, following the signs to the village of Canal Flats. On the eastern edge of town turn north on Granger Road and follow the signs to Canal Flats Provincial Park, just a few kilometres away. It is well-marked. The view north up the lake is splendid, and many varieties of birds nest in the marshes nearby.

The Flats

Since the first written description of the area is that of David Thompson, we begin with an entry from his diary dated May, 1810.

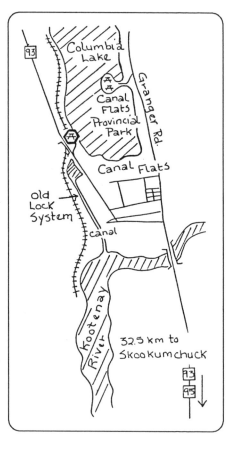

On the 14th we came to the head of the Columbia River 268 miles from our winter Hut. I could never pass this singular place without admiring it's [sic] situation, and romantic bold scenery which I have already described; other Rivers have their sources so ramified in Rills and Brooks that it is not easy to determine the parent stream, this is not the case with Columbia River, near the foot of a steep secondary mountain, surrounded by a fine grassy Plain, lies it's source, in a fine Lake of about eleven square miles of area, from which issues it's wild rapid Stream, yet navigable to the sea, it's descent is great. [Tyrell 1916:458]

The Canal

W. Adolphus Baillie-Grohman was a British entrepreneur of noble birth. His father was a Scot, but his mother was a Tyrolean

The Remains of the Old Canal

countess. In 1882 Adolphus had come to western Canada to search for big game. He was amazed at the proximity of the two great river systems separated by only a mile of gravel at the source of the Columbia. He had noticed the marshy land to the south of the long valley, lands rendered useless by the annual flooding of the Kootenay River. It occurred to him that all of that land could become agriculturally productive if a canal were built to connect the two rivers. This would force part of the Kootenay to flow north into the Columbia, since the lake is eleven feet lower than the river. His scheme appealed to the government, soon he had backers, and the construction of the short canal was underway.

The canal was completed before the project was blocked for good. The Canadian Pacific Railway line ran through the flats then, as it does now. CPR officials became concerned about the threat to the line posed by the canal, and used all the power of officialdom to influence the government of the time to rescind the canal's approval. The canal was opened in 1889 but rules and regulations began to proliferate and the canal was closed the same year.

It remained, however, the only route linking the two river systems and permitting passage north to south. A particularly adventurous captain, Frank Armstrong, piloted two steamboats through the canal after convincing the provincial government to make it navigable once again. He took the *Gwendoline* through in 1894, and the *North Star* in 1902. The *North Star* caused the ultimate demise of the canal, since the vessel was wider than the waterway. It took two weeks to get her through, and the canal was destroyed in the process. If you stand facing the historic marker on the highway you can see part of the old canal. Walk south in the grass below the marker for a little way, and you will come across some of the lumber left from the lock that once controlled the flow of the Kootenay River into the Columbia.

Things to eat

This is a canal picnic: each dish is associated with one of the great canals of the world.

Kiel Canal Sausage

The 61-mile Kiel Canal links the North and the Baltic Seas, and is still the most efficient route between the two. The canal was built between 1887 and 1895, and has since been enlarged to accommodate modern shipping needs.

Buy an assortment of German cold meats from a deli, and don't forget to buy some German mustard while you are there. Unsalted butter is also appropriate. Make sandwiches with the French bread.

Canal du Midi Bread

This canal is a masterpiece of early engineering. Built between 1666 and 1681, it links the Mediterranean to the Bay of Biscay, providing a short-cut through France and avoiding the necessity of ships circling Spain. The canal crosses a range of mountains, with 32 locks in 32 miles rising 206 feet from the Mediterranean, a 3-mile stretch across the summit, and descending 620 feet through 74 locks in 115 miles, to the Atlantic. The Canal du Midi boasts the first tunnel ever constructed as part of a canal; its creation also marked the first use of explosives in underground construction.

Bring along a couple of loaves of French bread, preferably the thin sticks called baguettes.

Suez Shishkabobs

The Suez Canal remains at sea level for its entire 100-mile length. It crosses the Suez Isthmus in Egypt, linking the Red Sea with the Mediterranean. It was opened in 1869.

Bring some bamboo sticks and let your picnickers make their own shishkabobs from a selection of mushrooms, cherry tomatoes, chunks of green and red peppers, wedges of onion, tiny tinned potatoes, and pineapple chunks. Cook over your portable barbecue. Drizzle occasionally with a basting mixture: combine 1/2 cup of olive oil, and 1 teaspoon of each of the following: rosemary, thyme and crushed garlic. Serve by placing the shishkabob stick inside a chunk of French bread and pulling out the stick. The result is delectable.

Venetian Grand Canal Beverage

Venice is the city of canals, and the Grand Canal is Main Street. The canal system links the more than 100 islands in the lagoon on the Gulf of Venice which compose this unusual and very beautiful city. The Grand Canal passes among exquisite historic palaces, many of which remain private homes as they have been for centuries. It is pleasant to rest back in your seat in a gondola, sipping a little wine and singing along with the gondolier should the spirit(s) move you.

Despite the allusions made by those who favour dry French wines that Italian wine is made from a base of old canal water, we like a nice Chianti on this picnic, complete with its provincial basket container. This is the right place for the Venetian glass wine goblets, if you happen to have any.

Panama Bananas

Although this canal is in Central America, it is owned and operated by the Government of the United States. Its strategic importance is considerable, since it links the Atlantic and Pacific Oceans, and precludes the need for the trip around the Cape. Many attempts to build a canal were made over the last two centuries, but often the schemes failed for lack of financing before the first sod was turned or were halted once begun because of malaria and yellow fever among the work crews. The 51-mile canal was finally opened in 1914.

Pass a banana to each picnicker, peel and eat. Swat mosquitoes as necessary, rejoicing that they do not carry malaria in Canal Flats.

Mosquitoes

The term mosquito, meaning little fly, refers to small delicate insects which inhabit diverse environments the world over. The 74 species found across Canada, which are dependent for their reproductive capability on a blood meal, are categorized as serious pests, and have been known to drive many a hardy picnicker out of the park. Some species do carry viruses which infect humans. The anophile species in Canada carried malaria in the early 1800s, but this parasite is now unheard of here. Other viruses can be transmitted by mosquitoes, but they do not commonly afflict humans. The largest threat from mosquitoes in Canada is discomfort from the bites of the females.

Mosquitoes belong to the order Diptera, and to the family Culicidae. Eggs are laid in moist ground or in standing water. The egg phase is one of seven phases the mosquito passes through before reaching adulthood. Most Canadian species will complete only one generation each year, but some complete two or three; the average life span is three weeks. Males feed on carbohydrates alone, and the common anautogenous female requires a carbohydrate meal — usually nectar — as well as a blood meal to initiate laying of her eggs. Usually females mate once immediately after reaching adulthood, and then begin the search for a blood meal.

Approaching a warm-blooded victim, the female will first be attracted by concentrations of carbon-dioxide, then she will sense the body heat. After landing on the host, the female will probe the skin with the proboscis, in search of a capillary. She will consume up to three times her body weight and wait twenty-four to thirty-six hours for digestion and appropriation of the blood meal. Then the female seeks a spot in which to lay her batch of eggs. She may subsequently repeat the process of feeding and laying eggs up to five times per generation — unless she is swatted.

28 Fisherville/Wild Horse Creek Cranbrook

A Prospector's Picnic

You will find no facilities here now such as there were in 1865, when the town of Fisherville had 5,000 residents with an unknown number of transients in its hotels and rooming houses. This picnic is set as close to the ghosts of the former residents as you can get: beside the ancient graveyard.

How to get there

Finding this site is a bit tricky. The picnic takes place at Wild Horse Burying Ground, just above the ghost town: it is up a logging road not far from Fort Steele. To get there, drive 1 km (.6 mi.) north of Fort Steele on Highway 93/95. There is a junction by the Fort Steele Resort store and gas station; turn east on the road to Bull River and the Kootenay Trout Hatchery. Drive past the campground on your left, over the Texas gate, and turn left onto the logging road. Follow the logging road up the mountain for almost 6 km (4 mi.), keeping to the right and looking out for logging trucks. You will come to a dirt road on your right which leads quickly to the Wild Horse Cemetery. Turn in and park. You will find a level place under the tree canopy at the top of the cemetery, just near the gate. This is our picnic site.

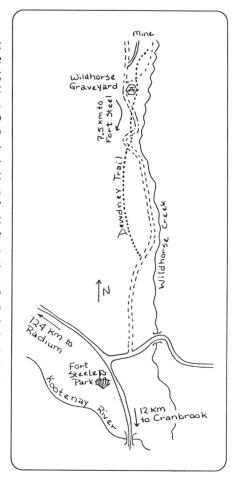

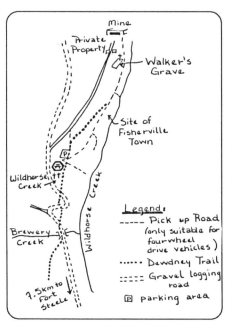

Legend:
---- Pick up Road (only suitable for four-wheel drive vehicles)
...... Dewdney Trail
===== Gravel logging road
Ⓟ parking area

Wild Horse Creek and Fisherville

In the summer of 1864 Jack Fisher found placer gold in Wild Horse Creek, and just a few months later Fisherville was a flourishing town below where the cemetery is now, and closer to the river. Fisherville didn't last long, because the miners discovered gold even in the gravel beneath the town, so the buildings were quickly torn down or burned, and only gravel piles remained. New cabins were built up the rise a bit, and the new town was called Kootenai, but was usually referred to as Wild Horse. After only two years the gold was exhausted and the miners moved on. The town of Kootenai struggled on for a few years, but eventually gave way to the forest.

You will find another cemetery nearby, that of the Chinese miners; it is empty now, as all the remains were eventually returned to China. The grave of Tom Walker can be visited further down the hill. Tom, a young Irish miner, died in a gun battle in 1864, at the age of just twenty-seven. His father made two trips out from Ireland in later years and attempted to find his son's grave, but he failed both times. Imagine how hard it would be to hunt through the thick undergrowth of the steep hillside in those days. If you take the recommended walk, however, you will find it quite easily. There is a guest book in a case nearby. Perhaps there is some justice, however. Tom's father didn't manage to visit this peaceful gravesite, but many hundreds of people have done so since, and paused to consider the violence and immediacy of frontier life.

Two important personages observed wild horses here. The first was David Thompson, who referred in his journal to the horses near what he called "Skirmish Brook"; the second was Jack Fisher, who christened the waterway Wild Horse Creek. There are no wild horses to be found now, only interesting ghosts. If you walk through the gate and down to the foot of the cemetery you will notice that the white crosses are all marked "unknown." The crosses are recent, bringing order to what was once a decaying piece of history.

Forestry Service Roads

Mysterious roads which lead up mountains are almost irresistible — but many of them are logging roads, and must be driven with caution. A pleasant family drive along a beautiful forestry service road can be spoiled, to say the least, by the sudden appearance of a rapidly approaching logging truck. This can be especially frightening when you realize that the road is only one lane wide, that logging trucks appear to be two lanes wides, and that logging trucks cannot stop. They travel these roads at speeds above eighty kph, and it is the responsibility of the non-industrial vehicle to get out of the way. There are usually widenings in the road, or pull-off spots here and there — watch for these, and be prepared to get to one quickly.

A number of measures can prevent an unexpected encounter between logging trucks and your small family car. Always stay on the right hand side of the road, even if it is narrow. Before embarking on an active logging road, check with the local forestry services office. They can advise you about which roads are safe, and when. Sometimes the logging trucks go up in the morning and down in the afternoon, so you are safer if you keep to this pattern. Logging trucks are radio controlled, but even if you have a citizens' band radio in your car, don't rely on it: logging companies often use frequencies which are inaccessible to the public.

Logging trucks have right-of-way by right-of-might, so stay alert, do not block the road, don't haul a travel-trailer, and obey all road signs.

The Dewdney Trail

The Dewdney Trail reached Fisherville in 1865, creating the final link from the coast, defining the southern route across B.C. The trail begins at Hope, the gateway to the interior, and was the route followed by the prospectors seeking Cariboo Gold. It first ended at Princeton (then Vermilion Forks), and was constructed to prevent all the gold from finding its way south to the United States by opening a route to a Canadian business centre — Victoria. The second part of the trail, from Hope to Wild Horse, was added for the same reason, following the discovery of gold in the East Kootenays. Edgar Dewdney was the young surveyor who worked on both sections of the trail, but was primarily responsible for the construction of the latter portion.

The Dewdney Trail was 576 km (360 mi.) long, and Dewdney was only 28 years old when he began work on it.

Graveyard at Wild Horse Creek

Things to do

1. Take the circle walk around the Fisherville/Wild Horse site by following the trail. There are signs along the way indicating what once stood, and where. Watch for the side trail to Tom Walker's grave — it is halfway down the hill, between the upper and lower town sites.

2. Continue on down to the river to see traces of the old mine workings. There is also evidence of the old hydraulic system. This system hastened the process of recovering gold by spraying cliffs above the creek with water under pressure, thereby forcing the gravel down to creek level. Since gold is heavier than other minerals, it fell to the bottom and was more easily recovered. This process has now been outlawed by the B.C. government because of the extensive environmental damage it causes. If you are lucky, you may find present-day placer miners down by the creek. With the increase in the price of gold in the past few decades many people feel that it is worthwhile to work over the old sites, and some gold has indeed been found here recently.

3. Walk back along the last two kilometres of the Dewdney Trail. You will have noticed various signs indicating access to other sections of the trail as you drove up the logging road. Our favourite place

to start walking is from the lower road, the old main street of Fisherville. You will see the trailhead marked, just beside the one remaining building.

4. Visit Fort Steele, a town restored to the glory it enjoyed in the 1890s. Fort Steele began as a cable ferry crossing to serve the miners in Fisherville. John Galbraith's investment paid off, and in 1877 Galbraith's Ferry became the home of Sam Steele's crack team of North-West Mounted Police for 13 months. In recognition of the "law and order" established by the Mounties, the citizens of Galbraith's Ferry changed the name of the town to Fort Steele. The town quickly became an important steamship harbour, and continued to grow until the Crowsnest Pass Branch of the railway passed through Cranbrook instead of through Fort Steele. As with many other transport-dependent towns, this advance in technology was the kiss of death. Nothing but a few ruined buildings were left standing in 1961, when the restoration process began. The site offers much information about the various stages of history on this part of the Kootenay River. Today over 60 reconstructed buildings can be seen at Fort Steele.

Things to eat

Here in Wild Horse — or Fisherville — we will have a miners' meal, featuring sourdough pancakes smothered in golden maple syrup and sour cream, with a little bit of history tucked in; bacon (we figure you can manage this part yourself); sweet mixed pickles to add a savory touch — buy these in advance; and fruit compote. This meal is quite authentic, as pork was preserved by making it into bacon, maple syrup was one of the few sweetening agents the miners had, and the fruit compote could be made from a variety of dried fruits.

Contrary to popular belief, miners did not exist solely on bannock and beans. Dry granular yeast is a relatively recent product. Before this, it was necessary to keep yeast alive. Next to his gold pan, a miner's most valuable possession was his sourdough starter. This had to be kept cool but never permitted to freeze. Starter should not be stored in a metal container, so miners often used old wooden buckets or hollowed-out logs as their sourdough containers.

Sourdough Starter

We offer the recipe, but if you can find someone who will share his starter, so much the better!

2 cups flour
2 cups warm water
1 packet dry granular yeast

Mix well and keep in a warm place overnight, out of drafts. In the morning the mixture should be bubbly and frothing, and is now called a "sponge." Place one half cup of the sponge in a jar with a tight cover. Store in the refrigerator; this is your sourdough starter for next time. Once you have made starter, you should never have to repeat this process again. (We have heard of present-day miners who claim to be using starter that dates from before the turn of the century.) A bit of starter makes a nice gift, along with recipes explaining what to do with it.

In order to preserve your own supply of starter, feed it before you use it each time.

How to feed your sourdough:

In a mixing bowl combine the 1/2 cup starter with 2 cups warm water and 2 cups flour. Beat well and set in a warm place, free from drafts, to develop overnight. Cut off 1/2 cup for the next time and proceed with your recipe.

Sourdough Hotcakes

(Serves 4 - 6)

To the remaining sponge add:
   2 eggs
   1 tsp. soda
   1 tsp. salt
   1 tsp. sugar
   2 Tbsp. oil

Blend together, bake on a hot, greased griddle.

For using the starter in muffins, waffles, bread and chocolate cake, see *The Northern Cookbook,* by Eleanor A. Ellis.

Fruit Compote

Select a mixture of prunes, dried apples, apricots, pears, peaches and a handful of raisins. Wash the fruit, place in saucepan, cover with water and soak overnight. Drain, rinse and add a few slivers of lemon rind, a cinnamon stick and some nutmeg, and 1/4 cup of honey for each pound of fruit. Cover with water and simmer for 10 to 15 minutes.

29 Crowsnest Pass Sparwood (Michel-Natal)
A Coal Miner's Picnic

This picnic is a striking mix of the past and the present. The mine which has always been the foundation of the economy here in the pass still exists; the town to which it gave rise does not. Our picnic site is in plain view of both the Westar mine and the site of the town of Natal.

How to get there

The picnic table is on the north side of Highway 3, 3.9 km (2 1/2 mi.) east of the Travel Info Centre in Sparwood. It is across the road from the Westar Mining Company Head Office Building. There is a large rock next to the site, and the single picnic table is on a small patch of grass facing part of the Westar strip mine (see photo). This spot, with its view of the industrial development, is a fine place to contemplate the history of the coal mining district of the West.

Picnic Site at Natal

The Pass

The Crowsnest Pass is one of the four major passes through the Rocky Mountains, and the last to be discovered by the Europeans, although it had been used for centuries by the Blackfoot and Cree. John Palliser knew of the pass from the Indians, but Michael Phillipps, a Hudson's Bay clerk, was likely the first European to visit the pass. Hunting for gold in the district in 1873, he found coal instead: soon to be called black gold because it proved almost as lucrative to some. In 1882 a geological survey was conducted, and the Crowsnest Pass Coal Company was incorporated in 1897. The Canadian Pacific Railway completed construction through the pass in 1898, making the exploitation of the coal resources feasible. Soon entrepreneurs arrived on the trains, as did immigrants from Slovakia, Wales, and many other places. Towns sprang up every mile or two through the pass. The major ones were Bellevue, Blairmore, Coleman, Sentinel, Frank, Hillcrest, and Michel-Natal. The economic bases of these towns were precarious, each dependent upon the fortunes of a nearby mine.

Michel-Natal

The settlement of Michel was established in 1898 to house the miners, and by 1903 more than 500 people were living there. In 1907 a new settlement was built just down the road from the old one. At first it was called New Michel, but the name was soon changed to Natal. Predictably, houses sprang up between the two settlements, and the resulting intermediate zone was called Middletown. The combined settlements reached their peak population in 1920, at over 2000 people. With the Depression the population began to decrease, and there was a sharp fall after the fire in 1937 which destroyed the colliery. But the community of Michel-Natal persevered despite these setbacks. It was not economic or natural disaster which finally caused the death of the town, but government edict. In the 1960s, when British Columbia began to encourage tourism in the province, it was decided that the Crowsnest Pass entrance to the province was an eyesore. In addition, there was concern that living adjacent to the mine created a health hazard for the residents of Michel-Natal, increasing the likelihood of lung disease. Amid considerable controversy, the residents of Michel-Natal were moved to a brand new townsite five miles down the road, and Sparwood was born. Michel-Natal was razed.

The picnic table is in a small park on the Natal townsite. Bodie Park was named in honour of the man who initiated reclamation on the Michel-Natal strip.

Sparwood

This relatively new town continues to be a coal mining centre. Several mining companies provide jobs in the various mines in the surrounding mountains. Since 1960 the area has been a principal supplier of coal to Japan. About 20,000 tons are taken from the ground daily.

Things to do

1. Tour the largest open pit coal mine in Canada, the Westar Mining, Balmer operation. Visitors should check at the Sparwood Travel Info Centre for tour schedule, or phone 425-2423. Make sure that you see the world's largest truck, the Terex Titan: 350 tons. Loaded, this truck weighs 1 million pounds! It is driven by a 3,300 horsepower, 16 cylinder locomotive engine. The tires are 11 feet high.

Things to eat

This is a picnic in the traditional sense of the word, offering unusual things from various places — all of them relating to Sparwood in some way. Since you are in the coal branch, purists will, of course, use their Coleman stoves. Alternatively, you can use charcoal briquets in your hibachi. The Japanese stir fry is complemented by a warm cup of saki. Why Japanese? Because the Japanese are the major buyers of Sparwood coal. The Flapper Pie is reminiscent of the 1920s, the heyday of Michel-Natal.

Japanese Stir-Fry

Prepare strips of beef or chicken, cabbage, carrots, onions, zucchini, and mushrooms, because, after all, this was a strip mine. (Dare we call this a "strippers' picnic"? No!)

To your stir-fry mix, add bean sprouts just before serving. To add zest, in addition to the usual soy sauce, add a generous portion of grated fresh grated ginger, and a few splashes of rice vinegar.

The easiest way to eat a stir-fry on a picnic is to tuck it into pocket bread, or pita, bread.

Flapper Pie

Flapper Pie has been chosen for dessert, since Michel-Natal was at its peak during the flapper era, a town of the roaring twenties.

Crust:
  22 crushed Graham wafers,

mixed with
>   *75 ml sugar*
>   *125 ml melted butter*

Set aside 250 ml for top of pie. Press the remainder into the bottom of an 8 inch (20 cm) pie pan, and chill.

Filling:

Mix in a double boiler
>   *500 ml milk*
>   *1 ml salt*
>   *170 ml sugar*
>   *60 ml corn starch*

Partially beat
>   *3 egg yolks*
and add to the mixture. Cook for 3 minutes.

Remove from heat and add:
>   *30 ml butter*
>   *5 ml vanilla*
Pour into crumb shell.

Meringue:

Beat until frothy
>   *3 egg whites*
>   *1 ml cream of tartar.*

Slowly add
>   *90 ml sugar*
beating until mixture stands in stiff peaks. Spread over the cream filling and sprinkle the remaining crumbs over the top.

Bake at 350 °F (180 °C) for 15 to 20 minutes.

30 Lake Windermere Invermere
The Map-Maker's Picnic

The picnic site is on one of the Wilmer promontories looking south down the length of Lake Windermere. Follow the map carefully to a spectacular spot — no facilities, but a view that more than compensates. You will be in a wildlife sanctuary just a few miles north of David Thompson's Fort, Kootenay House.

How to get there

If you are coming from Invermere, drive north toward Highway 93, but turn left on to the Toby Creek Road then right after crossing the bridge, and follow the signs to Wilmer.

If you are coming from Highway 93, turn west at the Athalmer/ Invermere exit. Drive through Athalmer and turn north at the sign for Wilmer/Panorama. This is Toby Creek Road. Follow the signs to Wilmer.

Drive through the town of Wilmer, staying on the main road despite the few turns, and out on the northeast side on the Westside Road, above the lake. After you leave the town you will cross over a Texas gate (a ditch in the road covered by steel pipes, forming a small bridge); check your odometer carefully here, because the next turnoff is easily missed. The site is exactly 0.7 km from the Texas gate. On the right is a small rutted track which is quite safe for your car. Follow it for a few metres to the promontory. Park anywhere and spread your blanket where you can enjoy the splendid vistas.

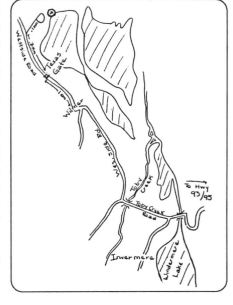

Ants

No picnic book would be complete without the mention of ants. The word "ant" refers to most of the insects of the family of Formicidae, order Hymenoptera. They are a most numerous, diverse and fascinating insect group. Ants are social insects, and although prehistoric ant colonies contained as few as twelve ants, modern colonies often contain millions. They live in a complex hierarchical society — usually, although not always, dwelling in the ground, and frequently beneath picnic blankets.

Although ants are fascinating to watch, they are not welcome guests at blanket picnics. Their tiny segmented bodies make them easy to recognize, and a few species do bite. Some species even fly. There is no sure way to avoid ants at your picnic, but some techniques work better than others. The first step to take is to scout out your spot very carefully and be sure to avoid setting up on top of — or near to — an ant colony. Avoid dousing yourself with bug repellent as this may repel other picnickers, but not the ants. Some people believe that ants can be distracted from a picnic by placing a bowl full of sugar and water four paces from the picnic blanket. The idea is that the ants will head for the sticky bowl instead of your iced tea glass. In reality, the ants still come marching across your salami.

Mapping the ancient highways

European explorers such as Alexander Mackenzie and David Thompson have been given credit for "discovering" the west. This is misleading, to say the least, since the land had already been occupied by native people for at least 10,000 years. In order to establish trading forts for their companies, the Hudson's Bay and the North West Company, it was necessary for traders to journey into the northwest of Canada to cultivate trading relationships with the Indians, the suppliers of furs. David Thompson spent an entire winter with the Peigans in what is now southwestern Alberta. Thompson is remembered as the "map-maker" for the painstaking measurements recorded in his daily journal which he later turned into valuable maps. Without his knowledge of several Indian languages and his carefully established friendships with the leaders of many Indian nations, the road to the Pacific through Howse Pass via the Athabasca River, and the route via the Columbia would have remained inaccessible to European traders for many more years.

Alexander Mackenzie was the first to write of the mighty Columbia River as a route to the Pacific. The brutal barrier of the Shining

Mountains, the Cree name for the Rockies, and the threatened enmity of the Peigan Indians, prevented traders from following Mackenzie's recommended route until 1807. It was David Thompson who finally persuaded the Kootenay Indians to guide him through this new pass to the big lake beyond. He established Kootenay House on the northern end of what is now called Windermere Lake, a widening of the Columbia River. It was some time, however, before Thompson realized that he had indeed reached the Columbia. Because it flowed north when he expected it to flow south to the Pacific he continued to seek information from the Indians about Mackenzie's now legendary Columbia River. In years to come he would follow and map the course of this great river and learn that its course does turn south eventually, and on to the Pacific.

The Peigans had tried to stop Thompson from trading with the Kootenay and Salish Indians farther west since, for as long as they were the only ones with guns the Peigans controlled the region. A trading post in the Kootenay district would quickly alter this balance. Thus, after several delays related to avoiding the Peigan tribesmen, Thompson and his party arrived at the mouth of the great river in July of 1811 only to find that an American expedition led by John Jacob Astor had arrived by travelling by boat around the tip of South America three months earlier. The land which Thompson had intended to claim for the British Empire had already been claimed for America; it was then called Astoria, and later Washington.

Things to do

1. Visit the site of Kootenay House. All that is left now are the chimneys. Even the water course has changed since 1807 when the lake was close enough for buckets to be lowered into it from the fort at night during a Peigan siege. However, it is clearly a fine site for a trading fort. Thompson and his men built a three-sided stockade, the fourth side being the cliff above the water. It was a sturdy stockade with loops here and there for muskets. Thompson, his wife Charlotte (daughter of an Irish Hudson's Bay factor and his Cree wife), and their children spent three winters here, trading with the Kootenay Indians.

David Thompson, surely Canada's greatest geographer, having travelled over 50,000 miles on foot, horseback and by canoe to map half a continent, was forgotten for over 70 years after his death. Even when his work was acknowledged, recognition came slowly. The monument at Kootenay House was the first to be erected, and that was not until 1922, 150 years after David and Charlotte Thompson had established the first trading post on the Columbia River.

2. Visit the "David Thompson Tree" on the point at the southwestern

corner of the town of Invermere. Follow the map carefully, and as you drive down the narrow, one-way street past little cottages tucked beneath the brow of the steep hill, you will notice a huge old tree stump, about 12 feet high. It has a burn mark at its base, and it was here that David Thompson's North West Company expedition first camped when they reached Lake Windermere in 1805. About 30 years ago the tree had to be cut down because it had become a danger to the surrounding houses. Axe marks were found in a nearby tree. Growth rings were counted back, and it seemed that someone with a steel-headed axe had been camping in the shelter of the cliff, and had lighted a campfire nearby in the year 1807. This coincides

The David Thompson Tree

exactly with the date in David Thompson's detailed journals on which he described alighting on the point and camping here. The campsite was abandoned for the actual site of Kootenay House, as it was more easily defended than the low land on the point. There is a sign on the tree stump explaining the history. It is right beside the road, but on private property, so be unobtrusive as you wander in the footsteps of the great map-maker.

3. The north Windermere Lake wetlands have been set aside as a place for observation and non-consumptive recreational activities. The wide variety of winter waterfowl and ungulates was noticed by David Thompson in his diary in January of 1809:

> January 5th. took a wood Canoe and went down to the little Lake, which had upwards of one hundred Ducks about one third of them Stock Ducks [mallards], the finest of Ducks. I killed one Stock and three fishing Ducks, the first very good, the latter bad tasted, but the Canadian[s] eat them; after this I frequently killed one of these ducks for a change.

January 11th. Two Swans came, but being disturbed again left us. The Birds about us are, the bald headed Eagle, a small Hawk, the Raven, and Magpies numerous: these with the Raven frequent the edge of the shore ice and make sad havoc among the small fry of fish. There are also some fine Woodpeckers with scarlet heads and rich plumage. As there was now plenty of shore ice of sufficient thickness, we made a Glacier for frozen meat. This is a square of about twelve feet, the bottom and sides lined with ice; in this we placed one hundred and sixty Thighs of Antelopes; this is necessary, for as soon as the fine weather comes on, the Deer of all species leave the low lands, and retire for fresh grass and shelter to the vallies of the high Hills. In these meat glaciers, a layer of Meat is laid on the ice, and then a layer of ice, and thus continued: when the warm weather comes on, it is covered with fine branches of the Pine, the ice is found so much thawed that the pieces are joined together, the meat is also thawed, but remains very sound, though [it] has lost it's juice and is dry eating. I have even seen the meat covered with a kind of moss but not in the least tainted. [Tyrell 1916:400-401]

We suggest that you spend a while identifying the birds that are inhabiting the wetlands while you are here. The picnic site is on a rise surrounded by marshes. As well as the birds listed by David Thompson, there are mud-swallows nesting in the cliffs, ospreys, falcons, blue herons and many geese.

4. Visit the Valley Pioneer Museum in Invermere. It is located on the north side of the main road as you enter Invermere from Athalmer. Among the precious items displayed here is a copy of *David Thompson's Narrative*, edited by J. Tyrell in 1916, and published in a limited edition of 500 copies. One of these is in the museum in a glass case, and the quotes from Thompson's Journal appear in this picnic courtesy of the museum staff. Another intriguing exhibit is the slice of the tree with the axe scar, reputedly made by one of the men on Thompson's first expedition into the Columbia valley. There are many other fascinating Kootenay and Salish artifacts.

5. Pick up a brochure at the museum and take a walking tour of the town of Invermere. There are several interesting old buildings worth seeing.

Things to eat

Although David Thompson waxes poetic in his journals about the exquisite taste of wild horse meat, the custom of eating horses in

Canada is a bit passé. Still, in keeping with his dependence on wild food, we suggest a gourmet feast of cold duck, roasted before the picnic and served chilled with a tart wild cranberry jam.

David Thompson Duck

Obtain hunting license. Shoot two ducks in season, and only where it is permitted. Have your dog retrieve them. Clean the ducks immediately by removing crops and innards. Upon reaching your cabin hang the duck in the shed for 24 to 48 hours. Pluck feathers from the ducks. To remove the pinfeathers more easily, singe them first by holding the duck by the legs over a candle flame; then pick the pinfeathers out with your forefingers and the tip of your knife. Check carefully for shot- or dog-damaged areas. Remove the oil sac from the base of the tail.

Wash the ducks, rub with salt. Place an onion in each cavity. Place on a spit and roast over hot coals for 15 to 25 minutes. If a crisp skin is desired, pour a little heated medicinal brandy over the skin when the duck is done. Allow the brandy to flame to burn off the spirits. (David Thompson was an abstainer.)

Alternatively, wrap ducks individually in heavy foil, and cook in very hot oven (500 °F) for 30 minutes.

A salad of orange slices and onion rings with a light poppy seed dressing will complement the duck.

Hunter's Salad

Place slices of peeled orange and grapefruit artfully on a bed of fresh young dandelion leaves (lettuce may be substituted if it is late in the summer). Place thin slices of red onion among the fruit, and drizzle with the following dressing:

Combine:
1/4 cup tarragon vinegar
2 Tbsp. water
1/2 cup salad oil
1 Tbsp. sugar
1 Tbsp. poppy seeds

The following cranberry sauce is tangy; some of us like to finish off by spreading it on Mrs. Marples' scones, as well as on the duck.

Charlotte's Cranberry Sauce

4 cups wild cranberries
1/2 cup water
3 cups sugar

Wash and pick over berries, combine ingredients and simmer until soft. Chill and serve.

We complete the meal by including a recipe from more recent history. Mrs. Marples' Scones are well known in the valley, and were sought after by miners and steamship captains alike as they passed through the valley just a few generations ago. This recipe is taken from the Windermere Historical Society's collection of pioneer recipes. Serve the scones with tea.

Mrs. Marples' Scones
(Makes 8)

2 cups flour
3 Tbsp. sugar
1 tsp. salt
4 Tbsp. raisins
4 tsp. baking powder
1 egg, beaten
3 Tbsp. shortening
1/2 to 2/3 cup milk

Mix dry ingredients. Cut in shortening. Beat egg, add to milk and add to dry ingredients.

Place on cookie sheet and pat down to about 1 inch thick. Score in pie-shaped wedges. Brush with milk. Bake at about 400 °F until light brown.

31 Cominco Gardens Kimberley

A Bavarian Company Picnic

This picnic carries the theme that the city has already chosen for itself. This is the self-proclaimed "Bavarian city of the Canadian Rockies." It is also very much a "company town," with Cominco providing many of the jobs for the residents. Thus, we are holding a company picnic in the Cominco Gardens — where else?

How to get there

From Highway 95A, which is also the main street, Ross Street, turn north on Wallinger Avenue, and drive 4 blocks; turn a sharp left, almost a U-turn, onto 4th Avenue, and follow the hill until you reach the Cominco Gardens parking lot.

The Sullivan Mine

Kimberley is truly a one-company town. Its history parallels the development of the mine. The original mine here was the old North Star, but records regarding it are scanty. The present mine was discovered in 1892 by Pat Sullivan, after whom it is named, but the original owners had difficulty processing the ore. The lead-zinc ore is complex, as is the processing technology. In 1913 Cominco purchased the mine, and began by sorting the ore by hand, according to lead content. It wasn't until 1920 that a satisfactory method for separating the lead and zinc components of the ore was discovered. This "differential flotation" process revolutionized the mine — and Cominco became a world leader in lead-zinc production.

The mine itself, among the largest lead, silver and zinc mines in the world, is just northwest of the city. Ore is mined by both open pit and underground methods. From there the ore is carried to the Sullivan Concentrator for processing, and then off to Trail for smelting. Cominco has grown over the years; the company now has a wide variety of interests in 13 different countries. It remains 94 per cent Canadian-held. In Kimberley Cominco employs about 1,200 people at the mine and the concentrator.

What's in a name?

Trivia nuts will be interested to know that the first settlement here in 1892 was called Mark Creek Crossing. In 1896 the name Kimberley was selected by one Colonel Redpath, an American mining entrepreneur. Perhaps he thought that by naming the place after the very profitable South African diamond mine at Kimberley, his investments would flourish. The South African Kimberley was named after the British Colonial Secretary in 1871, the first Earl of Kimberley, who placed the South African diamond mines under British "protection," thus ensuring that the profits of South African soil and toil would continue to leave the country.

The Cominco Gardens

Our picnic is set inside the gardens, at the tables across from the tea shop. There are only enough chairs for about 16 people, but others can bring folding chairs and blankets if your company picnic group exceeds this number. The garden is open to the public from June through September. It features brilliant floral displays with 48 varieties of flowers, and over 50,000 plants. The head gardener must use Elephant Brand fertilizer!

Things to do

1. Tour the Sullivan Mine. Tours leave the Info Centre near the Platzl weekdays in July and August at 9 a.m., returning at noon. Children must be at least 8 years old to go on this tour. The tour includes both pit and underground operations.

2. Check the fire hydrants in Kimberley! Each one is different, painted by Kimberley residents in an effort to beautify their little city. The fire hydrants keep bringing us back — we love the originality of the idea, and each of us has a favourite.

3. Walk from the gardens to the Platzl, in the centre of

A Fire Hydrant in Kimberley

town. The beginning of the walk is indicated by a sign in the garden. It takes about 10 minutes. The Platzl, a pedestrian precinct of Bavarian-inspired design, is well worth a visit. If you are close by the clock tower on the hour you can observe the operation of the biggest cuckoo clock in the world. Have a coffee and German pastry in a sidewalk cafe while you wait.

4. If you can be here in early July, try to attend the Old Time Accordion Championships. Check with the Info Centre or the Chamber of Commerce for exact dates.

The Biggest Cuckoo Clock in the World

Things to eat

You needn't be associated with any company, let alone Cominco, to picnic here in the gardens. It is open to everyone, for a small admission fee. We couldn't resist this opportunity, however, to supply a few recipes for larger groups, so here is the Company Picnic for a group of 40. For even larger groups, see the chapter entitled, "Loaves and Fishes."

The menu reflects the Bavarian theme of the city with German potato salad, frankfurters on buns, marinated cucumber salad, sauerkraut, and for dessert, Black Forest cake. Wash it all down with cold German pilsener.

Note: If planning a picnic for 40 people (or even fewer) causes you to shrink in terror, there is another way: call the tea house in advance and ask them to cater your picnic.

You will need to buy:

60 frankfurters
5 dozen hot dog buns
4 Black Forest cakes

If your group includes a large proportion of adolescent boys, double the above quantities. Don't forget a selection of mustards and relishes. We especially like green pepper Dijon mustard, but our kids prefer French's.

German Potato Salad for 40

12 pounds potatoes
4 dozen eggs (hard boiled)
2 cups finely chopped onion

1 cup finely chopped dill pickles
1/2 cup chopped pimento
1 cup chopped green pepper

Boil and cool potatoes. Peel and dice into a large bowl. Slice the eggs, and add remaining ingredients. Mix well.

To make the dressing, combine:
2 cups mayonnaise
1 cup hot bouillon
1 cup white vinegar

1/2 cup salad oil
1 Tbsp. dry mustard
salt and pepper to taste

Mix into the salad thoroughly, but gently. Let stand in refrigerator for at least 12 hours. Keep chilled until serving.

Cominco Cucumber Salad

(serves 40)

Place 16 large or 20 medium cucumbers, peeled and thinly sliced in a bowl with 6 tsp. salt, and let stand for 2 hours.

Make a sauce:
3 cups sour cream
4 Tbsp. sugar
4 Tbsp. vinegar
1/4 cup chopped green onion
pepper to taste

Mix gently with cucumbers and chill.

Sauerkraut

(serves more than 40 - take what you need)

Sauerkraut is the traditional way of pickling and preserving cabbage. Nowadays people buy it ready-made from their grocery store or deli. In case, however, your garden produced too many cabbages this year, the *Canadian Homestead Cookbook* by Jean Scargall provides the following:

Slice, chop, and dice:
25 lb. cabbage
1/2 large onion
3/4 cup salt
1/4 cup red pepper for colour

Press lightly into a crock and fill to cover with lukewarm water. Cover with a cloth and plate and set in a warm place.

Leave for 5 days, then bottle.

32 Sinclair Canyon
Radium
A Hiker's Picnic

The Sinclair Canyon, on the edge of the Kootenay National Park, is a narrow rock channel at the bottom of which runs the Vermilion River. The canyon forms one of the most spectacular passes through the Rocky Mountains, and was used by Indians for centuries before it became a trade route for the Hudson's Bay Company. Its popularity continues today not only because of the natural beauty of the place, but because of the famous hot springs which attract those who wish to "take of the waters."

We offer two picnic places, neither having the usual facilities, but both worth the possible inconvenience.

How to get there

The Sinclair Pass is at the south end of Highway 93, just a couple of kilometres before it joins Highway 95 at Radium. You will come upon the Hot Springs rather suddenly. Watch for the parking lot just across the street on the west side of Highway 93, and park there. Energetic picnickers can walk to the southwest corner of the parking lot and see the sign indicating the head of the Juniper Trail. It is a fairly easy walk one kilometre up the side of the canyon to the viewpoint at the top, from where you can see the magnificent Columbia Valley spread below. There is a bench at the top of the canyon, and this is where we like to stop and have our picnic. (Our children climbed up this trail with us when they were quite small.)

If you are, for some reason, unable to make the hike (as our frustrated researcher was, with a broken leg) an alternative, but equally lovely place can be found by walking south through the canyon from the parking lot. There are a couple of stopping places along the way, just off the paved path, that offer the aesthetic beauty of the canyon and the Vermilion River, and a bench for resting your tired (or broken) bones, and for enjoying your picnic.

If you have the time we highly recommend both walks, as the trek along the top of the chasm is dramatically different from the walk through the twisting, narrow canyon below.

Whichever picnic site you choose, the ending is the same. After you eat, collect your towel and bathing suit and cross the street to Radium Hot Springs for a relaxing soak in the soothing mineral pools.

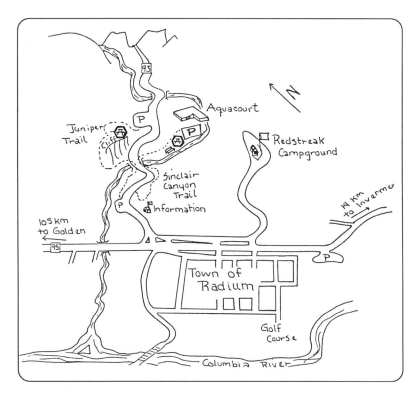

The history of the canyon

The Sinclair Canyon, a stunning valley of rock, was created some 75 million years ago. The texture of the colourful sedimentary layers of rock forming the canyon walls provides a striking contrast to the lush green vegetation beside the rushing spring that thunders along the bottom of the chasm. Despite the popularity of this place as a tourist attraction, the power of the chasm seems to eclipse the human presence, providing irrefutable evidence of the supremacy of nature. Erosion, continental drifting, the passage of glaciers, and winds, water and frost have molded this spectacular landscape.

Attracted not only by the accessibility of the pass, but also by the plentiful materials for making paint, both plains and mountain peoples have gathered here over the centuries. This was part of the route taken by the Kootenai mountains peoples when they travelled to the Great Plains for their biannual buffalo hunts. The pictographs on the canyon walls indicate that the hot springs were an attraction even then, providing a choice campsite. In fact, the word Kootenay means "stranger," or "someone who has come from beyond the mountains." By the 1800s Europeans were also using the ancient

Radium, Kootenay National Park

Indian trails through the pass to extend their fur supply territory.

By the middle of the nineteenth century the race for sovereignty of the west coast was on. American settlers were moving across the Oregon Trail by the hundreds. Sir George Simpson, Governor of the Hudson's Bay Company, attempted to counter this influx by sending Canadian settlers to Oregon. In 1854 James Sinclair, a third generation HBC employee, led a party of 23 Red River Métis families — 125 people — to Oregon by way of the pass which now bears his name. The settlers, however, were quickly absorbed by the overwhelming American majority.

The Indian trail that became a trade route is now a well-travelled highway through the Sinclair Canyon. The first road through the pass was built in 1922 by the Canadian government, in exchange for parkland ceded by the government of B.C. The Banff-Windermere Road, as it was called, was paved in 1952, and continues to serve as one of the more splendid passes through the mountains.

The Hot Springs

Although the first pool and bath house were built in 1911, and have been run by the park since 1922, the popularity of the mineral waters goes back through the centuries beyond recorded time. The mystical nature of the place has long been recognized by the Kootenay Indians. One legend tells of a young Kootenay boy named Amelu who had reached adolescence, and was seeking a sign from his spirit, his nipika, that he had passed from boyhood into manhood. The vision of his personal spirit appeared to him by the spring, investing him with maturity, courage, strength and, most importantly, peace of mind. The spring has always been a sacred place to the Indian people. When commercial development of the springs was first being considered in the early part of this century, the water was analyzed and found to contain more radium than did the famous pools at Bath, in England. Legends about the quality of the spring continues despite the commercialism, and white people as well as natives have claimed to be cured by the healing properties of the waters. The first such healing was the well-publicized case of St. John Harmsworth (Lord Northcliffe), a British millionaire who had become paraplegic as a result of an automobile accident. Repeated bathings in the pool restored some movement to his lower body. To this day people come to the springs seeking relief for the more prosaic aches and pains of arthritis, and whether or not you believe in the spirits or the special quality of the water, the view from the pools itself will certainly make you feel better!

Things to do

1. If you feel energetic after your picnic on the upper canyon trail, follow it along to the various other viewpoints towards the Columbia Valley. The Juniper Trail, considered "moderately strenuous," is 3 km long, and ends by the government Information Centre. You can do a pleasant circle tour by returning via the Sinclair Canyon Trail, which connects with the Redstreak Campground Trail and ends up back at the Aquacourt, and your parking place. (Trail maps can be picked up at the Information Centre.) The total length of the walk is about 6 km.

2. Stop and visit the chainsaw sculptor's shop on the main street of Radium. You can't miss it on the east side of the highway, just north of the junction with Highway 95. Samples of this unusual craft are exhibited outside, and wood carvings are sold in the gift shop.

Things to eat

This picnic is meant to be easy to carry on your short hike to the picnic spot. The following will fit in your day pack, and the more you eat, the less you have to carry down — at least, in your back pack. The menu is a Thermos of chilled cucumber soup, filling, but refreshing along with an eclectic selection of deli meats, cheeses and pickles, and fresh onion buns for the sandwich base. Bring an onion, a tomato, mustard, salt and pepper, and a sharp knife. Back Pack Squares may

give you the energy to explore the upper canyon trail.
Here is our favourite cold picnic soup, which we have been
making for years.

Cold Cucumber Soup

(4 - 6 servings)

2 Tbsp. butter	2 cups chicken broth
1/2 onion, finely chopped	1 tsp. sea salt
1 clove garlic finely chopped	3/4 cup yogurt
4 medium cucumbers, peeled,	1 Tbsp. snipped fresh dill weed
halved lengthwise, seeded	or 1 Tbsp. dry seeds
and chopped	1 tsp. grated lemon rind
3 Tbsp. unbleached white flour	1/8 tsp. mace

Heat the butter in a heavy skillet.Sauté onion, garlic and cucumbers until
onion is tender, about 10 minutes.

Sprinkle in flour, stirring well. Gradually stir in the broth and salt, and
bring to a boil. Cover and simmer until the cucumber is tender. Cool.

Purée the mixture in batches through an electric blender. Stir in the
yogurt, the dill, lemon rind and mace.

Chill several hours, and pack in wide-mouthed Thermos for transport to
picnic site.

Back Pack Squares

Mix together:

1 6-ounce can frozen orange juice	1/2 cup raisins
concentrate	1/2 cup chopped nuts
1/2 cup quick oats	1/4 cup chopped dates
1/2 cup dried apricots, chopped	1/4 cup wheat germ
1/2 cup pitted prunes, chopped	1 tsp. sesame seeds

Cream together:

1/2 cup shortening	1/2 cup table molasses
1/2 cup brown sugar	1 egg

Sift together:

2 cups whole wheat flour	1 tsp. cinnamon
1/4 tsp. salt	1 tsp. powdered ginger
1 tsp. baking soda	

Stir dry ingredients into molasses mixture. Add fruit mixture and blend
well. Turn into a 13 x 9-inch greased pan and bake at 325 °F for 35 minutes.
Cool thoroughly. Cut into bars, wrap in waxed paper to store. Can be
frozen, if this stops your children from eating them ahead of the picnic.
(It never stopped ours.)

HIGH COUNTRY

33 The Canadian Pacific Craigellachie
A Trans-Canada Picnic

The last spike was driven on the far side of this track, opposite the place where the monument now stands, on November 7, 1885. This joined the eastern and the western links of the Canadian Pacific Railway and thereby produced a continuous ribbon of steel from Montreal to Port Moody. The journey across the continent could now be made in six days.

How to get there

The site is on the Trans-Canada Highway. It is 43 km (26 mi.) west of Revelstoke, or 25.5 km (16 mi.) east of Sicamous.

There are several picnic tables near the parking lot, but there is also one down by the monument in the shade. That is our favourite.

The history

At an obscure siding with a Scottish name in the Eagle Pass in the Monashee Mountains, on November 7, 1885, the longest railway in the world was completed. The terms of Confederation were fulfilled, and Canada became a nation. "Craigellachie" was named after the rock which marked the meeting place of the Scottish clans from which both Donald Smith (the chief factor of the Hudson's Bay Company and a director of the Canadian Pacific Railway) and George Stephen (the first president of the railway), had come. The completion of a transcontinental railway in only four years was an impressive accomplishment, and the general manager, William Van

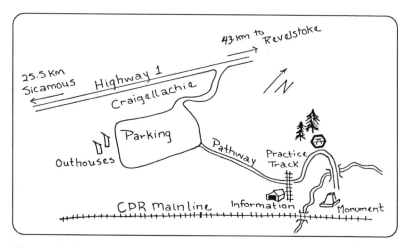

Horne, had every reason to be proud. The first train to travel all the way from Montreal to Port Moody reached its destination July 4, 1886, following a 6-day trip.

Much of the railway was funded by the federal government, although the Canadian Pacific Railway is a private organization. In 1871, British Columbia entered confederation on the condition that construction would begin within two years, and be completed within ten. Delays in financing caused that province to threaten secession several times in the decade which followed. By the time the last link of track joining the eastern and western sections was completed at Craigellachie, the eastern branch had already proved its worth. In the spring of that year the Riel Rebellion had broken out on the prairies, and soldiers were transported by the first train through to Saskatchewan to quell the outbreak. This incident proved the value of the railway to the Canadian public in the east, and funds for the completion of the railway were immediately forthcoming from Parliament.

Things to do

1. Have your picture taken with the 1880s hammer beside the rail at the information booth, and gain a sense of what driving the last spike must have been like: that hammer is heavy! Smith wasn't such a good shot, either, and he bent his first spike — it now lies in the National Museum of Science and Technology in Ottawa, a gift from Smith's great grandson on the 100th anniversary of the event.

2. Read the inscriptions on the monument, and talk to Florence Boyes or Dave Ritchie in the information booth. They are the couple dressed in 1880s costume. They are happy to give you what Dave calls "a dull, boring speech" in which he recreates the history and

Lord Strathcona driving the last spike, November 7, 1885

sense of occasion of this special Canadian event. It's an opportunity you shouldn't pass up!

3. Just across the highway is a short hiking trail. It takes about half an hour, and is suitable for people from 3 to 83. The trail was constructed by the provincial forestry ministry, and features benches, waterfalls and an old trapper's cabin.

4. Drive the 7 km (5 mi.) east to the Eagle River Fish Hatchery, a federal operation for breeding salmon. It is open from 8 a.m. to 4 p.m. weekdays, and tours are available. (Check at the office.) The site is set up so that tours are not really necessary. Excellent interpretive signs explain the life cycle of the salmon and the breeding operation.

5. There is good fishing in any of the streams in the area.

Things to eat

The stones supporting the monument set the theme for the menu of this picnic; there is one from each of the ten provinces, and one from Craigellachie, Scotland. This is a Trans-Canada menu.

Pickled Herring from New Brunswick with toothpick spikes
Habitant Pea Soup from Quebec
Buns from Saskatchewan Wheat

**Fillet of Sole from Newfoundland, garnished with
Manitoba Dandelion Greens
Alberta Fillet of Beef
Fiddlehead Greens from Nova Scotia
Wild Rice from Ontario
Buttered New Potatoes from Prince Edward Island
British Columbia Cherries Jubilee
Chinese Fortune Cookies**

Scotch whisky, preferably from the Craigellachie region of Scotland, is sipped throughout the meal. The Chinese fortune cookies should be sold at a dollar apiece, in tribute to the large number of Chinese Canadians who worked on the railway for one dollar a day.

The pickled herring and tooth picks (make sure they are from B.C. spruce) can be picked up in most grocery stores.

Quebec Pea Soup

Cover with water and soak overnight
   2 cups yellow split peas

Place in a large kettle with cold water to cover
   1 ham bone
Simmer for 1 1/2 hours, keeping the lid tightly closed. Then, add the peas and
   1 medium onion, chopped
   2 carrots, diced
   3 celery stalks, diced

Simmer on low heat for 2 to 3 hours, or until peas are soft. Season to taste with salt and pepper. Remove soup bone and serve hot. Carry to the picnic site in a Thermos. Yields 10 - 12 servings.

Saskatchewan Buns

Purists may choose to order flour from friends in Saskatchewan, or better still, order wheat, and hand-grind it. We prefer to assume that most of our whole grain bread, unless it is imported from the States, likely has Saskatchewan wheat in it. Buy brown whole wheat buns.

Come-by-Chance Sole

Place 1/2 cup water, 1/4 cup white wine, 1 tsp. butter, pinch of tarragon, and 1 Tbsp. finely chopped onion in the frying pan, and simmer for few minutes. Add the sole fillets to the liquid and poach until fillets are firm to the touch. Serve with lemon sections and butter on a bed of Manitoba

Dandelion Greens.

Manitoba Dandelion Greens

Collect sweet, tender young leaves of the dandelion. Wash carefully, drain and chill to make crisp. Use as a serving bed for the sole.

Alberta Fillet of Beef

For beef cooking instructions refer to Falkland picnic.

Western Shore Fiddlehead Greens — Nova Scotia

Wash fiddleheads thoroughly in several changes of water until all the brown papery shreds are removed. Steam in a sieve over boiling water for 10 to 15 minutes. Salt lightly, serve with butter and lemon juice.

Ontario Indian Wild Rice

(yield - 3 cups)

Wild rice, a unique Canadian food harvested by the Indians long ago, is not really rice. It is a wild grass, from which we eat the seeds.
Wash the kernels, cover with cold water and soak overnight. Drain, but do not rinse. Place 1 cup wild rice in saucepan with 4 cups water and 1/2 tsp. salt. Bring to a boil, simmer for 15 minutes. Drain and serve.

Green Gable Potatoes

Select uniformly sized fresh new potatoes, cover with water, add a pinch of salt, and boil until they are cooked. Do not overcook, or they will become mushy. Test with a fork. Drain and drizzle melted butter over them. Garnish with Green Parsley.

British Columbia Cherries Jubilee

Heat
  1 cup preserved, pitted, bing cherries.

Add, and then ignite
  1/4 cup warmed brandy.

When the flame has died down, add
  2 Tbsp. Kirsch.

Serve hot on
  Vanilla ice cream.

34 Pillar Lake
Falkland / Chase
Tidbits of the Old West Picnic

A lake, a legend, and a restful spot away from the main highways combine to make Pillar Lake a special picnic spot.

How to get there

The road by Pillar Lake runs between Chase and Falkland. An interesting diversion for those heading west on the Trans-Canada Highway 1 can be created by heading south at Monte Creek on Highway 97. At Monte Creek you are near the site of Canada's Great Train Robbery. At Westwold (38 km [24 mi.] from Monte Creek) in 1905, the last of the B.C. camels died. And Falkland (54 km [34 mi.] from Monte Creek), now a quiet farming and logging community, is also the site of B.C.'s largest gypsum mine. Turn left (north) at Falkland along the Chase-Falkland Road. Pillar Lake is 12 km (8 mi.) along this road, Chase is 40 km (25 mi.). Alternatively, picnickers travelling west on the Trans-Canada can do the whole tour in reverse, starting at Chase and driving the 28 km (18 mi.) to Pillar Lake. There is no specific site here, although we were told that soon there may be tables. There is a road below the highway along the lake. Here, by the lake and below the Pillar is where we set our portable picnic table.

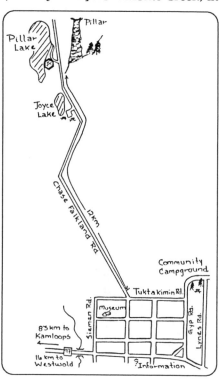

The legend of the Falkland pillar

Across the highway from the lake a short distance into the woods (there is a path and it is signed) stands a lone sentinel, a ninety foot (30 metre) pillar of clay and fine gravel packed as hard as granite and topped with a large round boulder. If you look up the path from the road you can see the pillar, or you can ascend the short, steep trail to its base. Geologists explain this formation, which they call a hoodoo, as the result of differential erosion, with the stone cap preventing the lower layers from wearing away. However, members of the tribe which

The Falkland Pillar

has lived on the shores of this lake for centuries have a better story.

The Pillar of Happiness

Once there lived, in the village on the shores of the lake, a beautiful Indian girl named To-no-ana. This maiden loved the cool, pellucid waters of the lake. Often she would paddle her canoe to the centre of the lake and there, while the canoe drifted gently with the wind, she would peer intently into the crystal depths. Gradually the spell of the Water Spirit, Ton-ug-nik-nik reached out to her; stronger and stronger grew the call of the Spirit until it totally encompassed her and drew her deep into the waters to his underwater world. That day To-no-ana did not return from her canoe trip and her canoe was found floating empty on the lake.

Deep was the lamentation of her parents and the tribe. The wails of grief and the calls for her return reached even down to Ton-ug-nik-nik. It worried him that his action had brought sadness into the lives of the Indians.

Creeping onto the shore of the lake, the Water Spirit constructed a giant pillar and carefully placed a rock on the very top. When he had finished he summoned the parents of the girl and said to them:

"Weep no more for To-no-ana. She is happy with me. The instant that she is not happy or that I cause her the slightest tremble of fear, that rock will fall. Then I will send To-no-ana back to you."

The Spirit returned to the lake. The aged parents returned to the camp solaced. The pillar remained during their lifetime, and during the ages since. The word of the Water Spirit has not been broken. The rock is balanced on the slender shaft to this very day.

Regional Tidbits

Bill Miner — Gentleman Train Robber

In 1904, British Columbia suffered its first train robbery; three men held up the CPR at Mission and made off with $7,000. The following year in Washington the Great Northern Railway was robbed of $30,000. In each case the leader of the robbers was a polite, silver-haired gentleman.

In 1906 the three men held up the CPR near Monte Creek, but this time luck was not with them. First, they held up the wrong train; the mail that they were expecting to find was on the following train. Second, they missed $40,000 in bank notes on a shelf and only managed to find and steal $15. Worst of all, during a scuffle the leader's mask came off and several people got a look at the gentlemanly train robber.

A posse was quickly formed and the three were tracked to their camp on Douglas Lake, 50 mi. southeast of Kamloops. Bill Miner was arrested and tried for train robbery.

Bill Miner, a pleasant, polite fellow in his sixties, had come to Princeton several years before and was generally known as the nice gentleman who played the fiddle at the local dances, and took the village children for horse rides. In fact, so well-liked was Bill that during his first trial, the jurors could not believe that he was actually a notorious train robber — so they were unable to reach a verdict. The jurors at the second trial did not have that problem and Bill was sentenced to life imprisonment at the New Westminster Prison. After one year at the prison he tunnelled his way out, and fled to the States. There he was caught, tried for the other train robberies, and again sentenced to prison. After two unsuccessful escape attempts, he died in the Georgia State Prison in 1913.

The Cariboo Camels

In 1862, Frank Laumeister, a Victoria "braumeister" turned ex-pressman, brought 21 camels to the Fraser Canyon from the construction camps in Arizona. It was Frank's idea to use the beasts as pack animals along the Cariboo Waggon Road.

Unfortunately, the idea did not prove to be very workable. The haughty camel has a powerful smell, and does not mix well with other animals. On the road mules, packhorses, and oxen would usually refuse to pass these odoriferous beasts, and when a camel train was met, pandemonium was the result, with horses and mules bolting into the woods and leaping into the river.

A Cariboo Camel

The other packers came to hate the work camel and sued Laumeister for damages. Laumeister was forced to abandon the enterprise and turned the camels loose on the Thompson Flats near Cache Creek. They reared no offspring and the last one, pictured in this archival photo, died at Westwold in 1905.

Gypsum — Anhydrite

Although the Falkland gypsum deposit was discovered sometime before 1894, the major development of the property did not come until 1925, when the Kamloops to Vernon Railway line was completed. The gypsum mined was shipped to a plant in Port Mann where it was used to manufacture plaster of Paris, plaster board, and tiles for lath and plaster construction. Since then the mine has operated intermittently, the peak production being in 1951 when 80,000 tons of ore were shipped. It is now used occasionally by Canada Cement Lafarge Ltd. to supply their cement plants at Kamloops and Richmond. The gypsum mine is located up the hill to the north of the town. Until 1941 the gypsum was transported by aerial tramway from the mine, over the town, and to the railway siding.

The Douglas Lake Cattle Company

For those who like to wander the back roads, the road south from Westwold will take you onto the Douglas Plateau and to the Douglas

Lake Cattle Company. Established in 1884, this is Canada's largest cattle operation and the largest one in the British Commonwealth. Its 14,000 head of cattle range over half a million acres (200,000 hectares) and are contained by 960 km (600 mi.) of wire fence. The ranch ships 3,200 head of cattle to market each year. A general store sells souvenirs and books about the ranch. Check at the local travel infocentre for bus tours. The Douglas Lake Road continues on until it joins highway 5A about 27.5 km (17 mi.) east of Merritt. The total length of the diversion is about 80 km (50 mi.).

Things to do and see

1. Fish, swim, boat, on any of the numerous lakes within a 16 kilometre radius of Falkland.

2. For the rockhound, the area around Pinaus Lake has jasperized wood, geodes, jasper agate, banded agate, silicated lava, and calcites.

Things to eat

Since this is near cattle country, the appropriate feast is a barbecue, with steaks, baked potatoes, steamed vegetables, and a Woodland Salad.

The best steaks for barbecuing should be selected from the following cuts: fillet, sirloin, T-bone, Porterhouse, wing, rib.

Steak Cooking Times (minutes per side)

Thickness	Rare	Med.	Well-done
2.5 cm (1")	5-7	7-9	9-11
4 cm (1 1/2")	8-10	10-12	16-20
5 cm (2")	13-15	15-17	24-30

The flavour and tenderness of steak is often improved by a marinade.

Marinade

(Enough for 1 kg or 2.2 lbs. of meat)

1/2 cup salad oil
1/2 cup lemon juice
1 small onion, chopped
1 clove garlic, crushed
dash of Worcestershire sauce

1/4 cup soy sauce
1 tsp. dry mustard
1 tsp. oregano
coarse ground pepper to taste

Combine all ingredients and blend well. Pour over the meat in a shallow dish and allow to stand at room temperature for 2 hours or in the refrigerator overnight, turning occasionally.

Barbecued Vegetables

Vegetables wrapped in pockets of heavy aluminum foil and baked on a barbecue grill are easy to prepare in advance, and scrumptious to eat.

Vegetable	Preparation	Time
Carrots	Peel and cut to sticks. For each pound of carrots combine 1 Tbsp. brown sugar, 1 Tbsp. lemon juice, 1 tsp. salt, 2 tsp. powdered ginger, 1 Tbsp. melted butter. Mix together in a bowl, divide into four equal portions and wrap each loosely in aluminum foil, sealing the edges tightly.	60 minutes
Mushrooms	Wrap one pound of large mushrooms in foil with butter, salt and pepper.	20-25 min.
Potatoes	Brush each medium sized potato with oil and wrap in foil.	45-60 min.

Woodland Salad

Salads can be boring bowls of lettuce, or they can be fascinating combinations of vegetables served with imagination. To provide you with a little inspiration, the following chart includes some of our favourite salad things. The worst that can happen is a guest's exclaiming, "I never thought of putting pine nuts in a salad before!" This may be said to cover the fact that the guest has never heard of pine nuts before. But what better garnish for a Woodland Salad? So:

Select crisp fresh lettuce — butter, bib, leaf, or the usual iceberg, or a combination of these. For fresh salads it is best to do the final preparation at the picnic table just before announcing dinner. Take along a small cutting board for your last minute salad preparations. At home, wash lettuce leaves in cold water, dry in a dish towel (or use one of those magic lettuce-drying machines). Place the lettuce in a plastic bag with a piece of paper towelling to absorb any extra moisture, and chill in the fridge for several hours before the picnic.

Other Vegetables

Wash well and take along several tomatoes, some green onions, a couple of stalks of celery, a cucumber and a green pepper.

Just before the steaks go on the barbecue, chop the vegetables in the sizes that most please you (large chunks for a picnic which includes one or more teen-aged boys who are impressed only by quantity and potential speed of ingestion; thinner slices and diced pieces will suit a more refined group).

Tear bite-sized pieces of lettuce into the salad bowl, and mix well with the other vegetables. A spoon and a fork will work, but we find it much easier to toss a salad with the wide-bladed, short-handled salad servers which are part of our picnic kit. Once the salad is mixed, shake the dressing and pour it over, tossing just a little bit more.

Garnish with a handful of pine nuts (available in the bulk section of large grocery stores, or in health food stores). They add a sweet, woodsy flavour to the salad, along with lots of protein.

French Dressing

Combine the following ingredients in a blender, and when mixed place in a screw-top jar in the picnic basket. Always dress the salad just before serving it at the picnic to prevent wilting.

1/2 cup olive oil
2 Tbsp. red wine vinegar
2 Tbsp. lemon juice
2 tsp. sugar
1/2 tsp. salt
1/2 tsp. dry mustard
1/2 tsp. paprika
dash of cayenne

Garlic Dressing

Make ahead at home, dress at the picnic.
1 cup salad or olive oil
1/4 cup white wine vinegar
1 clove garlic, minced
1 tsp. sugar
1/4 tsp. black pepper
1/2 tsp. salt
3/4 tsp. dry mustard

35 Mount Revelstoke Revelstoke
A Mountain Meadow Picnic

Near Revelstoke there is a true alpine meadow that is accessible by car! Some people assume they will never see a mountain meadow, because they are not likely to hike for several hours uphill to get to one. The road to the top of Mount Revelstoke is easy to drive, and the flowers and vistas are well worth the trip.

How to get there

The road up the mountain leaves Highway 1 just east of Revelstoke. The exit is well marked. The drive to the top is 26 km (16 mi.) and has an elevation gain of one mile. The Balsam Lake picnic area that we have chosen is just 1 km before the summit, on a road leading off to the left.

(Bring an axe and paper for starting your fire in the shelter stove. Insect repellent is a must for any walks, but you can eat inside the screened shelter. It can be windy up here, so bring a windbreaker and long pants, just in case.)

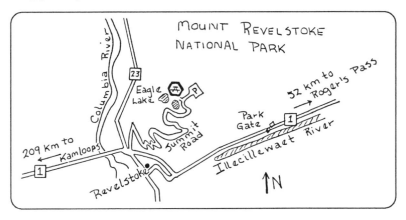

The meadow

Photographs cannot convey the wonder of an alpine meadow, the variety and brilliance of the colours of the miniature blossoms against a backdrop of mountain peaks and glaciers. Mount Revelstoke National Park was established in 1914. It did not become well

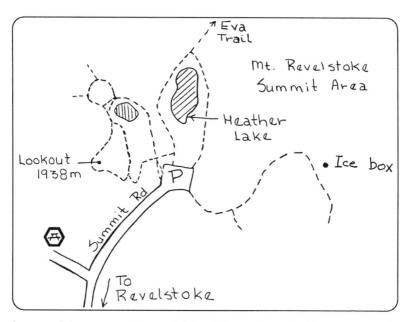

known, however, until much later. Then a tragedy began as people misused and abused the meadow, not realizing the effects of their casual behaviour on the fragile ecology of an alpine meadow.

This is the ultimate in rock gardens, as these plants live on thin layers of soil or moss, on a foundation of bedrock. Because of the altitude, the growing season is extremely short. The small size of alpine plants allows them to be adaptive because they hug the ground to avoid the high winds which predominate in such altitudes throughout much of the year. Plants must also adapt to the shortage of water, and many have pulpy leaves for storing this scarce resource. Others, like the avalanche lily, burst into bloom in the early spring, pushing right through the snow to take full advantage of the melting water. Growth of even the tiniest plants takes many years, and they remain miniature, compared to the plants of lower ecozones. When there are trees, they too, are stunted. Thus it takes very few feet treading on the plants to destroy what took many years to create. Park staff have now marked off the trails very carefully so that it is easy for people to follow them—and to remain on them. As you walk you will see many areas of damage, places where little side trails inadvertently destroyed the vegetation. The park program to regenerate one of the few readily accessible meadows is underway.

Things to do

1. Take the self-guiding summit trail. There is a profusion of

A Bench in the Meadow

alpine flowers, at their peak in early August. The loop trail is about 1 km in length, and begins and ends at the summit parking lot. To assist you in flower identification we advise stopping at the Rogers Pass Interpretive Center first to purchase a copy of *Mount Revelstoke National Park Wildflowers,* by James H. Soper and Adam F. Szczawinski. This useful Parks Canada publication has excellent colour photos of the flowers, arranged by colour for easy identification. The book is handy to have on hikes in other mountain regions as well. Among the flowers we identified recently were yellow arnica, pink and white valerian, Indian paintbrush — both salmon and deep red, alpine heather, monkshood, and several varieties of saxifrage.

2. Practise your nature photography here. Try close-ups of the flowers with the Selkirk or Monashee Mountains as a backdrop. A telephoto lens is excellent for catching the detail of the tiny alpine flowers. Authorities suggest that photographing the flowers on an overcast or rainy day produces more brilliant colours. Take an umbrella along!

3. Cool off by the "Icebox," a peculiar ice formation at the edge of the meadow which disseminates cool air even on the hottest summer day. Watch for it just to the side of the Mountain Meadows Trail.

Things to eat

It can be cool on the top of the mountain, so we want something warm and substantial to eat. Start off this picnic with a Thermos of hot cheddar cheese soup, followed by a main course of cold garlic chicken and Mountain Meadow Potato Salad, and finish up with a tribute to the Icebox, that perennial favourite, Icebox Cookies. The meal is accompanied by a Thermos of hot tea.

Cheddar Cheese Soup

(Serves 6)

Melt in a sauce pan:
> *1/4 cup butter or margarine*

Add:
> *1/2 cup minced onion*

Cover and cook on low heat till onions are transparent.

Stir in:
> *2 Tbsp. flour*

Simmer for another 3 minutes.

In a separate container, dissolve:
> *1/2 tsp. dry mustard in 1 Tbsp. cold water*

Add the mustard solution to the onion mixture and
> *3 cups chicken broth*
> *1/2 tsp. paprika*
> *1/4 tsp. freshly ground pepper*
> *dash cayenne*

Add:
> *1 cup light cream or 1/2 cup milk and 1/2 cup sour cream*
> *1/2 pound grated cheddar cheese*
> *1 cup dark ale or beer*

Simmer, stirring constantly, until the cheese is melted and the soup is heated through. Do not allow to boil.

Place in a wide-mouthed Thermos for transport to the picnic.

Garlic Chicken

(allow 1 chicken for four people)

Wash and dry
> *1 3-pound roasting chicken.*

Liberally sprinkle rosemary inside the cavity.

Prepare a sauce of:
  1 *clove garlic, minced*
  1/2 *cup melted butter*
  1 *tsp. rosemary*
  coarse ground pepper
Paint the sauce over the chicken.

Bake the chicken on a rack in the oven at 400°F for 1 hour. Place a pan beneath the rack to catch the sauce drippings, and baste frequently with the sauce.

Mountain Meadow Potato Salad

(serves 10)

Combine in a bowl:
  10 *medium cooked, diced potatoes*
  1 *peeled, diced cucumber*
  1 *medium onion, chopped (red, if possible)*
  1 *green pepper, chopped*
  2 *eggs, hard-boiled and coarsely chopped*
  1 *small tin pimento, chopped*
  1 1/2 *tsp. salt*
  3/4 *tsp. celery seed*
  1/4 *tsp. pepper*
  1 *tsp. fresh summer savory*
  4 *leaves fresh basil, snipped*
Mix well and chill.

Prepare a dressing of:
  1/2 *cup whipping cream*
  1/2 *cup mayonnaise*
  1/4 *cup vinegar*
  1 *Tbsp. prepared mustard*

Shake well in sealed jar and carry to picnic site. Toss with potato mixture 1/2 hour before serving. Garnish with raw, unsalted sunflower seeds and fresh, snipped parsley.

Icebox Cookies

(Makes about 2 dozen)

Combine in a bowl
  1 *cup sugar*
  1/2 *cup butter or margarine*
Blend until creamy.

Mix in:
> 1 *beaten egg*
> 1 *tsp. vanilla.*

Sift together:
> 1 1/2 *cups flour*
> 1/4 *tsp. salt*
> 1 1/2 *tsp. double-acting baking powder*

Stir the dry ingredients into the wet ones. Form into a 2-inch diameter roll on a piece of waxed paper. Wrap, seal the ends and refrigerate 12 to 24 hours. A day later, if there is still any dough left (if you have children, this is unlikely) retrieve it and slice it into 1/4 inch thick cookies. Bake in 400°F oven on greased cookie sheet for 8 to 10 minutes. Cool and pack. Hide until picnic time.

36 Glacier House
Rogers Pass
A Swiss Guide's Picnic

To encourage revenue from tourism the Canadian Pacific Railway built a string of hotels along the railway line through the mountains in the late 1800s. Among these were, Chateau Lake Louise, the Banff Springs Hotel, and Glacier House. A few pieces of foundation are all that remain of Glacier House now, in a field inhabited by gophers and the ghosts of the past.

How to get there

The picnic site is just a little way from Highway 1, 2.4 km (1.5 mi.) west of the summit of the pass. Watch carefully for the sign to the Illecillewaet Campground. Turn in, and drive past the campground and up to the T-junction at the top of the hill, by the Youth Hostel. Turn right, and drive along for a few metres until you come to a parking area, next to some interpretive signs showing old photos of Glacier House and the Swiss Guides. Park here, and carry your picnic supplies across the meadow, following the footpath, until you reach a large pile of rocks at the far left-hand corner of the meadow. This is where we sit, on a piece of the old hotel, and enjoy our Swiss Cheese fondue.

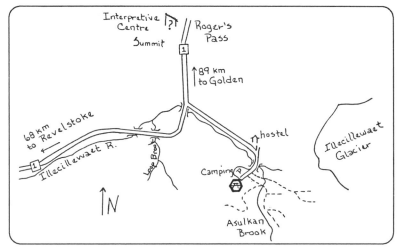

The railway and the pass

The pass was discovered in 1882 by an American surveyor, Major A.B. Rogers, while the CPR was working under pressure to provide the transcontinental service promised to the Province of British Columbia in 1871. This may be the only pass through the mountains that was found without the leadership of the native people. It is little wonder that they have historically avoided this area. Sandford Fleming, a member of the railway survey crew, describes the hardships of bushwhacking in the Illecillewaet valley in graphic detail:

> The walking is dreadful, we climb over and creep under fallen trees of great size and the men soon show that they feel the weight of their burdens. Their halts for rest are frequent. It is hot work for us all. The dripping rain from the bush and branches saturates us from above. Tall ferns sometimes reaching to the shoulders and Devil's Clubs through which we had to crush our way make us feel as if dragged through a horsepond and our perspiration is that of a Turkish bath. We meet with obstacles of every description. The Devil's Clubs may be numbered by millions and they are perpetually wounding us with their spikes against which we strike. We halt frequently for rest. Our advance is varied by ascending rocky slopes and slippery masses, and again descending to a lower level. We wade through Alder swamps and tread down Skunk Cabbage and Prickly Aralias, and so we continue until half-past four, when the tired-out men are able to go no further...
> *Snow War: A Guide to the History of Rogers Pass.* Environment Canada Publication, 1986

Avalanches

The hazards of working in the pass were not limited to the thick growth of underbrush in the summer. Winter's avalanche hazards were even more dangerous, and many lives have been lost in the pass since 1881. As twentieth century technology has advanced the danger has been lessened, but it can never be eradicated.

The first attempts to mitigate the effects of the mountains of snow which raced down without warning were the avalanche sheds. There were 31, of varying lengths, when the railway was first constructed. Bridges were also an important part of the strategy; the track crossed the Illecillewaet River three times in order to avoid the most common avalanche paths. Many creeks had to be bridged, as well, and one of the more spectacular bridges was the trestle at Mountain Creek. At the time it was built in 1885, it was the largest structure on the CPR,

Mountain Weather

It may seem ridiculous to pack a range of clothing from shorts and T-shirt to down-filled jacket and mitts for a simple picnic on a hot August day, until one picnics in the mountains. On one childhood excursion in the Rogers Pass, we started out sweltering in shorts, but as we climbed higher up the mountain, it began to rain. Out came the sweatshirts and rain gear: just in time for the snow storm. Our picnic was very short as most of us kids had neglected to pack our jackets and mitts, and we were sharing Mother's pair of gloves as we ate our peanut butter sandwiches in a blizzard.

Mountain weather is unpredictable, and there can be four seasons of mountain weather in one afternoon. It is possible, and not uncommon, to sit on a mountain top and watch a thunderstorm in a valley to your left, and people sunning on a beach in a valley to your right. The weather forecast for one town may be completely different from another only 20 kilometres away, and the weather may change despite the predictions.

So, if it is sunny and warm when you start your picnic in the mountains, wear your shorts and T-shirt, but pack long trousers, a long-sleeved T-shirt, rain gear, gloves or mitts and a warm jacket (down-filled takes up the least space). A survival blanket, available in any camping supply store, doesn't take up much room but comes in very handy in any sort of emergency. Dress in layers, and bring a day pack to carry extra layers of clothing. Even if the weather is blazing hot and the weatherman predicts sun for a week, do not be deceived as you head into the high country.

measuring 331 m (1,075 ft.) in length, and 50 m (163 ft.) in height. One of the old stone bridges can still be seen if you stop at the Mountain Bridges Viewpoint, 7.2 km (4 1/2 mi.) east of the Rogers Pass Interpretive Centre. The chronology of technical advances continued, with the completion of the Connaught Tunnel in 1916. It was the longest railway tunnel in Canada, 8 km (5 mi.) in length, and it bypassed some of the more dangerous terrain altogether.

Contemporary travellers have the choice of train or car. The Trans-Canada Highway was extended through Rogers Pass in 1962. Even now, the highway may be closed without notice for avalanche dangers. A system of avalanche predictions operates in the pass, and in some cases avalanches can be controlled. This is done by preempting their development process! Under certain conditions an avalanche can be made to happen by the firing of the great Howitzers (field

Swiss Guide with Climbers on the Illecillewaet Glacier

artillery guns) that are deployed by the Royal Canadian Horse Artillery. (You will notice the firing pads along the highway as you drive. They look like big targets.) The road is closed, the gun is fired, the avalanche roars down and the snow is cleared away. Between 1885 and 1911 over 200 people died in the pass; since the highway opened 25 years ago there have been only 2 deaths. Technology has indeed advanced, but the power of the snow has not been tamed.

The Swiss guides

The CPR spared no expense in creating luxuriously appointed hotels and dining rooms for its passengers. Glacier House was built in 1887 and operated until 1925. At first the train stopped here for lunch, thus avoiding the need to haul heavy dining cars over the pass. The alpine beauty of the place attracted so many tourists that the facility was quickly expanded to include 90 hotel rooms. Guests would meet the group of professional Swiss Guides who had been especially brought here by the railway officials to serve the more adventurous tourists. It was the job of Edward Feuz, Christian Hasler and the others to take the tourists up to the toe of the Illecillewaet Glacier, and through the more dangerous mountain trails above. Years later one of the guides noted that there was never a serious accident while they were guiding. Many of the trails that still exist in the region were built by these men a century ago. The Illecillewaet Glacier has receded about 1.5 km (1 mile) up the valley in the past 75 years — it was just a twenty-minute walk to the glacier then! (You have a splendid view of the glacier from the campground.)

Things to do

1. Take a hike. There is a short walk along the path at the top of the meadow which leads to "The Meeting of the Waters." This is an easy and pleasant walk, 1 kilometre or half an hour round trip. You will see the confluence of the Illecillewaet River and Asulkan Brook. Those with lots of time and energy can hike to the toe of the Illecillewaet Glacier. Wear proper hiking gear, and take extra clothing, as the weather changes quickly in this pass. The hike is 4.8 km (2.8 mi.) each way, with an elevation gain of 1250 to 1935 m, depending upon whether you choose to climb the shale for an extra hour and get right to the glacier snout. It is about 5 or 6 hours return. Both of these hikes can also be made with a Park Naturalist — check the notice board in the campground for the schedule.

2. Visit the Loop Brook Interpretive Trail, 5.4 km (3 mi.) west of the Rogers Pass summit on Highway 1. Turn in at the Loop Brook Campground sign. The Great Loop was a remarkable engineering achievement. The trains could not cope with more than a 4% grade, and yet it was necessary to change the elevation of the track crossing the Illecillewaet River within too short a distance for the usual gradual slope. And so a series of loops was built, extending the track by 5 km. The train travelled around the gentle slope and thus gained the additional distance required to climb — or descend — an otherwise impossible grade. The abandoned rail bed, a portion of an original loop, is now part of a pleasant and gentle hiking trail 1.6 km (1 mile) long.

3. Spend some time at the Interpretive Centre at the top of Rogers Pass. The centre looks like an avalanche shed, not unlike the several that you drive through west of the pass. There are films of interest to history and nature buffs, and displays concerning the building of the railway through the pass. The framed photos in the coffee shop in the hotel just across the parking lot make the danger of avalanches seem quite real!

4. Try yodelling.

Things to eat

The Swiss have always understood the need for high protein mountain food. If you are going to walk to the glacier you'll need all the high energy food you can get. We therefore recommend that you always have a Toblerone chocolate bar in your pocket for quick energy (we prefer the triangular ones).

Our picnic, on the site of the old Glacier House Hotel, features a Swiss Fondue, of course. You'll need to bring your fondue forks from home for this one. A fondue pot is great, but a saucepan on a Coleman stove works as well. If you find the cheese is burning, rig a double boiler.

Swiss Cheese Fondue

Mix together:
  8 ounces grated Swiss cheese
  8 ounces grated Gruyere cheese
  2 1/2 Tbsp. flour

Rub the fondue pot with 1 clove garlic, and leave the clove in the pot. Put 1 1/2 cups dry white wine into the pot and turn on the heat. (You will, of course, be carrying a suitable vintage from one of the Okanagan estates.) As soon as the wine begins to bubble, reduce the heat gradually, and add the cheeses, a bit at a time, stirring constantly with a wooden spoon or clean stick. When all the cheese has melted, grind in some fresh black pepper, and add 2 - 4 Tbsp. Kirsch. If you like it, add even more Kirsch.

Dip large cubes of fresh French bread into the sauce with your fork, eat and enjoy, while sipping the rest of the white wine.

The Oxford dictionary assures us that a "fool" is a creamy liquid of fruit, stewed, crushed, and mixed with milk, cream, custard, etc. Illy-silly is our family code name for the glacier just above this picnic site.

Illy-Silly Fool

The pure fool is a mixture of wild raspberries, blueberries, strawberries and huckleberries, stewed and served on ice cream.

The lazy fool involves purchasing a tin of fruit cocktail, mashing it with a fork, and pouring it over tinned custard.

The average fool requires bringing a jar of stewed rhubarb from home, heating it at the picnic site, and serving with ice cream. Sprinkle a handful of Muesli over the top — this is the traditional cereal of Switzerland, and of health nuts the world over.

37 Shuswap Lake Sicamous

A Houseboat Picnic

Shuswap Lake is renowned for its houseboats, and so we have planned a picnic that takes place on board a boat on the lake; either a houseboat, if you want to rent one for a day and be a captain, or on board the mail boat, the *Phoebe Ann*, while she makes her run from Sicamous to Seymour Arm.

How to get there

Sicamous is on Trans-Canada Highway 1, on the narrows between Mara Lake and Shuswap Lake. To get to the berth of the *Phoebe Ann*, turn south on Gill Ave., west on Finlayson Street, and find a parking place at the junction of Young Avenue. The *Phoebe Ann* is easy to see ahead of you in the harbour.

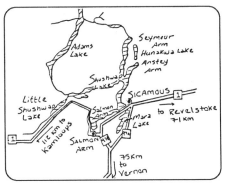

If you decide to rent your own houseboat: only a few companies rent them for the day, and then only if they can't get a longer charter; but you may be lucky. Try Portside International Houseboat Charters. To get there, turn south from Finlayson St. onto Riverside Ave., and drive a block and a half. You will see Portside on your right. Prices are bound to change, but when we inquired the daily rental cost was about $70.

The Shuswap Lakes

Long the preserve of Indian peoples and named for the Shuswap Indians, a northern branch of the Salish peoples, the Shuswap Lakes had their period of economic importance. Before trains and trucks forced them into retirement, steam-powered paddlewheelers moved people and supplies along this crucial waterway, supplying the gold fields, the railway construction sites, the settlements, and the logging camps with food and equipment, and pulling the log booms to the mills. The sternwheelers provided essential transportation in the

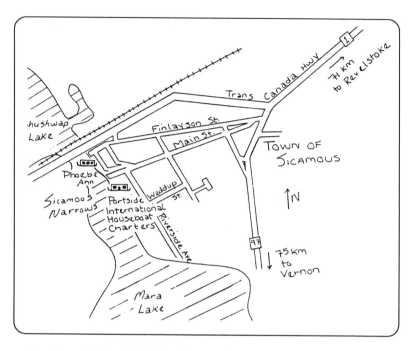

region from 1866 to 1916. For the most part, mail freight and passenger services are supplied now by other means. But the mail is still carried by boat to Seymour Arm three times each week.

The *Phoebe Ann* and the mail run

The *Phoebe Ann* was built in 1971, and is named after the owner's grandmother, Phoebe Ann Kelly. The boat, a shallow draft, single deck vessel of all steel construction, is powered by a diesel engine, but also boasts a paddle wheel. Three days a week, Monday, Wednesday and Friday, she pushes the mail barge all the way up to the tip of Seymour Arm, stopping to make deliveries as necessary. This is an all-day outing, since the trip takes 4 hours each way, with an additional hour and a half stop in Seymour Arm. This village offers a quiet beach, a neighbourhood pub and a tea house. Along the way you will enjoy the ever-changing beauty of the mountain lake, and even see ancient Indian pictographs on the rocks in Anstey Arm and Mara Lake.

There is plenty of room on board, inside or out on deck. Snack foods are available for sale, and passengers are welcome from June to September. Be at the dock well before 8 in the morning, or book ahead by calling 836-2200, or writing Box 370, Sicamous, B.C.

For those who prefer to take a shorter cruise on the *Phoebe Ann*,

The Phoebe Ann

several are available in July and August. There is a 2 hour cruise on Tuesdays, from 1-3 p.m.; a lunch cruise on Thursdays to St. Ives, 9:30 a.m. to 3:30 p.m., and a four-hour cruise on Sundays through the Cinnemousun Narrows, 1-5 p.m. Reservations are advisable.

Houseboats

Sicamous is the "Houseboat Capital of the Shuswap." Houseboat vacations on the Shuswap have become extremely popular over the past decade or so, and as you drive along the shore you will see dozens of them on a clear day. You don't have to have papers and certificates to become the captain of a houseboat. A bit of advice from the renter, a measure of common sense, and away you go for a day on the lake. There are grocery stores on the docks here and there, if you need picnic supplies. There are about 2 dozen campground/picnic sites on the Shuswap/Mara Lakes, many of them water-accessible. Many have picnic tables, fire pits and other facilities, if you choose to take your picnic ashore.

Things to do

1. Fish. We would not presume to tell a fisherman how or where to fish, but we have it on good authority that there are fine fish to be had in the lake, as long as you fish deep.

2. Explore the shore as you pass by. You will see ruined old buildings, relics from the mining days; exquisite waterfalls, splendid for swimming or fishing; and Indian pictographs, ancient paintings on the rocks just above the water level. Many of these things are accessible only from the water, so keep your eyes open, perhaps scan now and then with your binoculars, and find your own private beach, or undiscovered traces of the past.

3. Skinny dip! (Not from the *Phoebe Ann*, but from your houseboat)

4. Go on an evening picnic and star-gaze. The view of the heavens from out on the lake is unsurpassed, matched only by being at sea at night. Lie on your back on deck, and wish upon a star!

Things to eat

You can shop at the floating General Store, a barge just at the narrows, for your picnic supplies.

Alternatively, the *Phoebe Ann* usually stops at Ron's Catering, just past Cinnemousun Narrows. You can order ahead by VHF Channel 12, or BC Tel radio phone, and your picnic lunch will be delivered to the boat. The same service is available for houseboats, and it is a nice run from Sicamous — check your navigation charts, Captain!

38 Yellowhead Pass
Mount Terry Fox Provincial Park
An Overlander's Picnic

An overland route through the mountains — how elementary this sounds to those of us who blithely drive in our cars from Edmonton overland to Vancouver in 16 hours or so. This pass has not been so easily crossed through history, however. Determined explorers, seeking cheaper and more direct routes for transporting furs back to the East came this way, guided by the Indians to whom the pass had long been a familiar trail. In 1862 a particularly courageous group of people, remembered as "The Overlanders" for their trouble, passed this way in search of the gold of the Cariboo. And not so long ago, in 1980, young Terry Fox tried to cross the continent overland, with the same kind of courage and determination, but seeking a different kind of gold, the kind that would support research on the disease from which he would never recover. Contemporary overlanders gaze at the powerful beauty of Mount Robson, and occasionally one or two of them might even see the top, without that ubiquitous little white cloud.

How to get there

Mount Terry Fox Provincial Park is just at the edge of Mount Robson Provincial Park. This quiet and beautiful place was set aside in honour of the famous runner in June 1982. The picnic spot, with its fabulous views of both mountains, is off Highway 16, 10 km (6 mi.) north of Valemount. Several picnic tables offer the splendid view.

The Overlanders

Word of Billy Barker's gold discovery in the Cariboo in the spring of 1862 quickly reached Toronto and Montreal. Thousands of people set out for the west, among them a group of 150 men, one woman and three children who were to walk into history as the "Overlanders." Public transportation in the form of ships and the American trains carried them as far west as Fort Garry, but there they had to switch to the less comfortable Red River carts to Fort Edmonton. From there they had to walk. And they did. Six died along the way, others turned back. Of those that persevered, some only stayed a while in the Cariboo, and then directly or indirectly found their ways back East.

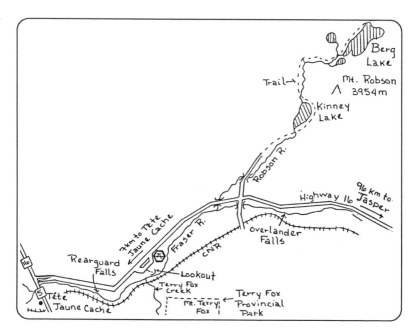

A few remained to make their fortunes, some larger than others, and to become leaders of the emerging British Columbia society.

Terry Fox

In 1980, a twenty-one-year-old man who'd lost one leg to cancer, decided to run across Canada from the Atlantic to the Pacific Ocean, in order to raise funds for cancer research. His journey lasted 20 weeks, and unlike the earlier Overlanders, he was met at every town and village with crowds offering enthusiastic encouragement. He was averaging 40 km (25 mi.) per day, and had covered 5,373 km (3,358 mi.) when his disease overtook him, and he was forced to end his epic journey in Thunder Bay. But he had already accomplished part of his goal. He had raised $1.7 million for cancer research, which quickly became $24.7 million from additional donations from Canadians inspired by the hope of this man. In the years to follow hundreds of communities across Canada have carried on the tradition, holding an annual Terry Fox Run and contributing the proceeds to the Terry Fox Fund. Terry's Marathon of Hope continues.

The Mountains

Mount Terry Fox is 2,650 m (8,600 ft.) high. Mount Robson reaches 3,954 m (12,859 ft.) into the clouds, the highest peak in the

Mount Robson

Canadian Rockies. There are several men called Robson in British Columbia history after whom the mountain may have been named; which one it was is lost in the clouds of time. The headwaters of the mighty Fraser River can be found in the southwest corner of Mt. Robson Park, a deceptively gentle forerunner of the torrent it soon becomes.

The Dos and Don'ts of Bears

Whenever I walk in a London street,
I'm ever so careful to watch my feet;
And I keep in the squares,
And the masses of bears,
Who wait at the corner all ready to eat
The sillies who tread on the lines of the street,
Go back to their lairs,
And I say to them, "Bears,
Just look how I'm walking in all of the squares!"

And the little bears growl to each other, "He's mine,
As soon as he's silly and steps on a line."
And some of the bigger bears try to pretend
That they came round the corner to look for a friend;
And they try to pretend that nobody cares
Whether you walk on the lines or squares.
But only the sillies believe their talk;
It's ever so portant how you walk.
And it's ever so jolly to call out, "Bears,
Just watch me walking in all the squares!"

A.A.Milne

The poem of the previous page contains some good advice for avoiding bears — follow the safety rules: if you are in London, walk only in the squares; if you are in the British Columbia wilderness, follow the rules listed below. We always call out to the bears when we are in the woods, so that we don't inadvertently interrupt a teddy bears' picnic. Perhaps it works — we have never encountered a bear in all our time in the wilderness!

Do not feed a bear, whether it be from your car, or at a picnic site. They are quick to acquire a taste for human food, and will come searching for more.

Avoid bear cubs. They are curious and playful, but Mom is always nearby. A protective mother bear may attack in response to a perceived threat to her young. Steer clear of a cub or cubs: do not stop and play, or take photographs, but make a wide circle around where they may be feeding or playing.

Don't take your dog for a walk in bear country. Dogs are safer in the car — accidents happen when people try to protect their dogs from bears who are trying to protect their young from dogs.

Make plenty of noise to warn an approaching bear that you are there. We wear bear bells and sing as we walk, if we think we are in bear country. There is safety in numbers as two people make more noise and smell than one does. Remember that a stream may drown out your noise, and a wind may obscure your scent from a bear upwind.

If you come upon a bear by surprise, don't panic. In an encounter the animal is generally as shocked and frightened as you are. If you stand your ground, make noise and slowly back up, more often than not, the bear will turn and bolt.

Keep your food in airtight containers, leaving no odours to attract the bears. If your food is all in one place in your pack, you can take off your pack, and drop it to distract the bear while you slowly make a retreat.

If you take the above precautions, you should be able to avoid any confrontations with angry, frightened bears.

Things to do

1. Drive to the viewpoint on Highway 16 at Rearguard Falls, especially if you are lucky enough to be in the area in August or September. This is the farthest point of migration of the Pacific salmon, which have travelled upstream from the ocean almost a thousand miles to spawn, and to die.

2. Drive to the Mount Robson viewpoint by the Information Centre, park, and follow the signs to the Berg Lake trailhead. Cross the bridge and enjoy the cool spray of the Robson River. There is a picnic area here, too, with a shelter.

Things to eat

For the Overlanders the going was rough and the food spartan. By pickling chunks of beef in salt solution they could keep meat from rotting during the heat of the summer months, as they walked from Fort Garry to the Cariboo. Corned beef was boiled and served with vegetables. Leftovers were chopped and made into hash, for a nourishing and simple meal.

Corned Beef

To corn beef, rub with salt the surfaces of a 2-kg brisket or rump of beef. Place in plastic or stone crock and cover with a super-saturated solution consisting of:

2 L. water
1/2 kg salt
1/4 kg sugar
1 bay leaf
6 peppercorns
10 ml mixed pickling spice

Make sure that the solution covers the meat. It is necessary to keep the meat completely submerged in the solution throughout the corning process. To do this, place a dish inside the crock on top of the meat, with a weight on it. Store in the refrigerator for 4 to 6 weeks, checking to ensure that the meat remains submerged and turning the beef every three to four days.

Remove meat from brine and rinse. Place in kettle, cover with water, and simmer approximately four hours, or until meat is tender through to centre.

Overlander Hash

(4 - 6 servings)

500 ml diced, cooked potatoes
500 ml chopped, cooked corned beef
1 medium onion, chopped
10 ml prepared mustard
1 egg, beaten
freshly ground pepper

Mix ingredients together and form into patties, or pat into greased frying pan. Fry until crispy brown on the edges, and serve topped with a fried egg, sunny-side up.

Serve this with:

Cariboo Corn Relish

(Makes 5 - 6 pints)

kernels from 18 ears corn
4 large onions, chopped
2 green peppers, chopped
1 sweet red pepper, chopped
1 lb. light brown sugar
1/4 cup salt
3 Tbsp. celery seed
4 Tbsp. dry mustard
2 qts. vinegar

Combine the ingredients in a large kettle, cook slowly for twenty minutes, pack in sterilized jars and seal at once.

For dessert, since fresh fruit was impossible to carry, Overlanders ate raisins, both for sweetness and for high energy. Drop by the bakery in Valemount or Jasper and buy some butter tarts.

CARIBOO COUNTRY

39 Barkerville Waggon Road
A Gold Digger's Picnic

Over a century ago Barkerville proclaimed itself the biggest city north of San Francisco and west of Chicago! And now it has become legendary again, because it is an authentic ghost town — not reconstructed, but much of it still there, as it was in 1870. The past is tangible in Barkerville, just like the big gold nuggets that Billy Barker found in Williams Creek.

How to get there

Just follow the highway maps, to the middle of nowhere and beyond. Barkerville is east of Quesnel at the end of Highway 26; follow the "Waggon Road" signs.

The area is open year round, but the interpretive programs run only in July and August. There is an admission charge to the townsite in July and August, but none to the picnic area.

The picnic area is right across from the parking lot. Pick any table, and slip back into the history of a hundred years ago, when Barkerville was a city with 20 saloons!

The men who moil for gold

The romance of the gold rush has all but obliterated the reality of life in the mining camps of a century ago. We hear the names of a few of the characters of the time, but many who were also drawn to the Cariboo by the boom that made cities appear — and then disappear

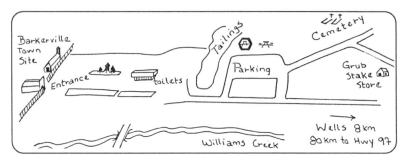

— have been all but forgotten. At this picnic you will meet the ubiquitous Billy Barker, of course, but you will also meet a few of the other men who were drawn by the lustre of gold, or by the services demanded by the miners — the Stagecoach driver, the Chinese grocer, and even the bandit.

Billy Barker

Fame and fortune came quickly in the gold fields of the Cariboo, but for many only fame was to last. Creeks, mountains and towns were named after those who came first. Williams Creek, Cameron-town, Likely and Stanleyville are just a few examples. Although Billy Barker, like so many others, died poor, the town which bears his name lives on.

Billy Barker was not the first to come to the Cariboo in search of gold; by 1861 gold estimated at well over $2 million had already been taken from the Cariboo. It was word of Barker's bonanza in 1862 on Williams Creek that started the rush to the region in earnest. Barker had worked hard for his reward. He had arrived from England on a boat in 1858. It wasn't until 1861 that he went to the Cariboo, following the thousands who had already trekked to the interior. All of the successful claims were farther up Williams Creek, and the land below was thought to be worthless. Since this was all that was available, Billy Barker worked 6 claims in turn, and was all but convinced that the lower claims were indeed worth nothing. It was likely a mix of hopelessness and stubbornness that kept Billy going on that last claim — he had to sink a shaft 52 feet before he struck gold, but when he did there was lots of it. In the first few days he was pulling out gold worth about $5 a pan; then he hit a crevice from which he drew $1,000 of pure rich gold. After drawing about $500,000 in gold from the claim, he left the Cariboo to spend Christmas back in Victoria. It was quite a holiday, and included Billy's marriage to a widow, Elizabeth Collyer — a different kind of gold-digger — who returned with him to Barkerville.

Some blame Elizabeth's extravagance, some blame Billy's gullibility in the saloons; in any case, the fortune was soon gone, and so

The Cariboo Waggon Road

was Elizabeth. Billy had to borrow money for his stage fare out of the Cariboo, and though he did a bit more prospecting, he never struck it rich again. In 1894 he died in Victoria, a pauper. But his last claim, still there, on the main street of Barkerville, served as an incentive to the 10,000 people who followed Billy to the Cariboo. There were the legendary yields of $2,000, or $6,500, or on one occasion $38,000, in a day. In the boom years about $50 million was mined in the Barkerville district. Many men became rich, some several times over, but most lacked the practical ability to conserve some of their sudden wealth for a distant old age.

William Parker of the BX Stagecoach

Among the unsung heroes of the Cariboo are the highly skilled drivers of the stagecoaches, who were commissioned by the British Columbia government to carry the mail between Yale and Barkerville. The Barnard Express Company, soon widely known as the BX, was incorporated in 1868, and under various owners served the Cariboo for 50 years (see also the Yale/Fraser Canyon picnic). The stages also carried passengers, and in the mining season, gold dust was often transported in the safe or the treasure bag under the driver's seat!

The earliest stagecoaches were brought from California. Soon they were being made in Yale, still following the design of the California Concord thorough brace model, but more rugged to withstand the extreme conditions of the Cariboo Waggon Road. Even more important than the coach itself were the horses; teams of two to six horses, specially selected and trained, pulled the stage the 280 miles (450 km) along the trail from Ashcroft to Barkerville, taking four days each way. The teams sometimes averaged 6 miles per hour, and were changed for fresh teams every 18 miles. The horses were the special responsibility of each driver, and he relied on them for his own safety and that of his passengers, and for fulfilling the commitment to get the mail through on time. A skilled driver could crack a whip in such a way as to encourage only one of his lead horses, without disturbing the others at all. He knew his horses, and knew how to harness them so that each was in the position best suited to its strength and capability. Older horses, for instance, would be placed back, closest to the coach, since their years of experience on the Waggon Road had developed sound reflexes for restrained and safe passage along the icy winter roads, and through the muck of spring flooding. In winter the road became a ribbon of packed snow, from six to twenty feet above the summer road level in some places. When a stage horse went off the road it would sink to shoulder level in deep snow; rather than panicking and fighting the snow, these horses would stand very still and wait confidently to be dug out. Such was the level of training of the stagecoach teams, and the level of skill of the BX drivers.

William Parker was the driver of the Cariboo stage on September 16, 1890, the date of the first hold-up of a BX stage. As he guided his team slowly up the 4-mile-long hill near 99 mile, he was surprised by a bandit demanding the safe and the treasure bag. (Hold-ups invariably took place on hills, when the horses couldn't speed up and get away.) Parker knew that the gold had been divided between the two containers, so he managed to convince the robber that the treasure bag contained only waybills and other documents and was not worth bothering about. The bandit made off with $4,500 worth of gold dust in the safe, but Parker's bluff had at least saved the dust in the treasure bag, worth at least $2,500.

Now, there were two things that Cariboo stagecoach robbers

needed to remember: one was the difficulty of escaping, since the only route out was the Waggon Road; the other was the fact that gold dust is identifiable! An experienced Gold Commissioner could tell from which creek any gold dust had been taken because of differences in colour and texture. Martin Van Buren Rowland erred in both areas. First, he didn't leave the Cariboo immediately, but went only as far as Ashcroft, and was later recognized by people who had seen him playing poker the night before the robbery; and second, he eventually sent a sizeable amount of the gold back to Barkerville, requesting that it be made into bullion. It was the Gold Commissioner in Barkerville who identified a sample of the dust as being part of the shipment the stage had been carrying on the day of the robbery. Rowland was arrested and convicted for possession of stolen gold on the basis of this evidence.

The Chinese community and Kwong Lee

The Americans and eastern Canadians who rushed to the Cariboo in the 1860s were looking for big caches; they were not interested in fine dust or small nuggets, and they were an impatient lot. Not so the Chinese who followed them. These people came as indentured labourers, and were hired by the white miners at abysmal wages. At first they were favoured immigrants, as the Canadian government was anxious to counter the influx of Americans to prevent a sovereignty issue from arising over western land. Later, as racism became overt, Chinese immigrants were taxed $100 by the Immigration Department upon entering Canada. They often found work providing services needed in boom towns like Barkerville, such as laundry and cooking. Although they often began as service people, many stayed to rework the gravel piles abandoned by the Argonauts.

The Chinese community developed in Barkerville at the south end of town. Here they established the services for the community itself, the Chinese grocery store, the herbalist, the butcher shop. Many Chinese people became entrepreneurs in the wider community, running a hotel and the sporting-houses frequented by the white miners. One such entrepreneur was Kwong Lee, an immigrant from Hong Kong, who started the first "chain store" in B.C. He began in Victoria in 1858 with an import-export business. He dealt in general merchandise, including opium, the general use of which was legal then. He was successful, and soon opened branches in half a dozen other places in B.C., including Barkerville in 1866.

The Chinese community had a character all its own. Traditions from China continued; opium was smoked by many of the older men, and was sold freely in Chinatown to white and Chinese residents alike. The Chinese Masonic Hall, which was built in the 1870s and survives as one of the oldest buildings in Barkerville, housed a secret society called a Tong, which had as its main purpose the overthrow of the Chinese government. The fraternal societies were important to the Chinese community in a variety of ways, reaching far beyond the political arena of distant China. The Chinese members chose to align their society with a North American association, and the Freemasons were selected. The Tongs were powerful organizations in Barkerville, and legal justice was dispensed through them to Chinese citizens, rather than through the then recently-imposed British justice system.

Unlike the names of Billy Barker and the other legendary miners, the names of most of the Chinese miners have not been preserved, but stories of their perseverance persist. There is the story of the Twelve Foot Davis claim, where Davis, noticing that two claims had been staked incorrectly, claimed the extra twelve feet for himself, and sluiced out about $15,000 in gold. Sure that the claim was all but exhausted, he sold to another miner, who took out $12,000. He in turn sold the claim to a Chinese miner, who took out yet another $25,000 in gold. All this from a claim was only twelve feet wide. No wonder Williams Creek attracted the Billy Barkers, the William Parkers, the Chinese miners and merchants like Kwong Lee, and yes, even the stagecoach robbers like Rowland!

Things to do

1. Walk up the hill to the graveyard, 800 metres beyond the picnic area. The cemetery began with the grave of Peter Gibson in 1863. There are many interesting old headstones. In the Appendix to Richard Thomas Wright's book, *Discover Barkerville*, there is information about the lives of many of the people buried here. The book is available at the townsite, or in the Grubstake Store just past the cemetery.

2. Attend the live theatre performances during the summer months at the Theatre Royal. This building used to be the town's fire hall, and has been reconstructed in keeping with photographs of the original which was built by the Cariboo Dramatic Society in 1863. It was burned in the great fire of 1868.

3. If you are coming to Barkerville in July, try to attend the old-fashioned Pic-Nic. It features a pie baking contest, races for the kids, and all the other things associated with a traditional picnic. Call ahead to confirm the exact date (604) 994-3332.

4. Visit Cottonwood House, 60 km (37 1/2 mi.) from Barkerville, just 30 km (19 mi.) east of Quesnel. Now a museum, the house, built in 1864, served as a road-house and stopping place on the Waggon

Road to Barkerville. Take a ride on an authentic BX stagecoach along part of the old Cariboo Waggon Road.

5. Visit the nearby town of Wells; there are many interesting old buildings, a museum and a working gold mine.

6. Go canoeing at the Bowron Lakes, 28 km (17 mi.) from Barkerville. There is a picnic site beside the first lake. This is a very famous canoeing site, and attracts thousands of people every year. (To paddle the chain circle takes about one week.)

Things to eat

Lentil stew (we'll supply a recipe, but it is also available for takeout at the Wake-up Jake Cafe), poppy seed buns (to pay lip-service to the opium trade), and pie and bannock, bought fresh from the bakery on the main street. Chinese herbal tea is an appropriate drink.

Lentil Stew

(Serves 6)

Lentils, dry pulses, were a staple of mining camps because they were easily transported, and kept indefinitely. Their high protein and vitamin content still make them a popular choice for a meal.

Combine in a kettle:
1/2 pound lentils
5 cups water
2 carrots, cut into chunks
1 small onion, cut into quarters
Cook until the lentils are tender, about 45 minutes.

Add:
6 green onions, chopped
1 clove garlic, crushed
1 1/2 cups tomato juice
1/2 cup minced parsley
1 Tbsp. vegetable oil
1 tsp. salt
1/2 tsp. freshly ground pepper
1/2 tsp. oregano

Simmer until desired thickness — it will vary from soup to stew over time, or with neglect. Stir in just before serving:
1 Tbsp. wine vinegar or lemon juice

Provide a side dish of yogurt for dollops.

40 Chasm Provincial Park
Clinton

A Cariboo Picnic

This is another of our picnics in magical places with few facilities. You will spread your blanket under a very big old tree on part of the original 1865 Cariboo Waggon Road, overlooking a magnificent box canyon.

How to get there

Signs direct you to the chasm, which is a couple of kilometres east of Highway #97, 10 mi. north of Clinton, or at about 60 Mile. (It is hard to think in kilometres here, since the Cariboo Waggon Road landmarks were set out long before Canada adopted the metric system; i.e. the town of 100 Mile House has not been renamed to 160 Kilometre House.) Just after you cross the tracks you will see a parking area. Leave your car there, and proceed along the top of the canyon to your left, toward a very big old tree, which probably witnessed the passage of thousands of men on their way to the gold fields. Select just the right spot beneath the tree and spread your picnic blanket so that you can see down the canyon.

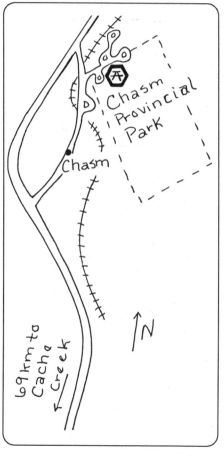

The chasm

Dr. Walter Butler Cheadle commented in his diary about the chasm as he rode by in October, 1863, on his way down the Waggon Road to Victoria:

> Passed this morning a curious chasm in the earth 300 or 400 yards wide height 200 or 300 feet perpendicular. Valley sides as if cut with knife, commencing in a gradual depression & ending abruptly in a valley to the south.
>
> *Gold Rush to the Cariboo* 1987:69

This observation is especially important because Dr. Cheadle's very presence seems to belie the legend of the origin of the chasm. According to the legend it was dug by a Scottish miner on his way north who had inadvertently dropped a penny and was hunting for it. Dr. Cheadle's description, however, gives the impression that the chasm has been there a lot longer. In fact, geologists say that it was created about 10,000 years ago following the last glaciation.

Reflections of sunlight on the walls of the chasm reveal many colours, traces of the minerals within the rock walls. The edge of the chasm is fenced to keep children back from the precipice. If you walk along the path at the top of the cliff, past the picnic site, you will come to a tiny creek, all that remains of the powerful cataract which once helped to carve the chasm.

The fences

As you drive to and from the chasm site, you will notice the variety of fences which line the road from Highway #97. We counted

eight different styles in 2.5 km. They represent the innovative solutions to the problem of sinking posts into the hard, gravelly ground of the Cariboo country. Some of the pioneer fences are constructed without nails or wire, and still rival any modern fence for durability. This is ranch land, and the fencing is constructed almost entirely of lodgepole pine, with the obvious exceptions of the milled rails and the barbed wire.

The snake rail fence, one of the several kinds you will notice, zigzags across the landscape, made entirely of logs. There are no posts or stakes in the early versions. A modified version of it, the Russell fence, is straight, with the lower rails suspended from tripods with loops of wire. A Russell fence is often made from an older snake rail fence. There are several versions of the snake rail fence; watch for the one that is stacked at right angles, making a crenellated pattern instead of the diagonals. You will notice more up-to-date fencing methods, too — the picket fence, the 2 x 6 rail fence, the barbed wire fence, and the ingenious Texas gate or cattle guard, a series of metal pipes laid across a ditch, which effectively prevents cattle or wild game from crossing, but permits vehicles to cross easily.

Things to do

1. Visit Clinton's museum on the main street of the town (which is also Highway #97). It is in the Old Court House where the famous Judge Begbie meted out justice to the frontier. His desk and chair are on display in the museum. Don't miss seeing the freight wagons in the shed behind the museum — these are the wagons that carried supplies to the prospectors at the northern end of the Cariboo Waggon Road. The museum is open May to September, 9 a.m. to 8 p.m. daily.

2. Take a walking tour of Clinton. You can pick up a brochure with a map and guide to the old buildings at the museum. Clinton is about half way between Ashcroft and the gold fields, and had a thriving hotel and outfitting business in the 1860s. The town was originally called "47 Mile," then it was briefly called "Junction" when the road linking the Fraser Canyon reached here, and finally in 1863 Queen Victoria selected the name "Clinton" in honour of Sir Henry Pelham Clinton, her Colonial Secretary from 1859 to 1964.

3. Wander among the tombstones in the old graveyard just north of town. As you drive out of the town on Highway #97 north, watch for the graveyard on a hill on the east side of the road. The entrance is a dirt road just to the right of the entrance to the Lone Pine Ranch. The first burial in the graveyard was in 1861.

Things to eat

This is a stopping house picnic. Stopping houses, offering meals and a bed to travellers along the Waggon Road, sprang up every 12 miles or so. One of the larger ones was the Clinton Hotel at 47 Mile. Stopping houses competed with one another, and some had legendary menus. One of the most famous dishes of the Cariboo was Mulligan, easily made ahead for a picnic on a cool autumn afternoon. The hosts at the stopping houses wasted nothing, and offered yesterday's leftovers as cold cuts, or incorporated them into stews and soups. A meal would include several choices of meat dishes, many kinds of bread and muffins, and as many as five desserts, several pies, cakes and cobblers. We leave the selection up to you, but offer a couple of special recipes.

Mulligan

(6 - 8 servings)

Brown in hot lard
  2 kg cubed meat
Add
  3 large sliced onions
and continue browning.

Stir in
  80 ml flour
  a handful of navy beans,
cover with water and simmer for 3 hours.

Add vegetables:
  turnips, cubed
  carrots, chunked
  potatoes, quartered
  parsnips, chunked

Season to taste with:
  Worcestershire sauce
  salt and pepper

Simmer for another half hour. Transport this in your Dutch oven and reheat on your portable stove at the top of the chasm.

For the cold meats, if you brought some along, the *British Columbia Heritage Cookbook* offers the following:

Cariboo Milehouse Mustard

250 ml dry mustard
125 ml brown sugar
5 ml salt
1 ml turmeric
5 ml white wine vinegar
75 ml flat beer

Mix mustard, sugar, salt and turmeric together in a bowl. Sprinkle with the vinegar to moisten. Continue moistening with flat beer. Mix together until mustard is thick and creamy. Keep chilled in jar with tight-fitting lid.

Saskatoon Pie

For pastry recipe, see Aunt Nell's Pie Crust recipe. You will need enough for a two-crust pie, or more if you are providing a Stopping House selection. We supply one recipe, and you can use some of your own, or select pie recipes from other picnics in this book.

Line a greased pie pan with pastry, poking it with a fork several times to release steam during baking.

Place in a saucepan
4 cups Saskatoon berries
(also called service berries in some places), washed and sorted, and
1/4 cup water
Cover and simmer for 10 minutes.

Add to this
2 Tbsp. vinegar or lemon juice

Stir into the berries
3/4 cup sugar
3 Tbsp. flour.

Pour berry mixture into the pie crust and cover with top crust, making steam holes in your favourite pattern. Bake at 425°F for 10 minutes, then reduce heat to 350°F and continue baking for 30 minutes.

Loaves and Fishes *or* Feeding the Multitude

This chapter is for that fortunate individual who has just been elected or appointed Social Convenor, or equivalent, of a group or club and is now responsible for the planning and conduct of the annual picnic.

Reunions, companies, unions, churches, communities, and lots of other groups hold picnics for their members and families. The planning required for such events is quite detailed, but with reasonable care you can indeed keep everything under control — except, of course, the weather.

In this chapter we will describe the generic large group picnic, covering a variety of concerns such as theme, supplies, games and activities, recipes for preparing large quantities of food, and we will provide an answer to that worrisome question, "how many potatoes in a potato salad for 100?" The chapter is mainly one long and involved checklist, with some games and recipes tacked on. You have undertaken an awesome and daunting task, one that would overcome a lesser individual, but we hope to provide enough suggestions that you may enjoy the afternoon and even volunteer to do it again!

☐ 1 What happened last year?

Did the picnickers enjoy themselves? Was the location OK? Who booked it and from whom. . . is she still in town? Was Mrs. Brown's Potato Salad the hit of the picnic, or the basis of the food fight that broke out? Will you be a hero by just repeating what was done before, or were many people dissatisfied? Organizations are often very bad at this type of history, but some conscientious digging can probably head off a lot of hurt feelings, and make the picnic fun for all.

☐ 2 The occasion

Picnics are often associated with an event, such as the completion of spring planting in rural communities, or a harvest festival. Certainly the fall bazaar or fair is still a common occurrence in many rural and urban communities alike. Work parties are another good reason for a picnic — it used to be barn-raising, but now it is sometimes garage-raising or developing the community ball field.

Picnics can be planned around a theme, although this is not at all necessary. Some suggestions to spark your imagination are as follows:

Canada Day	Summer solstice
Christmas in July	50th birthday
a wedding	retirement
end of school	end of summer

☐ 3 The group

The first step is to recognize the composition of the group since this will influence all the other factors: the food, the activities, the facilities, and so on. With old, established picnics this is fairly well understood, but with new groups, watch out. This may be the group of boys that you bowl with on Wednesday nights, but the picnic will include their families, too . . . . What do you know about them? What are the ages of their children? Do they like a primitive but beautiful site or are they happiest in an urban park? Do they have teenagers, or little kids, or is this an adult group (which, on a picnic, may be counted on to behave as a lot of aging adolescents)? This last group is especially hard to deal with as you can count on several bad sprains and possibly a broken bone or two as the picnickers try to convince their 40-year-old bodies that they can still play football like they did when they were 20. Even if it is the same group as last year, remember that a year has gone by, and while it may not have changed you or your friends much, the children might have metamorphosed from fun-seeking kids to very self-conscious teenagers.

□ 4 The facilities: Where to hold the picnic

Municipal and provincial parks usually provide pleasant settings for large picnics, and some provide special places and facilities for large groups. Once you have selected a likely spot, visit the site and check to see that there is enough space for the activities you are planning, shelter in case of rain, sanitary facilities and a water source. If these are missing, portable toilets can be rented, and a water supply can be carried, but both of these arrangements require lead time and planning.

If you intend to serve alcoholic beverages, check first to make sure that this is legal in the site you have selected. The consumption of alcohol is usually forbidden in public parks, but sometimes you can obtain a permit, particularly if you are using a community hall as a base.

It is a good idea to notify the local police department about the event, as well. You may need assistance with traffic control, or help in dealing with unruly guests — or you may need nothing at all. This is just part of the ounce of prevention which beats a pound of cure.

If you are booking a park as the site of your picnic, you might wish to be weather-safe, and book an alternative venue, such as a community hall or church, in case of rain. Sometimes groups set up an alternate date, assuming that if the first day is rainy, the second won't be. The invitation or announcement might read, "Social services department picnic at Kinsmen Park on Saturday, July 6th, or, in case of rain-out, Saturday, July 13th." Make sure you book both dates with the parks department, or appropriate authority.

□ 5 Equipment

You will need supplies for decorating the picnic site, such as balloons and streamers. In larger centres these can be found by checking the Yellow Pages under "balloons," "helium" or "giftwares." Helium machines can be rented for a nominal fee, and even outdoor sites look more festive when there are brightly coloured balloons flying from the trees and telephone poles.

You will need prizes for any contests or races — and make sure that you have plenty. We usually give at least three prizes for all children's contests, and, if possible, a prize to everyone. Ribbons for first, second, third, fourth, and so on, are usually available at the same place where you bought the balloons.

You will need to buy, borrow or make the equipment for any races or contests: barrels for barrel races, strong ties for three-legged races, bags (green garbage, perhaps) for the sack race, eggs for an egg toss, and so on.

Finally, there will be the cleanup afterward. Rakes, brooms, shovels, or maybe just a lot of garbage bags will be needed, and line up your work crew ahead of time.

☐ 6   First aid equipment

We have found it wise to bring a complete industrial first aid kit. These can be purchased from any industrial supply store, and come in a water-proof metal box.

Alternatively, you can put together a kit for yourself with a minimum of the following:

Band-aids of various sizes	sterile 2" and 4" gauze pads
low-allergy adhesive tape	skin disinfectant
lots of clean cotton balls	scissors
elastic bandage for sprains	sling
safety pins	burn ointment
insect repellant	

In any case, make sure that you have an adequate first aid kit at the picnic.

☐ 7   Activities

Games

Think back to the picnics of your childhood — what games did you play? I'll bet that you, like us, have trouble remembering the rules. Later in the chapter are the rules for some of the games we remember, but we have found that there are regional variations. Alter them to suit your own recollection.

Contests

Contests are fun, if they are not taken too seriously. Pies seem to offer the most versatility for contests: there are pie-baking contests, pie-throwing contests, and pie-eating contests. There are also barrel-rolling contests, where the contestants line up on their barrels (empty oil barrels are fine) at the starting line, and the prize goes to the person who reaches the finish line first without touching ground, or to the person who goes farthest. There are arm-wrestling contests. There are spelling bees. Prizes can also be given for the best decorated bike, the scariest costume, and the most lovable dog. If you are at a beach for your picnic, there could be a sand-castle building contest.

Searches

Treasure hunts of various sorts are lots of fun, and work well as team activities. Each team is given a list of things to find, and the winning team is the one which first collects everything on the list. Alternatively, quantities of a particular item, eggs, or specially wrapped candies, or tokens of some sort, can be secreted about the picnic site, and the prize can go to the team — or individual — who finds the most.

Team Sports

The old reliables, the baseball game, the touch football game, or for some groups, a rousing round of croquet always go better if someone remembers to bring the bats, balls, mallets, hoops, and base sacks. Delegate the responsibility to someone else.

Kite flying

If your picnic site has a big enough field, and no power wires nearby, you can ask people to bring their kites; alternatively, you can supply some. This only works in a big space, and only a few people can fly kites at the same time, since the strings easily become entangled. If the picnickers know and understand the rules for kite fighting, that is also an interesting pastime.

Balloon rides

Hot-air ballooning has become very popular in the last few years. Many balloon owners are willing to attend community events or private functions to provide balloon rides — for a fee. Some groups have even rented helicopters for the afternoon, and sold rides to the picnickers.

Guided hikes

If the picnic is in a rural setting, a park just outside town, or even some of the larger city parks, guided hikes for groups of picnickers can be a welcome diversion, especially for senior citizens. Identify someone in the group who has special knowledge of birds, plants, animals, or all three. Ask your guide in advance, so that he or she can brush up if necessary. Limit the hikes to no more than an hour — and perhaps less, depending on who you expect to participate.

Camp-fire sing-songs

Most effective after dark, sing-songs provide a quiet ending to an exciting afternoon. Everyone slows down and relaxes, little children fall asleep on blankets by the fire, and adults feel that sense of warmth and companionship which can only happen by a fire. Make sure that you provide at least one guitar or accordian player who has a wide repertoire appropriate to the ages of your group. Consider having song sheets available, if you think people will be able to see them. Alternatively, brain-storm with your accompanist in advance, and prepare a list of tunes for which most people already know the words, so that awkward silences and false starts will be avoided.

Fireworks

Fireworks have made a big come-back in the last few years, much to the chagrin of many parents. Nonetheless, they make a marvelous display when carefully selected and responsibly detonated.

☐ 8 Things to eat

Donations

There are many factories in most cities and larger towns which will be happy to donate some of their product for your picnic, in exchange for recognition in the announcement or invitation. Others will donate, but prefer to remain anonymous to stem the tide of subsequent requests. Some may prefer to give a small cash donation. Think about what you will need in the way of food, and then consider which companies are represented in your community. Most have a public relations officer to respond to such requests. It is certainly worth a try.

Supplies for food preparation

If you are using a community hall or equivalent as a base for your food preparation, arrange to visit the place to assess the number and capacity of mixing and serving bowls, pots and pans, and so on. If you are going to be working in a park, preparing hot dogs and hamburgers, make sure that you book enough barbecues and frying pans, or whatever else you will need. Nothing is worse than a bottleneck in the food production area when everyone is hungry. The easiest system is to select cold foods, and to have them prepared by individuals in their homes in advance. This is the ideal time for a pot-luck dinner, in true "picnickian" style, with everyone contributing to the feast. We have found that it isn't even necessary to direct people about what to bring — you will get several potato salads, but this is a popular dish anyway, and most of it will be eaten. You will also get some of the specialty salads that people like to make for such events, and the variety is endless. The most direction we have ever given is to request either a salad, casserole, dessert or bread. Usually the picnic organizers provide the beverages, in the form of juice or pop. Have water on hand for those who want it.

Most important, make sure you have enough. Err on the side of too much! To help you, we provide selected recipes.

Chicken Salad

(100 Servings)

8 qts. cooked chicken, cut into small pieces
8 cups chopped celery
2 Tbsp. salt
2 Tbsp. pepper
2 qts. mayonnaise or salad cream
6 green peppers, chopped
16 hard cooked eggs, sliced

Mix ingredients together, and keep well-chilled until serving time. It is best to prepare this the day of the picnic. You can maintain a safe temperature by placing the serving bowls in a tub of ice on the picnic table.

Salmon Loaf

(100 Servings)

Mix together:
    20-1 lb. cans of salmon
    6 qts. bread crumbs

Scald:
    8 qts. milk

And mix with:
    3 cups melted butter
    5 1/2 cups flour
    1 tsp. paprika
    4 Tbsp. salt

Cook for 15 minutes.

Combine the sauce with the fish, blend together, and pour into greased loaf pans. Sprinkle with buttered bread crumbs and bake at 350 °F for 30 minutes.

Cole Slaw

(100 Servings)

Combine:
    10 lbs. cabbage, shredded
    3 lbs. carrots, shredded
    3 lbs. celery, diced
    1 pt. mayonnaise or salad cream

1 *cup salad oil*
1/2 *cup vinegar*
celery seed, salt and pepper to taste

Potato Salad

(100 Servings)

28 *lbs. potatoes, cooked and diced*
10 *doz. hard cooked eggs, sliced*   Dress with:
2 *cups onions, finely chopped*   2 *cups salad oil*
5 *sweet red peppers, chopped*   1/2 *cup vinegar*
5 *green peppers chopped*   2 *tsp. dry mustard.*
salt and pepper to taste   1 *qt. mayonnaise*

Mix ingredients together and chill well. As with the chicken salad, it is best to prepare this the day of the picnic, and to keep it chilled while serving.

Group Picnic Checklist

The following can be used as a rough guide, or as a plan of action, assigning committee members to each task and setting scheduled dates of completion.

Select date for picnic, and alternate date, if appropriate
Select site.
Visit site to check for:

water	ball diamond
toilets	games/races area
number of picnic tables	electricity
shelter	nearest telephone
cooking facilities	nearest hospital
fire wood	

Book site.
Get liquor permit, if needed.
Develop supply list:

prizes	plastic cutlery
ribbons	serviettes
safety pins	garbage bags
string	garbage buckets
rope	lawn chairs for seniors
tape	barbecues
fireworks	fuel
paper cups	pots and pans
paper plates	cooking implements

pot holders, oven mitts
first aid kit
water buckets
List food requirements:
  snacks
  main course
  salads
  buns or bread
List beverage requirements:
  drinks for little kids
  drinks for teenagers
  drinks for adults
  coffee, tea, cocoa, milk
  cups to drink from

felt pens and cardboard
  for signs

casseroles
desserts
cookies
pies

Games for Groups

Elves, Giants and Wizards
Materials: none
People: ten, to a large crowd

Directions:
Two roughly equal groups of people should be formed. They should then be taught the three basic positions of the game:
- an elf is little with two little horns on his head (so the person squats with hands behind head)
- a giant is huge (so the person puts arms way above the head and walks on tiptoe)
- wizards are sneaky fellows, always shooting rays of magic lightening out of their fingers. A wizard sort of person, therefore, looks sneaky and is always pointing his arms in the direction of the other groups.

To play the game, each group has a secret meeting and decides which of the three characters it will be. A first plan and a back-up plan should be chosen. Then the groups face each other, about five metres apart, on a large field. There should be designated safe zones at each end of the field since the participants are going to chase each other up and down the field.

Once facing each other, and conducted by the games' mistress or master, they all chant together three times in a row, "elves, giants, wizards" with the action for each word. After the third chant each group then chants its planned word. The result will be the two groups

yelling the same, or different characters. This seems pointless unless you know that:
- elves can run under wizards' cloaks and pull the hair on their legs;
- wizards can shoot magic rays that will destroy giants;
- that giants can stomp on elves' heads.

Thus whenever the first planned word called out by each team is different, there will be a winner (a chaser) and a loser (who will get chased). For example, if one side calls elves, and the other wizards, the elves are the winners and get to chase the wizards. So also, wizards chase giants, and giants chase elves. Anyone tagged before getting to a safe zone has to join the other team. If the first planned word is the same for both teams, then each should immediately chant their back-up plan word.

Kick-the-Can
Materials: one can
People: four, to a crowd

Directions
This is a fast-paced game a lot like hide-and-go-seek. One person is chosen to be It. The can is kicked by someone and this is the signal for everyone except It to race off, within the prescribed boundary, and hide. It retrieves the can, takes it home, and then with closed eyes, counts slowly to 60 out loud. It then goes to find the others without letting anyone get home undetected. When a person is discovered It runs to the can and says, "1, 2, 3 on (name of person)." The person should be named correctly, but with a large group, when names may not be known by all participants, this rule can be relaxed. There will often be a race to the can, and hidden persons who get there first shout, "Home Free," and are safe. Once a lot of people are at the can, both caught and safe, the last people out can try to sneak home and "Kick the Can." This action would free all the people at home to run and hide again. If no-one kicks the can, then the first person caught is It for the next round. No on can be It more than twice in a row.

Dragon
Materials: a blindfold, and a treasure (a shoe, a box, a coin, etc.)
People: Seven or more

Description:
Millions and hundred of years ago, dragons roamed the earth .. . and these dragons had great treasures. It seems that not all the dragons died off; one still lives, and he is the richest dragon of all time. This dragon has been collecting money and jewels for centuries

and has caves full of treasure. He is a very ferocious dragon, but he is blind. However, because of this, his hearing is especially good. Is there anyone in the group who is stealthy enough to steal the dragon's treasure?

Select one person to be the dragon and blindfold that person. The dragon sits on the ground with his or her legs spread out. The treasure rests on the ground between the dragon's legs, but not touching the dragon. Have the group sit in a circle around the dragon. The leader will point to one person who will try to steal in and take the treasure. If the dragon hears something it will point at the sound, and the intruder will be zapped by magic dragon fire. The dragon can only point at sounds. The group should be very quiet, and only one person may try at a time to steal the treasure. Sometimes, the group can make rain noise by rubbing hands together. When the treasure is stolen, appoint a new dragon and continue.

References

Akrigg, G.P.V., and Helen B. Akrigg 1969 *1001 British Columbia Place Names*. Vancouver: Discovery Press.

Anderson, Frank 1973 *Sheriffs and Outlaws of Western Canada*. Calgary: Frontier Publishing.

Assiniwi, Bernard 1972 *Indian Recipes*. Toronto: Copp Clark.

Baird, Elizabeth 1974 *Classic Canadian Cooking*. Toronto: James Lorimer.

Bandoni, R.J. and A.F. Szezawinski 1975 *Guide to Common Mushrooms of British Columbia*. Handbook No. 24. Victoria: British Columbia Provincial Museum.

Bars, Beulah 1983 *Come'n Get It*. Saskatoon: Western Producer Prairie Books.

Bennett, Jennifer 1987 *Becoming Legacy*. Equinox VI(32):34-44.

Blake, Don 1985 *This is Beautiful British Columbia: The Book of B.C. Trivia*. British Columbia Heritage Trust.

Bodsworth, Fred 1970 "The Pacific Coast." *The Illustrated Natural History of Canada*. Toronto: N.S.L. Natural Science of Canada Limited.

Bowers, Dan 1978 *Exploring the Southern Okanagan and Cathedral Provincial Park*. Vancouver: Douglas & McIntyre.

Cashman, Tony 1971 *An Illustrated History of Western Canada*. Edmonton: Hurtig.

Charlebois, Peter 1978 *Sternwheelers & Sidewheelers: The romance of steamdriven paddleboats in Canada*. Toronto: NC Press.

Clark, Cecil 1986 *B.C. Provincial Police Stories*. Surrey, B.C: Heritage House.

Cooperman, Jim and Mary Zoretich 1988 *Shuswap Chronicles*. Celista, B.C: North Shuswap Historical Society.

Downs, Art 1960 *Wagon Road North*. Surrey, B.C: Heritage House Publishing.

Downs, Art, Ed. 1977 *Pioneer Days in British Columbia*. Vol. 1. Surrey: Heritage House.

Downs, Art, Ed. 1975 *Pioneer Days in British Columbia*. Vol. 2. Surrey: Heritage House.

Edwards, R. Yorke 1970 "The Mountain Barrier." A volume in *The Illustrated Natural History of Canada*. Toronto: Natural Science of Canada Limited.

Ellis, Eleanor A. 1967 *Northern Cookbook*. Ottawa: Queen's Printer.

Evans-Atkinson, Mary 1984 *British Columbia Heritage Cookbook*. North Vancouver: Whitecap Books.

Fitzharris, Tim 1983 *The Island: A Natural History of Vancouver Island*. Toronto: Oxford University Press.

Florin, Lambert 1967 *A Guide to Western Ghost Towns*. Seattle, Washington: Superior Publishing.

Freeman, Roger and Ethel Freeman 1985 *Exploring Vancouver's North Shore Mountains*. Vancouver: Federation of Mountain Clubs of British Columbia.

Frideres, James S. 1983 *Native People in Canada: Contemporary conflicts*. Scarborough: Prentice-Hall Canada.

Hancock, David, Lyn Hancock and David Stirling 1974 *Pacific Wilderness*. Saanichton, B.C: Hancock House.

Hardy, W.G. 1959 *From Sea Unto Sea*. Garden City, N.Y: Doubleday.

Harris, Lorraine 1984 *Gold Along the Fraser*. Surrey, B.C: Hancock House.

Harris, W. Howard 1984 *Ten Golden Years: Barkerville-Wells, 1932-1942*. Quesnel, B.C: Little Shepherd Publications Ltd.

Hearne, G. and D. Wilkie 1980 "The K & S Railway." In *The Best of Canada West*. Langley, B.C: Mr. Paperback.

Hewitt, Jean 1971 *The New York Times Natural Foods Cookbook*. New York: Avon.

Hill, Beth 1975 *Guide to Indian Rock Carvings of the Pacific Northwest Coast*. Surrey, B.C: Hancock House.

Hill, Douglas 1967 *The Opening of the Canadian West*. Don Mills, Ontario: Academic Press.

Howay, F..C., E.O.S. Scholefield, and William G.R. Hind 1987 *Cariboo Gold Rush*. Surrey, B.C: Heritage House.

Johnson, E. Pauline (Tekahionwake) 1986 *Legends of Vancouver*. (First published in 1911.) Toronto: McClelland & Stewart.

Kananen, Leona 1975 *Yukon Cookbook*. Vancouver: Douglas & McIntyre.

Kootenay Journal 1988 No.1. Winlaw, B.C: Polestar Press.

Langshaw, Rick 1983 *Naturally: Medicinal herbs and edible plants of the Canadian Rockies*. Banff: Summerthought.

Lee, Barrie 1979 *Victoria on Foot*. Victoria: Terrapin.

Luard, Elizabeth 1987 *The Old World Kitchen*. Toronto: Bantam.

Ludditt, Fred W. 1972 *Campfire Sketches of the Cariboo*. Penticton, B.C: Fred W. Ludditt.

1980 *Barkerville Days*. Langley, B.C: Mr. Paperback.

May, Dave 1986 *Sandon: The mining centre of the silvery slocan*. Kaslo, B.C: Dave May.

McFeat, Tom, Ed. 1969 *Indians of the North Pacific Coast*. The Carleton Library no. 25. Toronto: McClelland and Stewart.

McGill, David E. 1979 *126 Stops of Interest in Beautiful British Columbia*. Aldergrove, B.C: Frontier Publishing.

Michener, James A. 1968 *Iberia*. New York: Fawcett Crest.

Milne, A.A. 1976 *When We Were Very Young.* New York: Dell.
Morton, W.L. 1963 *The Kingdom of Canada.* Toronto: McClelland & Stewart.
Neering, Rosemary 1974 *Settlement of the West.* Toronto: Fitzhenry and Whiteside.
Nicol, Eric 1970 *Vancouver.* Toronto: Doubleday.
O'Neail, Hazel 1962 *Doukhobor Daze.* Sidney, B.C: Gray's Publishing.
Ormsby, Margaret A. 1958 *British Columbia: A History.* Toronto: Macmillan of Canada.
Ortiz, Elisabeth Lambert 1976 *The Complete Book of Japanese Cooking.* New York: M. Evans & Co.
Paquet, Maggie 1986 *The B.C. Parks Explorer.* North Vancouver: Whitecap Books.
Paterson, T.W. 1980 "Billy Barker." In *The Best of Canada West.* Langley, B.C: Mr. Paperback.
Perrin, Tim ND *More Exploring By Bicycle: Vancouver Island, Vancouver and the Fraser Valley.* Vancouver: J.J. Douglas.
Ramsey, Bruce 1963 *Ghost Towns of British Columbia.* Vancouver: Mitchell Press.
Reksten, Terry 1986 *"More English than the English": A very social history of Victoria.* Victoria: Orca Book Publishers.
Roden, Claudia 1984 *Everything Tastes Better Outdoors.* New York: Alfred A. Knopf.
Rohner, Ronald P. and Evelyn C. Rohner 1970 *The Kwakiutl Indians of British Columbia.* New York: Holt, Rinehart and Winston.
Rombauer, Irma S. and Marion Rombauer Becker 1984 *The Joy of Cooking.* Indianapolis: Bobbs-Merrill.
Root, Waverley 1980 *Food.* New York: Simon & Schuster.
Sandford, Barry 1977 *McCullough's Wonder: The story of the Kettle Valley Railway.* West Vancouver: Whitecap.
Scargall, Jeanne 1980 *Canadian Homestead Cookbook.* Toronto: Methuen.
Scott, David and Edna H. Hanic 1974 *East Kootenay Saga.* New Westminster, B.C: Nunaga Publishing.
Shoreacres Ladies Club ND *Doukhobor Favorites.* Winnipeg: Gateway.
Soper, James H. and Adam F. Szczawinski 1976 *Mount Revelstoke National Park Wildflowers.* Natural History Series No. 3. Victoria: British Columbia Provincial Museum.
Stewart, Dave 1977 *Okanagan Back Roads.* Sidney, B.C: Saltaire Publishing.
Symons, Harry 1974 *Fences.* Toronto: McGraw-Hill Ryerson.
Tyrell, J.B., Ed. 1916 *David Thompson's Narrative on His Explorations in Western America 1784-1812.* Toronto: The Champlain Society.
Usukawa, Saeko, Ed. 1984 *Sound Heritage: Voices from British Columbia.* Vancouver: Douglas & McIntyre.
Wade, Mark 1981 *The Overlanders of '62.* (First published in 1931.) Surrey, B.C: Heritage House.

Walbran, Captain John T. 1971 *British Columbia Coast Names 1592-1906: Their origin and history.* Vancouver: J.J. Douglas.

Walker, Marilyn 1984 *Harvesting the Northern Wild.* Yellowknife: Outcrop Ltd.

West, Willis J. 1985 *Stagecoach and Sternwheel Days in the Cariboo and Central B.C.* Surrey, B.C: Heritage House.

Wherry, Joseph H. 1964 *The Totem Pole Indians.* New York: Funk & Wagnalls.

White, Derryll 1988 *Fort Steele: Here history lives.* Surrey, B.C: Heritage House.

White, Howard 1983 *Raincoast Chronicles Six/Ten.* Madiera Park: Harbour Publishing.

Whitney, Stephen 1985 *Western Forests.* New York: Alfred A. Knopf.

Wood, Kerry 1957 *The Map-Maker: The story of David Thompson.* Toronto: Macmillan.

Woods, John G. 1987 *Glacier Country: Mount Revelstoke and Glacier National Parks.* Vancouver: Douglas and McIntyre.

Wright, Richard Thomas 1984 *Discover Barkerville: A Gold Rush Adventure.* Vancouver: Special Interest Publications.

Yee, Rhoda 1982 *Szechwan and Northern Cooking: From hot to cold.* San Francisco: Taylor and Ng.

Other

Beautiful British Columbia Magazine Guidebook. 1988 Vol. I. Vancouver.

British Columbia Recreation Atlas 1978 Victoria: Province of British Columbia Ministry of Recreation and Conservation.

Buckskin Cookery 1957 Vol. 1: The Pioneer Section. Williams Lake, B.C: Gwen Lewis.

The Canadian Encyclopedia 1985 Edmonton: Hurtig.

The Concise Oxford Dictionary of Current English. 1983 7th Ed. Oxford: Clarendon Press.

The Dewdney Trail: Hope to Fort Steele. 1987 Surrey, B.C: Heritage House.

Fraser & Thompson River Canyons 1986 Surrey, B.C: Heritage House.

Gold Creeks and Ghost Towns 1978 Summerland, B.C: Canada West Magazine.

Opportunities for wildlife and recreation development in the 1983 Columbia River wetlands. A report prepared for the Fish and Wildlife Branch, British Columbia, Ducks Unlimited (Canada), Canadian Wildlife Service by Pedology Consultants et al.

Recipes of British Columbia. 1984 Vol. 1. B.C: Beautiful British Columbia Magazine.

Photo Credits

John Whittaker
Pacific Rim p. 33, Butchart Gardens of Victoria p. 43, Ft. Rodd p. 48, Granville Island p. 95, Spanish Banks in Vancouver p. 100, Stanley Park p. 103, Ambleside Park p. 113, Yale p. 124, Osoyoos p. 136, Jade Beach p. 141, S. S. Moyie p. 156, Mt. Revelstoke p. 213, The Phoebe Ann p. 225, Mt. Robson p. 229, Nanaimo - petroglyph illustration

Carolyn Whittaker
Pit House - Zuckerburg Island p. 150, Canal Flats p. 169, Wildhorse Creek p. 176, Michel-Natal p. 179, Invermere p. 186, Kimberley p. 191-2

Nancy Gibson
Radium p. 196

Diana Gibson
Port Alberni p. 37, Laurel Point p. 51, Gibsons p. 59, Othello Quintette Tunnels near Hope p. 69, Shannon Falls p. 88, Emory Creek p. 120, Keremeos p. 133, Falkland Pillar p. 205, Harrison Hot Springs — sasquatch illustration, Chasm — fence illustration

McGraw-Hill Ryerson
C.W. Jefferys drawing, Barkerville

BC Archives
Pauline Johnson p. 104, Craigellachie p. 201, Cariboo Road p. 207, Illecillewaet p. 220

BC Tourism
Fort Langley p. 75, Capilano Canyon p. 84

Kootenay Lake Historical Society
Kaslo p. 162

Alberta Archives
Picnic Athabasca p. 246

Nancy Gibson and John Whittaker

About the Authors

The search for the perfect picnic has been an all-consuming passion of the Gibson-Whittaker family. The search has been conducted on five continents and included mountaintops in India, riverbanks in Africa, castles and olive groves in Spain, and buffalo jumps and ghost towns in Canada. Nancy is a cultural anthropologist, gardener, management consultant, author and university lecturer. John is a cook, management consultant, author and professor of engineering management.

Recipe Index